State College

at

Framingham

7500-1-64-932122

The Moulding of Modern Man

T. H. PEAR

The Moulding of
Modern Man

A PSYCHOLOGIST'S VIEW OF
INFORMATION, PERSUASION AND
MENTAL COERCION TODAY

London
GEORGE ALLEN & UNWIN LTD
RUSKIN HOUSE MUSEUM STREET

PRINTED IN GREAT BRITAIN
in 11 on 12 pt. Juliana
BY SIMSON SHAND LTD
LONDON, HERTFORD AND HARLOW

3/65

TO

MORRIS GINSBERG

PREFACE

Though there are innumerable treatments of this book's subject, it does not appear to have been examined recently by a psychologist. I have tried to discuss modern encroachments on personal freedom, and attempts to belittle the individual. Examination of such activities led to realization of relatively new problems, e.g. the psychological nature of the individual today, and, perhaps, tomorrow: his consciousness of co-operation and conflict with other persons, perceived or imagined, and the ways in which such experiences change with variations in the social pattern, especially those caused by technological and educational developments.

The present book may be compared with one by a social anthropologist, reporting observations made in many places and in different contexts, in the hope that others with special training may be stimulated to theorize about them.

Part I (Chapters 1 to 3) deals with the nature of the individual person acting in a social environment. The possibility has been kept in mind that when a human being travels alone through space with no light or sound, his perception of self will be extensively altered. Experiments show that sensory deprivation alone will produce amazing results.

Part II (Chapters 4 to 12) treats of the individual as he reacts to society, accepting, ignoring or rejecting its laws, customs and conventions, displaying social skill and clumsiness. Current ideas of 'social adjustment' are discussed, with glances at other cultures.

The slippery concept of the 'intellectual' has been handled as firmly as possible. The gap alleged to exist between intellectuals and scientists is discussed, with accounts of the intellectual and anti-intellectual in different countries. Conflicting claims on the loyalties of the professional thinker are examined.

Chapter 8 describes forcible indoctrination, 'thought reform' and 'brainwashing'.

The influence on personal beliefs of advertising and 'public relations' are considered in detail, and the relation of culture to the mass media, here and in America, is discussed.

A great deal of Part II describes hindrances to individual freedom of thought and action. Discussion of the many ways in which the fight for freedom is being waged would have obscured the issues described here.

It seemed unnecessary, even impertinent, to interrupt by frequent recitals of my creed, though personal views have been stated where clarity necessitated this. I hope that the book will not convey the general impression of a Laodicean attitude towards tragically important issues. The technique of polemic composition is easier to acquire than the unlearning of psychology which it necessitates. Of the emotion-provoking subjects of brainwashing and advertising, loyalties, treachery and treason, aspects of psychological importance have been selected for discussion. The psychologist is inured to the comment that some of his remarks are platitudes: still, many platitudes are true, important and not generally respected, and some require to be nailed to the counter.

Psychologists may regret that while the book's bibliography contains few studies reported in the technical journals, much attention is paid to facts, views and opinions reported in the Press and on the air. My professional colleagues will understand my estimation of the importance of public opinion, even if uninformed. The general reader will encounter few technical terms: these are explained.

My thanks are offered to friends for supplying material from very different sources: to Mr Philip Unwin, who suggested a psychological discussion of encroachments on individual freedom; to Mr E. M. Eppel for sympathetic reading of the first drafts and many helpful comments and deserved warnings; to the late Dr E. B. Strauss for permission to quote from his discussion of treachery and treason; to Professor Magdalen D. Vernon and Dr N. F. Dixon for similar permission in connection with subception; to Dr P. L. Short for help in the treatment of advertising; and to Professors Robert J. Lifton and Edgar H. Schein, who have kindly allowed me to summarize data from their reports; and to the editors of *Psychiatry* and the *Journal of Asian Studies* for permission to quote. Professor Alexander Kennedy generously allowed me to read, in advance of publication, notes of his Royal Institution discourse on brainwashing.

I acknowledge gratefully gifts of relevant publications from

Professors Gordon W. Allport and Reuel Denney, Dr Erving Goffman, Professor Harold Guetzkow, Dr Marie Jahoda and Professor David Riesman, and encouragement from Mr J. Hutton Hynd, who invited me to speak on the subject at Conway Hall meetings. Thanks for valued help are given to the librarians of the English-Speaking Union, London (Miss Barbara W. Appleton and Miss Norma Hatcher), and the National Institute of Industrial Psychology (Mrs Rosemary Rabe), to Mrs K. Whittaker, who typed the scripts with her usual care and patience, and to Mr and Mrs John Beadle, who read the proofs.

T. H. PEAR
Woodchurch, Kent
June, 1961

CONTENTS

PART I

CHAPTER ONE

The Moulding of Modern Man

A completely solitary human being is rarely found: social forces continually mould the ordinary person's thoughts and character. In our lifetime, the rate of this modification has accelerated immeasurably. Fifty years ago in England few persons even looked at a national daily paper. Advertising, recognizable as such, was sporadic; it was not the chief force in changing attitudes towards buying, nor did it express the desires of large organized groups.

Today, here and in America, few families are without newspaper, radio or television. They are constantly exposed to the influence of news, straight or slanted, opinions and persuasive advertising. Most periodicals, especially the illustrated ones, depend for their existence on large payments from advertisers. Many educational systems imply character-formation: concerning their desirability sharp differences of opinion exist.

About these social forces much is known: about the nature of the persons being moulded, less. This obviously psychological subject is relevant to any discussion about the alleged antithesis between Man and Society. Some philosophers and sociologists who debate this remember that almost invariably personality is felt as uniquely one's own. Yet mystical awareness, illusions and delusions caused by drugs and sensory deprivation, 'cut-off' experiences at high altitudes, suggest that barriers between Self and non-Self are permeable to an unexpected extent. Since today the earth's surface is not the only plane on which important journeys are made, it is time to reconsider the perception, conception and 'management' of the Self.

To regard the individual person as important is unfashionable among many physical scientists and some psychologists who borrow their methods. For this, a common defence is the assertion 'Science does not deal with individual cases'. This view is only one among others. The scientific study of personality attempts, by experiment and test, to isolate traits or factors, to measure them and their interaction; yet few modern psychologi-

B

cal books on personality study refer to any identifiable living persons. If it be objected that to do this is unscientific, the reply is that there are other kinds of Science.

With the increase in the number and directions of forces influencing the individual, some concepts, e.g. of his loyalties and his right to privacy, are being challenged and re-examined. These problems, ethically and politically important, are at bottom psychological, and an attempt will be made to see them in that light.

The views expressed in this book are those of a psychologist interested in sociology and anthropology. After reading many discussions of personality in the last twenty years, I conclude that to regard the individual as important is unfashionable among psychologists: with some notable exceptions they seem content to hand over the subject to columnists, novelists and some historians.

Many physical scientists know that henceforth almost every advance in their subject will create social problems, and that to plead that 'politics' must never interfere with 'science' is to appeal to an increasingly sceptical public. To substitute in this sentence 'politicians' and 'scientists' might bring the social psychologist nearer to the present facts of life. In their writings, physical scientists usually disregard the human individual, and some resent speculation concerning his motives. Beyond the Iron Curtain, the 'cult of personality' is discouraged. In the social sciences, including economics, it is orthodox to search for 'trends' and to designate the stray sheep as deviant, maladjusted or neurotic.

A certain professor of philosophy, who loathed teaching, used to ask students, at the first meeting of a class, 'What do you hope to get from this course?' Any positive reply elicited a weary 'Oh, no, you won't!' Forty years ago, if a student had mentioned that by reading psychological works he would increase his understanding of persons, some teachers would have discouraged him. Have we changed all that? Not all. There exist in abundance, and interesting they are, medians, modes, ticks against printed 'Yes'-es, 'No'-es and 'Don't Know's', ruthless squashings of heterogeneous persons into socio-economic brackets, accounts of human behaviour with no description of any one person who behaves, of the 'sense of taste' with no reference to national and class preferences, of 'smell' with no hint of human motives which make the fortunes of fashionable scent manufacturers.

As children, many of us were forbidden to point: social psychologists who forget this prohibition incur severe criticism or pained disapproval from colleagues. I know that a certain botanist's eyes glaze with boredom at the mention of an actual flower, since moulds are his dearest love, yet he knows more about different kinds of flowers than psychologists do about the varieties of *genus homo* in their immediate vicinity. Is there a fear, in part unconscious, that some facts which obviously interest millions of non-psychologists, many of them educated, might wreck an elegant theory?

Today Personality is studied scientifically, and it is claimed that its structure and dimensions are being mapped. This is theoretically interesting, but what if the 'subject' cannot read or, though erudite, is bored, even if the enthusiastic tester thinks he ought not to be, by jigsaw puzzles, wallpaper patterns or tests of 'perseveration'? Mental 'factors' are mathematically analysed from data collected by asking subjects, not face-to-face, but, to ensure objectivity, *in absentia*, to tick or cross out printed statements. Since countless English words convey, to the native at least, several meanings—or where would our poets and humorists be?—questionnaire-framers strive, not always successfully, to avoid ambiguities. Yet to anyone who professionally judges a personality or character, many questionnaires and experiments seem unduly constricted by considerations of mathematical techniques to which the results are to be subjected. The profile that launched a thousand ships was not the top of a test-score histogram.

Pencil-and-paper methods are convenient and cheap, and examine many people simultaneously: this fact does not endear them to introverts. Such constrictions of method do not allow ambivalent reactions to be adequately described: these may occur in answers to questions about hunting, gambling, Sunday observance, 'thrillers' and the H-bomb. Readiness to reply quickly and definitely—a profitable ability in quiz competitions —need not depend on amount or depth of knowledge or respect for truth.

Obviously important in the world outside the laboratory are beauty, charm, gaiety, wit, humour, bonhomie: these are seldom mentioned in the indexes of books claiming to describe Personality. If these traits were passed through a statistical mangle, would not some of them emerge deplorably, if tidily, flattened?

Psychologists' tendencies to study groups rather than individuals may be due in part to the last twenty years' demands from the Forces. Except in special and secret work, armies seldom encourage the expression of marked individuality, and this, as scientists have found in two wars, may be disregarded by higher authority.

These criticisms take into account the great increase in the number of clinical psychologists, yet eyebrows rise occasionally at this extended use of 'clinical', which originally meant 'at the bedside'. The customary reply that, in the psychological world, 'clinical' has ceased to have medical overtones, is unconvincing: in the 1957 *American Psychologist*, resentment was expressed at a tendencious definition of psychiatry as *the* science of mind.

Let us look over that fence, or wide-meshed net, said to divide sociology from psychology. Some sociologists regard their study as explicitly excluding the individual; yet, were they with us, would Durkheim or Le Bon be the worse for studying patients in a modern mental hospital, or crowds at Wembley, Twickenham and Wimbledon?

Not long ago, after a famous sociologist had lectured to a learned society on trends, tendencies and group characteristics, one psychologist commented 'I hope he's training pupils to explain his ideas to us.' 'As if I were on the ground, wondering what those smoke-trails in the sky mean,' said another. A third remarked, 'All the time, I was hoping to hear something about Mrs Jones.' Yet some sociologists take a less dim view of her; for example, Professor David Riesman, in *Faces in the Crowd*, and Professor Edward Shils, who, discussing American Mass Culture, asserts that few of its disapproving critics know much about it at first hand. He doubts if, unless they change their ways, many empirical sociologists will get such knowledge.

'Precise and orderly as their observations might be, they are made outside a matrix of intimate experience, without the sense of empathic affinity which would enable the events which they observe to be understood as they actually occur in the lives of those who experience them.'

In America, so far as this casual reader can observe, no love is lost between novelists and sociologists. Some psychologists champion the aims of an impersonal treatment of Personality, an unsentimental view of Sentiment, not overtly, however, of an unintelligent handling of Intelligence. Physicists can describe music objectively ('Sound,' said one, 'isn't interesting; it's all arithmetic') but they are not employed, in that capacity, as music-critics. Can psychologists regard the description and assessment of a personality as the prerogative of novelists, playwrights and chair-borne library workers? Recently a literary critic praised a biography of Admiral Lord Nelson for its 'freedom from psychological probings': another, discussing Sir Harold Nicolson's *Good Behaviour*,[118] exclaimed, uncontradicted by the team, 'If a sociologist had treated this subject, how dull it would have been!' 'To an inquisitive Psychologist' was the original title of a poem which Amy Lowell dedicated to her friend Professor Walter V. Bingham.

Undiscouraged by the present cold climate, some psychological toughs remind us that psychology is the study of experience as well as of behaviour, that psychology has not gone out of its mind, or its mind out of psychology. Comparatively little light is thrown, by psychologists, on an individual's experiences of social differences, perceived, imagined or conceived, between himself and others. If we may judge from his letters, William James, that renowned introspectionist, seems to have taken for granted, and never thought of dissecting, his attitudes toward his social status and the colour of his skin. Yet—though few do—we can ask a friend who has risen in the social scale to tell us in confidence something of the processes of ascent; of scars received in the climb, prizes, pleasures, and views from the top. In some psychological quarters this phenomenological approach is once more becoming popular; Professor Robert B. MacLeod reminds us that this change is happening more rapidly in Europe than in America.

It need surprise nobody that gifted amateurs psychologize on the side-lines, using a long-focus candid camera. William H. Whyte Junior has studied middle and upper strata in America and given us the famous phrase, *The Organization Man*.[181] One editor described this book as 'peripheral' to psychology; at times while reading it I felt the storm coming nearer and that the next flash and clap might be simultaneous. Whyte maintains that Americans, once guided by the Protestant ethic, and proud of their rugged individualism, are now less rugged than they think, and so do not realize the strength and constancy of pressures tending to prevent not only the expression but even the experience of individuality. This is asserted of many American corporations, firms, universities, even churches. Integration into a group, social mixing, group-thinking (a dozen near-synonyms are in current use) contribute to a person's wordly success more than a belief that he is highly intelligent or intellectual. In floating a large research project the chief problem is how to 'sell the idea'—one has heard this phrase used of the Christian gospel—to a corporation or foundation.* This being achieved by the leader, 'other ranks' in the research army will do as they are told.

Off duty, the aspiring business executive may live in a 'packaged' community. He may expect to leave it again in two or three years, since his employers urge him to widen his experience, but this may have to be acquired in a similar community hundreds of miles away. To succeed, it is very useful to develop a 'company character'.

Whyte asserts that 'personality' tests originally designed for purely theoretical investigations are used by corporations to help to decide whether an employee who may have worked for the firm for years has the 'right personality'. The prospect of a test-ordeal on which so much depends may give him, in middle age, the jitters which afflict some children in test situations. Whyte believes that the chief aim of these tests, in certain hands, is to investigate loyalty to the firm.

A popular term, 'social engineering', begs more than one important question, for though man designs engines, no engine, so far, has designed a man.† It has been claimed that in America the spread of 'social engineering' has led, and leads, to a fiercely anti-intellectual attitude. 'Could this happen in Britain?' Whyte asked Professor Asa Briggs in a transatlantic radio discussion: his reply was that our intellectuals are still powerful and fairly deeply entrenched.

The term 'social adjustment' is less disturbing to contemplate.

---

* Cf. Chapter 8 of Jacques Barzun's *The House of Intellect*.[13]

† A friend remarks: 'Samuel Butler, indulging, in *Erewhon*, a fantasy on the evolution of machines, thought he was driving an argument to logical absurdity. The development of self-correcting and self-adapting machines may well turn our grins to grimaces.'

The most introverted railway passenger is expected to modify his behaviour to increase the comfort of the group of which he temporarily forms a part. A totalitarian regime demands much more than this. At the World Congress of Mental Health in 1953 in London, I was impressed by apparent unanimity about one aim; the individual's 'social adjustment'. To some psychiatrists who had recently been under military discipline it might have seemed the only proper social goal. Yet complete social adjustment of prisoners was the Chinese Communists' aim in the Korean war. Though old techniques were used, a new feature was the attempt to control, night and day, for months or years, a human being's material and mental environment. To survive with any comfort, the prisoner had to adjust entirely.

In most countries there is much study of the social forces tending to mould behaviour into similar forms. During the last twenty years, interest has increased in answers to such psychological questions as 'How is the Self felt?' 'What are its boundaries?' 'Do these vary, and in what ways in different ages and cultures?' 'Are developments in air and space-travel producing new problems in sociology?'

Lately, the public has been presented with more complicated practical problems of the Self, as in ethical and religious discussions of artificial insemination, of a Self's relations to Western or Eastern conventions; and now, not only to the earth, but to the sea, sky, and heavenly bodies. Dazzled by such impressive vistas, I suggest that since these subjects interest thousands of thinkers, they should not be regarded lightly by—of all people—social psychologists.

Let us now examine the present and future importance of the individual. Thousands of speakers have preached that he is important; surely, too, thousands of others believe in his utter insignificance. Eastern and Western philosophers differ on this vital issue, and every day the picture is complicated by clashes of upstart nationalism. A few reminders are revelant. In the last few years new ways have been devised of deliberately constricting the public personalities of some people and widening ('blowing-up') others. Contradictory pronouncements are made daily on the ethical, religious, moral and legal justifiability of such procedures. It therefore seemed opportune to describe psychologically some invasions of personality, in the hope that it may encourage others to discuss this vast subject. What word indicates its chief theme—'individual', 'person', 'self', 'ego'?

In previous books[130, 131] I have explained my reluctance to use 'personality' as a blanket term, obscuring many issues and encouraging avoidance of others, socially important.

'Self', 'ego' and adjectives derived from these often invite value-judgments, e.g. few people are flattered if they are called selfish or egotistical. 'Individual' serves the present purpose, even if to some minds 'individualist' is a term of praise, while to others it suggests a stiff-necked, self-willed prig, an eccentric—almost a paranoiac. What does it feel like to behave as an individual? Let me try to answer from my own experience, with no suggestion that it is important.

I choose to write these pages in a sunny garden rather than in a more convenient, quieter but darker study. It is time for tea : the decision that a good place for it is behind a hedge shows that society is not absent from my thoughts even if I want to be alone. No awareness of a promise clouds this present pleasure: I can stop writing, if I like, to admire a Constable sky. At this point of time I am unusually willing to distinguish the individual from society. Yet is this antithesis real? My present act of writing is not merely to clarify my thoughts: possible readers are kept in mind.

To set this age-old problem in a contemporary frame, I borrow from the writings of Professor Morris Ginsberg[57] and Mr Archibald Robertson.[142a] These represent contrasting, though not antithetical points of view.

Mr Robertson maintains that no real antithesis between Man and Society can be discovered, though we are familiar with phrases like 'Man is born free, but everywhere he is in chains'; 'Moral Man and Immoral Society'; and 'Individualism versus Socialism'. Readers of current books and newspapers (one might add listeners to radio talks) are often tempted to mistake the abstract for the concrete, and words for realities.* We mistake paper-opposites for real opposites, and believe that politics are about these paper-opposites. In fact, politics are about quite dif-

---

* The following story is told in more than one form : a London educational institution was described as 'that vast empire on which the concrete never settles'. The speaker, one recalls with affection, was renowned for his tendency to think abstractly.

ferent things.* Phrases like 'Man versus the State' express paper antitheses invented to conceal real opposition between certain people and certain other people.

Mr Robertson was born and bred among upper middle-class families, very much at ease in Victorian England. Asked if they were individualists or socialists, they would have chosen the individualist label. Yet in our war with the Boers people of his class enthusiastically supported the State. Any who opposed it were pro-Boers, traitors who were lucky not to be shot, and when they had to run for their lives, got no more than their deserts.

'The very word "society" means different things to different classes. To the circle in which I was brought up, "society" meant people of a certain exclusive level of means and refinement. To a working man, his "society" means his trade union.'

Professor Ginsberg, discussing this question, writes that it is fashionable to say the old antithesis is outworn:

'Nevertheless, the frequency with which this repudiation of the antithesis is repeated shows that it is far from discarded. Its continuing influence can be seen in the current arguments as to the place of psychology in the explanation of social phenomena, in the new antithesis between culture and personality, or between individual and social character. It can be seen above all in political discussions, where it appears in the form of a contrast between the good of individuals and the good of the state. We are told repeatedly that the ultimate source of conflict in the world today is to be found in the struggle between two opposed ideals, that which attached supreme value to the individual and that which subordinated his good to that of the community. While originally the term individualism seems to have been coined in express opposition to socialism, the revival of individualism in our own time is often directly intended to express opposition to "totalitarianism". In both cases there is an underlying assumption that

* A famous member of scientific committees, when asked on the radio about the wisdom of suspending H-bomb tests, replied simply that it would halt the progress of science, which ought to be kept clear of politics. Capital and small letters are hard to distinguish in spoken language, but one gathered that for him Science had a large S and politics a small p.

the opposed terms between them exhaust the possibilities, and that no midway is open.'

He adds that 'individualism' has been used to mean a feeling or attitude, or a number of traits, 'such as a tendency to turn inwards, a desire for independence, or freedom from external constraint, distinctiveness in self-expression, passing into self-will and self-absorption'.

(This suggests a speculation: might a 'tendency to turn inwards' sometimes be due, not to distaste for the physical presence of other human beings, but to the influence upon a person's thought-processes of his predominant mental imagery? Confronting a difficult situation, a verbalizer may recall maxims, regulations or laws which tell him what to do. A visualizer, activated by motives of which he may be clearly or only partially aware, may mentally turn inwards, to consult in imagination a living or dead person who, he believes, can abolish his perplexity. Then he may talk, actually or sub-vocally, to himself, his father, his God, and from this meditation emerge with a verbalized resolve leading to action. A person of this mental type may seldom wish for complete independence, but rather for clear instruction from trusted persons. He may be deemed simple by the philosophically trained thinker, but he exists in large numbers.)

When a concept of individualism dominates a sociological theory, society is conceived as an aggregate of individuals whose relations to each other are purely external. Ginsberg continues:

'The methodological theory which is dominated by individualism insists that in studying social phenomena it is best to begin with individual actions and to consider social wholes as complexes of social relationships, arising out of the behaviour of individuals, in so far as this is directed towards or away from other individuals.'

He cites an exposition of the individualist approach by Professor F. A. Hayek[70, 71] who insists that the only way to understand social phenomena is through an understanding of individual actions directed towards other people, and guided by their expected behaviour. This is surely a special use of 'understanding'. When Hayek writes, 'What we do in the social sciences is

to classify types of individual behaviour which we can understand', Ginsberg comments:

'It is interesting to note that those who consider that the aim of
the social sciences is to classify types of individual behaviour
which we can "understand" make no use of psychology. In order
to "understand" it is not necessary, we are told, to delve deeply
into human motives. We operate with motives familiar to us in
our own actions, and interpret other people's actions by analogy.
An action is directly "intelligible" if it corresponds to what we
would do in similar circumstances.

Like Professor Ginsberg, I doubt if we can interpret correctly
the actions of other people by analogy, whatever that word may
mean in this context. The actions of most romantic historical
figures were unlike those of a modern university scholar who
aspires to interpret them. How many of these students could
even interpet by analogy the screen-behaviour of a 'produced'
TV political speaker? Could an intellectually brilliant person,
living in a country not his own, really be convinced that his
motives are analogous to those of the natives?* It is entirely
arbitrary, says Ginsberg, to confine 'understanding' to what can
be learnt by unaided and untrained introspection.

Since no two human beings are alike, except perhaps in some
trait arbitrarily chosen by a psychologist, and have seldom been
reared in the same physical and mental environment and since all
perception is selective,

'In comparative sociology and psychology, the individual cannot be taken as a constant. The self consists largely of relations
to other selves, yet there is a core of individuality in each person
which is uniquely his own, and ... in the last resort is unsharable
and incommunicable. The question whether society is a sum of
its parts is meaningless; subtle internal relations involving mental references are not additive.

'When the good of the community is said to be opposed to the
good of the individual, it will be found that a sectional good is
parading in the guise of the good of the whole community, or
that the good has been falsely conceived to lie in ends which will

* In The English, are They Human?[140a] Professor G. J. Renier does not try.

not make life better for anyone, or that certain individuals claim the power to decide what is best for the rest of society.'

In this and other chapters of the present book the danger of false antitheses will be emphasized. I try to avoid them: where the reader notes failures, I trust he may take the will for the deed.

The effective study of small groups necessitates knowledge of the individual's mental processes. This fact is recognized by modern biographers, e.g. the account of Shackleton of the Antarctic by Margaret and James Fisher[50a] emphasizes a 'maternal' streak in his character. Popular discussion of Lord Montgomery's Memoirs immediately after their publication, and of his visits to Russia and Africa in April 1959, focused on his present personality, rather than on his past achievements. Yet many studies of groups seem to betray, if not a deliberate neglect, at least an unconcern with individual differences.

To assign correctly a number of individuals to a category chosen by the observer himself requires not only keen interest but also inside knowledge and psychological training. A newly-appointed parish priest may discover that the congregation of his village church is stratified socially, economically and culturally in ways which a town-dweller may find it difficult to perceive. Insulated groups, for example, may discuss affairs in words and tones intended to exclude the outsider.

A social observer, unless he has been trained to 'rub off his edges', is inevitably influenced by his bringing-up and education; e.g. a Marxist may perceive signs of what he has been taught to regard as class differences, and overlook important symbols in dress, speech and manners, if he has not moved extensively in the country which he describes, at times with assurance born of ignorance.

Many sociologists eschew the mention of personalities. Yet the relations between an individual and his group, as experienced both by him and by the other members, seem an essential consideration when attempting to understand group conduct. For example, in England, when, how and why do four strangers in a first-class railway compartment become a group?

Were I not a social psychologist, I might be baffled by many psychologists' lack of interest in the individual person. Even if the fundamental laws of mind, when discovered, prove to be identical in all humans ('At bottom, people are all alike' is a phrase which, understandably enough, amuses novelists) psychologists ought to be interested in the end-products, as well as the early manifestations of a person's basic 'drives', interacting with the physical and social environment. Professor D. W. Harding asks the disturbing question: why should early childhood experiences be assumed to be always all-important?[66]

Perhaps avoidance of considering the 'concrete particular' is partly an exhibition of intellectual pride. When conversing, many sophisticated people avoid *oratio recta*; ('I said . . . so he said . . .') knowing that actors use it to suggest that persons whose sentences they 'reproduce' are comic. (*Mrs Dale's Diary* leans heavily on this convention to distinguish middle from working class.) To render the gist of a conversation requires ability to abstract, generalize and verbalize: when this leads to a first-class Honours degree, a change in the graduate's personality sometimes follows. 'High-level' treatment of memories removes a narrator far from the reality which he may believe he is describing. A ten-minute conversation in a village group might be reported—correctly in one sense—as 'Defects in the local drains were deplored'. Yet, assuming a rate of 150 words spoken per minute, and, which is improbable, that all the speeches were solos, the total of 1,500 words probably included neither 'deplore' nor 'defective'. Condensation into *oratio obliqua* may express the formulator's personality: at times the paraphrase comments on the naïve verbosity of the person 'reported'.

We have already hinted at a tendency among psychologists, the older ones often recruited from philosophy and the younger from the physical sciences, to eschew not only the study but even the mention of the concrete case; to fear the social consequences of a reputation for liking the 'warmth and intimacy of experience', to prefer gray theory and smooth generalizations, at times insecurely supported, to regard even the true anecdote with suspicion. Few psychologists fearing an unfavourable buddy-rating would dare to speculate in print about the mental processes of some famous, well-marked but living personality, for he might ridicule the offender; and this generally silences any properly-brought-up Englishman. The use of ridicule as a means of social control is a favourite theme among anthropologists.

In contrast, the general public is so intensely interested in

persons that significant ideas for which they stand may be neglected or ignored. The organs of mass communication build up
many personalities. How many of the public who smiled at reading the reported remark of a famous scientist that he was depart-
ing to live in a free country, 'which this one isn't', were given
any idea of his valuable scientific experiments and readiness to
risk his life in causes which seemed good?

Any traveller in a country bus is compelled to hear conversation. Almost invariably it is about things and people, usually
named; hardly ever about ideas, theories, beliefs, apart from
persons alleged to hold or promulgate them. There is much
dramatization and use of direct oration. Richard Hoggart
writes:[76]

'The working-class splitting of the world into Us and Them is
. . . a symptom of their difficulty in meeting abstract or general
questions. Most people, of whatever social class, are simply not,
at any time, going to be interested in general ideas. . . . The most
important things in life, so far as the working class can see, are
other things.

'Even the simplest anecdote is told dramatically, with a wealth
of rhetorical questions, supplementary illustrations, significant
pauses and alterations of pitch. . . . They have an acute eye for
faces and ear for voices, an eye and ear which can sometimes be
fresher and truer than those of a person who filters his perceptions through his reading and discussion.'

Perhaps there is room here for a personal note. My working life
has been spent with university people of many types, in more
than one institution. One feature of their communal life, often
kind to the queer fish, cheerfully tolerated in ways unknown in
business houses, tends to promote, especially in the old don in a
male community, partial blindness and deafness to non-verbal
means of communication. In some ways, academic appearance
and ways of speech have been standardized: a gown at High
Table is expected; so is some form of 'received pronunciation'; if
this is not forthcoming, unusual speech may be tolerated, because
the deviant is now 'one of us', a member of the 'in-group'. Consequently, dons are most likely to study historical and geographical
implications of 'accent' than to evince interest in its social 'load-

ing', or in the effect this may have upon success in the outside world.

Today, middle-aged adults who enjoyed only brief schooling, no university life, but were educated in other ways, perhaps in the Forces, and abroad, may have acquired effective ways of judging personality. At times these may be more useful than those of any psychologist who sees persons through a mark-sheet darkly. The new-type university student may have increased, behind a counter or beside a restaurant table, a sensitivity, unnecessary in some common-rooms, to nuances of facial expression and voice. Many modern NCOs express themselves in ways subtler than those customary on the barrack-square, and many privates can interpret these. A country boy who 'joins up' may discover that a village girl's open countenance is easier to read than the painted face of the town dweller who learned from the 'flicks' how to 'register'. He may find her, for all that, a good sort.

Perhaps a don who is a bad mixer, an inefficient teacher, and proud of it, since it shows anxiety to get away to important works in library or laboratory, has never been so clearly aware of his persona (there are famous exceptions) as his brothers in the Navy, Army or Church, or his sister who 'models'.

Hoggart asserts that some historians overrate the part played in working-class life by political activity. These writers sometimes have an inadequate sense of the grass-roots of that life. 'The middle-class Marxist part pities and part patronizes working-class people beyond any sense of reality.'

So far as my middle-class, non-Marxist experience goes, I would agree. But a reader may suggest that this ignores the popularity, here and in America, of 'Digests'. Do they not increase interest in abstract ideas? To a certain extent they do, but ask an expert in any subject which has been 'digested' whether its coverage and fairness of judgment impressed him favourably. He may answer that most of the important 'ifs' and 'buts' have been omitted and that the thought patterns are not as elegant or well defined as the digester implied; moreover, that he knew this. Clifton Fadiman discusses the decline of attention to ideas and abstractions in America:[48a]

'. . . the faculty of attention in general is undergoing a wholesale displacement away from ideas and abstractions towards things

and techniques. .... Literary men ... (are) most gravely menaced
by the attrition or displacement of attention, but a larger class,
technicians, generals, James Burnham's "managers", certain
kinds of journalists, of government and labour bureaucrats, has
much to gain from the same phenomenon, and there is a very
large class indeed which simply feels more comfortable in a society
that does not demand from it any considerable systematic effort
of the mind. .....

'We are developing a magnificent mandarin class and a less
magnificent mental-coolie class. If the intermediate class is starved
out, a most unhealthy state of affairs will result.'

The revival of interest, by Dr Grey Walter and his colleagues[60a]
in the use, when thinking, of visual images and of words, makes
it timely to suggest, admittedly on insufficient evidence, that the
predominance of a particular type of imagery in a person may be
one basis for classifying him as a thing-thinker or a word-thinker.
Some concrete thinkers, visual and auditory, are 'bad with' words
and know it. Finding that the right words often fail to come into
consciousness when needed, such thinkers use substitutes as,
caught in a burning house, they might grab the nearest clothes.
They may suspect or envy people who use words easily.

Verbalizers and some mathematicians may regard words, numbers or symbols, because of their general import, as superior to
pictures in the mind's eye. Examiners who decide today which
child shall receive 'further education' require from him much
manipulation of words, numbers and formulae. Is it possible that
long-continued selection of verbalizers has increased the present
tendency of British philosophers to focus on the meanings of
words rather than upon man's present acts and future consequences?

To summarize: many studies of the person are being made at
present. Experiments and tests do not contribute to the understanding of unique personal experiences, and exclude the consideration of some important mental factors which elude measurement. Preference for the study of groups and neglect of the individual was officially encouraged in the last war and immediately
afterwards: it still exists. The enthusiasm for 'social adjustment'
and the multiplication of 'organization men' merit very careful
study. In contrast, bizarre experiences of self are being reported

in connection with travel under and above the earth's surface.

'Society' means very different things to different persons. In some quarters it is asserted that the concept of an antithesis between Man and Society is outworn, yet in sociology and psychology the individual cannot be regarded as a constant, since his social relations, which mean nearly everything to him, are constantly changing. While scientists tend to neglect the individual, the public interest in persons and personalities increases. This is fed, and often created, by the mass media. Their influence is partly due to the facts that abstractions and generalization are high-level mental processes and their development and practical application, products of education. Yet no social psychologist should overlook the adulation of persons and the public's readiness to accept statements of general import made by them with little or no evidence.

Having considered conflicting attitudes towards the self in different sections of society, we turn to discuss the nature of the self.

CHAPTER TWO

What is the Self?

Psychological (as distinct from metaphysical) questions are asked: How is the self experienced? In what ways is it perceived and conceived by different types of person? Introspective descriptions of the self in normal and drugged states are described. When space-travel makes new demands, how will the body-image be changed? Where is the 'empirical self' felt? Is a sharp division between awareness of self and of the environment, physical and social, an instance of verticality in a gradient usually oblique?

Such questions present themselves in new settings now that psychological relations between man, aircraft and space-ships are being actively investigated.

The following paragraph illustrates the different percepts and concepts of self which may present themselves in a few minutes.

A man is watching the gloomy results of a thaw. As he sees the slushy roads, he meditates 'I need fresh air and exercise; shall I tramp to the village? I don't want to buy anything there: I am reading comfortably and in shabby clothes. A cold wind is blowing and my tooth aches. Why not stay here? If I do, I shall feel disgraced—in my own eyes; perhaps in nobody else's. Won't an overcoat solve the difficulty about temperature and respectability? It's easier to stay here.' In this sequence of experiences, what different selves does this man perceive, imagine and conceive?

I would suggest as a first approximation to a definition of Self, 'the individual's awareness of his own existence'. Professor R. B. MacLeod writes:

'The Self is a phenomenal datum, not a category of phenomenal data. The Ego, in my thinking, is not a datum but a construct. Before we can have a sound theory of the Ego, we must have a careful phenomenology of the Self. . . .

Self and Personality are respectively the "inside" and the "outside" views of the person, not necessarily parallel. . . . The inescapable phenomenon of selfhood is the body; not the organism, but the body as it is at present in the phenomenal world. We have, tucked away in the literature of somaesthesis (awareness of the body) a great deal of information about the phenomenal body, although much of it will require interpretation. The Self has a unique characteristic; it is indispensable to all perception of objects. It is an ever-present anchorage point, about which the frameworks of space and time are organized. In a literal sense, it is the subject of all experience.'[105]

An officer of a ship which he knows is sinking, or a convalescent patient still under hospital discipline, can easily distinguish the awareness of personality[128,131] from that of Self. In both instances, he must consider not only what he feels about himself, but what spectators may see and hear in his behaviour. In this connection, observations of one's body-image are of great interest. An artist's model may have an unusually extensive image of the body. After lessons in skating and ski-running, I discovered thrilling additions to body-consciousness. To my (the writer's) focused awareness of eyes and hands was added that of thighs, hips, shoulder-blades and back. To this somaesthesis were added new varieties of kinaesthesis: they have now faded, but not irrevocably.* Recently, a walk on snow in rubber boots invited several incipient falls. As each slip was corrected, an old pride in body-control returned. A vivid body-image was described to me by a psychologist who, travelling in a plane, was warned that the wheels could not be lowered and a crash-landing was imminent.

A person's chief philosophical problems, often unverbalized, probably concern his relation to the physical world and to other humans. There is a type of individual to whom the second problem seldom presents itself vividly. To him, his Self is all-important: others are to be ignored, avoided, manipulated, trampled upon, treated like inanimate objects. He likes jokes about psychologists.

* This was written before Mr E. M. Eppel read the typescript and kindly called my attention to Wordsworth's evocation of the skater's heightened awareness of bodily sensation, in the poem 'Influence of Natural Objects', especially in the second half.[187]

Mention of the Self in a group of scientists is often regarded as in poor taste. Fifty years ago, to many minds, the declaration 'Science is objective' seemed crystal clear. To most schoolboys, and to many of their teachers, colours were 'really', or 'nothing but', ether waves. Recognition that men die to save 'the colours' might be made, but in hours devoted to religion, history, or 'Eng. Lit'. No colour-blind man (one in twenty-five) assumed that his inability to distinguish red from green was socially important, unless he proposed to drive a locomotive. It was widely believed that persons who saw or heard things that were 'not there' were themselves either 'not there' or saints. Had Joan of Arc appeared in 1910 the RAMC would probably have certified her as 'delusional', ensuring that she gave no trouble and got no publicity. An English letter-box in a dirty town was described as 'pillar-box red' even if years ago it had lost this claim. An astronomer would note details on the moon's surface, but he 'really' saw the same same moon as anyone else : he 'just' knew how and where to look. 'Real' things were in principle public property. Snow was white, though, to a 'trained' eye, it looked pink, yellow or blue; a coal-heap black, though parts of its surface flashed in the sun. How charmingly it all dates !

Before commenting on attempts to explain the relation of yourself and myself to other people and to the physical world— the selflessness of some metaphysicians' writings contrasts strikingly with their behaviour—I venture to describe ways in which, from time to time, this problem has presented itself to me. The reader may care to compare these experiences with his own.

I am writing, alone. Where is my self felt? Apparently in the eyes, which ache, and in fingers, unexpectedly stiff. The awareness makes me realize that these discomforts arise from a hitherto unnoticed electricity cut, making the room darker and colder. The locus of my self seems usually to be my head, perhaps because I conceive myself as a thinker, of sorts. I doubt if a farm worker's awareness of self is so narrow : probably it is located in his muscles, especially those which adjust him to his physical environment. He and I may regard each other ambivalently; shamefaced envy alternating with amused superiority. I wonder, when he surveys a vast neglected field, how he decides which part, and with what tools, he will tackle first. Does he use visual imagery? Or does he, waiting for orders, leave that to the master?

A recruit on parade, not yet accustomed to execute drill movements automatically, succeeds in moving off smartly: at that moment has he any awareness other than of his body and the cardinal points in his visual field? Yet imagine an old-style drill sergeant whose self 'resides' in his muscles—including those of speech—who is told that his methods must be modernized; what then will be his awareness of self? Presumably it will not resemble a barrister's who, even during his address, realizes that he must modify, unobtrusively, his line of pleading.

An unexpected injury may focus a patient's attention on a part of his body which, formerly the object of pride, is now regarded with repulsion, even hatred.

In Dr Margaret Mead's *Cultural Patterns and Technical Change*[110a] there are interesting details on the nature and limits of the body-and-self image. Such knowledge becomes highly relevant in the context of technical innovation in undeveloped societies. The supersession of the primitive hoe by the bulldozer would bring about changes in the body-image of the person trained to use both.

What is the periphery of the 'empirical self'? An easy answer is 'the skin'. Yet expensive substances are commonly applied to it by women: 'make-up' is clothing, fulfilling functions of protection, assertion of status and sex appeal. People who move from a fashionable city quarter to the country may at first perceive women's unpainted faces as unhealthy.

Whether hair is clothing is debatable, though artificial hair fulfils all the function of clothes. Hair is assumed to be part of the self, though there are different views concerning natural hair sometimes deemed 'superfluous'.[35] Some Americans smile at the 'dirty' wigs of our judges. Many persons feel slightly revolted to see their own hair when detached from the body, and in some societies, hair and nails, when removed, are destroyed or concealed lest by their use evil magic may be worked against their possessors. Here, perhaps, we see a transition from normal to fetishistic attitudes. Some mothers cherish a baby's lock of hair or first tooth. By many people, to wear a stranger's clothes is felt as personally degrading, and not everyone likes to hire clothes even for a ceremony. Yet a loved one's dress may be treasured.

Erving Goffman[59a] describes the social effects of 'stripping' poor patients who enter some mental hospitals, and the significant moment when a nun's worldly garments are confiscated. Shoes, however 'good', wear out, and with them may vanish important symbols of the class to which their wearer, if now poor, still refers herself. Note, too, the significance of clothes as gifts. Handkerchiefs, ties, gloves, scarves are regarded as only semi-intimate: to give 'inner' garments might be interpreted as a sign of desired closer relations. Flowers, though the recipient may wear them publicly (this act has its meaning), do not last, so their symbolism is less liable to be misunderstood: in some countries, gifts of flowers are expected on so many social occasions that their significance becomes trivial.

At first glance, it seems impossible to disbelieve that you or I are sharply distinguished from the outer world: can we not show our privacy by just walking indoors? Gardner Murphy points out that the gradient from person to person may be steep or gradual: this is suggested by data from many studies; physiology, genetics, behaviour psychology, the psychology of immediate experience.

Is there not an obvious spatial boundary between person and non-person: the capsule, the skin? In vital processes like respiration, the living system within the skin is not sharply separable from the non-living system in which it is bathed; the air in the red-blood cells can be regarded either as part of us or as part of our environment, indifferently. We are part of our environment, yet protecting ourselves against it through special inner patterns of physical forces.

To many, especially Western, thinkers, the gradient between the self and the environment seems vertical. A generation ago, many psychologists regarded all events as necessarily happening either inside or outside the self.

All proposed concepts of self seem certain to be disapproved by many thinkers, possibly for personal as well as general reasons. I think that though concepts of extraversion and introversion become increasingly complex, the underlying ideas help to explain personal enthusiasms for and antipathies to certain theories of self. Can we, for example, distinguish between the selflessness of some introverts and the unselfishness of some extraverts?

Murphy wrote 'The notion that we tend to melt into our en-

vironment aroused opposition; perhaps proportional to our culturally ingrained conviction that there must be something utterly
our own', before excitement was noticeable when the public
realized that artificial insemination by an anonymous donor, a
practice praised in treatment of the lower animals, raised, in its
relevance to human relations, not only general religious, ethical,
legal and aesthetic problems, but disturbing personal-psycho-
logical questions.

Murphy says that in considering the ways in which you or I
view the barrier, we encounter the problem of the awareness of
our own individuality . . . the consciousness of self.

How does this awareness develop? Murphy says 'through the
observation of body surfaces, muscular contractions, the sound
of the voice. . . . By constant comparison of them with other
entities observed in other persons, an empirical self is woven and
given abiding structure. This self . . . represents a relative continuity from the cradle to the grave, is given a name, a social position and a sense of responsibility, and around it in time cluster
the goals, values and norms and ideals which give meaningful
purposive continuity to life . . . the self becomes a loved object;
Freud's narcissism being the clearest of the Western formulations
of such self-love.'cf. 168

'There is, however, constant reciprocity between the image of
the self and the image of others; and this means that fundamentally, from the point of view of an empirical psychology, the con-
tours of the self are often blurred, and the distinction between the
self and the not-self indistinct.'

In this connection, the symbiosis of lovers comes to mind. But
is a sharp delineation of one's self ever achieved? Extreme mental
illness may perhaps cause it. Professor D. O. Hebb reports that

'merely taking away from a healthy university student for a few
days the usual sights, sounds and bodily contact can shake him
right down to the base, can disturb his personal identity, so that
he is aware of two bodies (one hallucinatory), and cannot say
which is his own, or perceives his personal self as vague and ill-
defined; something separate from his body, looking down on

where it is lying on the bed, and can disturb his capacity for critical judgement, making him eager to listen to and believe any sort of preposterous nonsense'.

In all societies which have been scientifically studied, many types of awareness exist in which the self is not distinctly differentiated, and sharp isolation is an extreme instance. Many psychologists are reluctant to investigate such phenomena. Some causes of their feet-dragging may be the vigorous individualism of Western history, the tendency to leave such problems to philosophers and students of religion, and fear of losing caste among positivist scientists. 'In this instance, and in so many others in the history of science, fear can actually cripple the types of investigation which would give true unity and resolution to what have proved otherwise to be insoluble problems.'[116]

Psychologists may learn much about the boundaries of the self from airmen, including gliders. It is not easy for a landlubber to decide the point at which an airman's self-awareness, described by writers of different types—Exupery, Hillary, Shute—become of special psychological interest. In World War I, high-ranking officers concerned with discipline had unusually anxious moments, for so much depended on the skill, rapid reaction, dash and recklessness of boys with a life-expectation of a few weeks. Nearly forty years ago, a scientist seconded to the Royal Flying Corps told me that on the darkest days of the war some officers, too old to fly, may have encouraged in the boys the attitude of 'let us eat and drink for tomorrow we die', and assumed that a pilot's personal loyalties would be attached closely to his nearest colleagues. Investigation of group-morale had not reached the complexity now familiar to psychologists. One reads that in World War II, some members of an aircrew tended to regard it as their social unit, and members even of similar crews as outsiders. Contrast the nature and distribution of the sentiments of a married man with a family, in peace-time, with those of a boy fighter-pilot in war. Some city clerks and bank employees today could make such a comparison between their own sentiments in 1940 and 1961.

Numerous novels, plays and radio-scripts describe the wartime airmen's and airwomen's feelings and complicated social relationships. Oftener than most people they had to relate their selves to a rapidly changed physical and social environment. In August 1958 it was authoritatively stated that in this country good air stewards are harder to find than good air 'hostesses'. The glamorization of the latter, assisted by attractive-coloured pictures and courses in voice control,* is an interesting subject.

An article, 'The Psychological Relationship between Man and Aircraft', by T. H. G. Ward,[176] outlines problems and hints at others which arise when the bird-man's unusual life is considered. We learn, unsurprised, that few air pilots are naturally introspective. Deviants would find, did they not suspect it, that their group's inhibitions and conventions hardly encourage Proustian descriptions of experience. Scratch an airman: you may find the stage-personality of Jimmy Edwards.

Mr Ward, knowing his Freud and accepting 'Eros' in the spirit in which it was meant, agrees that the love of flying may have erotic roots. Acquaintance with early airmen's affectionate terms for parts of their apparatus and equipment makes one reluctant to question this.

It is believed that many instruments, if employed expertly and habitually, in time come to be regarded as extensions of the user's body. Instances are the tailor's scissors, the painter's brush, the skater's blade. Ward asserts that for successful flying this feeling of 'one-ness' with the machine is necessary, especially in a beginner's simple aircraft. When learners are introduced to planes progressively larger and more complex, the feeling of harmony with the machine, now regarded as the not-self, may be more like that of an expert dancer with his partner. They are, in a sense, equals, and though at times they seem a unity, each can break away or control the number and nature of signals to the other. But when a pilot enters a huge modern plane, he must not regard it as an inimical person, threatening inescapable constrictions on his freedom, but as a collection of inanimate objects, each one of which, if all is well, will behave predictably. Consequently the ritual, by others or by himself, of inspecting, adjusting and checking the machine's parts becomes impressive and obsessive. Perhaps the movements in such 'readying', indispensable even if

* In September 1959, talent scouts were said to be preferring air-hostesses with Scottish and North-country accents. An impression of greater friendliness and intelligibility seemed to be sought for; a tribute perhaps to Gracie Fields, Wilfred Pickles and other personalities.

simple, resemble processes in danger-areas of a certain war-time ordnance filling factory, where there was an impressive resemblance between the attitudes of the girl making these adjustments, and that of a celebrant in a religious rite.

If some readers grumble 'Keep psycho-pathology out of this; a successful aviator is surely the antithesis of a neurotic!' this illustrates the ambiguity of 'neurotic'. Ward mentions the 'indispensable' rabbit's-foot—a distinguished pilot refused to fly unless his own was found—and the spot of chewing-gum which 'must' be on the dashboard.

Pierre Janet indicated that many religious rituals are socially approved obsessions, which enable a believer, when amongst believers, to behave 'sanely'. Some people believe that to belong to a highly ritualized body, like the Jews or Roman Catholics, wards off worries which in a non-religious person might become obsessive. Many a believer does not hesitate to inconvenience others if this allows him to obtain satisfaction by carrying out his religious duties. An orthodox Jewish member of a non-religious committee may request that Saturday meetings shall be held after sunset. Though on a Sunday a Scot may be prepared to fight a battle, he may deny himself and others the pleasure of a game of golf.* The characteristic technically known as intolerance of ambiguity may be regarded by some as a sign of strong will; by others as undue fear of mental conflict.

A feeling of physical separation from the earth, sometimes experienced by air pilots at high altitudes, is discussed by B. Clark and A. Graybiel.[36] A hundred and thirty-seven jet pilots were interviewed. All had flown solo above 40,000 feet. Thirty-five per cent had experienced 'break-off'; only twenty-three per cent had heard it discussed. A number asserted that the experience was very personal, not the sort of thing that pilots talk about. Some feared that to confess to such an experience would evoke descriptions like 'corny' or 'silly': one said, 'I haven't got that poetic yet.'

They described being isolated, detached, or physically separated from the earth: 'It seems so peaceful—like you are in another world.' 'I feel like . . . I have broken the bonds from the terres-

* A friend adds that in the Outer Hebrides during the early part of World War II many of the islanders were incensed at the troops working on Sundays, even at the height of the Battle of the Atlantic.

trial sphere.' 'I feel like a giant.' 'I feel something like a king.'
Three reported that they felt nearer to God. Some were unhappy
until they got to a lower altitude, needing an important objective
to take the mind off the new experience.

W. Bridgeman's description[28] is interesting:

'61,000. I have left the world. There is only the ship to identify
myself with; her vibrations are my own. I feel them as intensely
as those of my body. There is a kind of unreality mixed with
reality that I cannot explain to myself . . .'

'What is my Self?' is harder to answer today than it was fifty
years ago, since many scientists outside psychological circles are
studying the Self.

It is unlikely that any member of an academic psychology
department could cover the USA to collect information on any
subject in the ways available to the *New Yorker's* 'Reporter
at Large'. One of these, Daniel Lang, reports exciting researches,
in the Armed Forces, aircraft firms and universities (the order is
perhaps significant) into the nature of the Self. 'Scientists are
puzzled about what to do with the one technically unimprovable
element in space-travel: Man.' So psychologists are reminded of
their proper study.

What sort of person is specially suitable for this new locomo-
tion? Mice, dogs and monkeys keep any introspections to themselves, even though two of the last-named who arrived back
from space on May 28, 1959, were described (by man) as having
been happy.* In selecting a space-man or woman the volunteer's
motives are of importance, both for theory and practice. At different levels in different persons, self-sacrifice may express clear
self-awareness, yet psychiatrists, Army officers and expedition
leaders know that behind the decision may lie a mixture of conscious and unconscious motives. A desirable space-passenger will

* On this, Mr E. M. Eppel comments: 'The claim that the monkeys were happy
is interesting. (One died soon after return.) One monkey was trained by Pavlovian technique to press a morse key. She didn't do it (on the journey). Yet,
according to "learning theory", the only thing that can rapidly bring about
the complete extinction of a well-established conditioned reflex is a severe
trauma (or brain shock). It appears then, that the monkey was both "happy"
or "unaffected" and at the same time severely traumatized. This seems a remarkable piece of "double-think".'

remain sane for a long time, though assailed by unpredictable, terrifying changes, not only in the environment but in himself. In a set-up which makes a fun-fair's haunted house seem homely, who knows what *mens sana in corpore sano* can mean?

Anyone who has worked with introverted scientific researchers knows that to them prolonged physical and mental contact with human beings whom they have not chosen as companions may be repellent, even terrifying. If a proposed 'huddle' is to last for weeks, selectors may find it useful to consult explorers, prisoners of war and others about the type of person who 'sticks it' best, and about means which they have devised for keeping themselves sane.* To quote communications from survivors who experienced World War I, a mathematician found solace in studying Heisenberg's Principle of Uncertainty: a journalist enjoyed Colette's more predictable sketches of Paris life.

Put in popular terms, the chief question is 'What kind of person is to be sought?' Researchers have distinguished many types of body structure and function, temperament, character and disposition, but little correlation between these patterns of 'factors' has been demonstrated. A few common-sense hypotheses are available, though in this very uncommon space-world, earth-dwellers' pretensions are to be supported. A terrestrial business chief who lives to a tight five-minute schedule, though miserable in an environment where the clock is irrelevant, might be adaptable to a sedentary life, yet, since the journey could be long, a Buddhist monk or an Eskimo might be a safer bet.

Now that *Nautilus* has sailed under the North Pole, much is known about social requirements if a large crew, in unusual circumstances, is to be happy. What size ought the space-ship's crew to be? In a group of five or more, other things being equal, desires to conform produce a stable social pattern, but in a smaller group individuals 'tend to attack the business in hand with greater zest and intelligence'.

In submarine crews, the mood seems to be chiefly boredom, interrupted by moments of stark terror. But all the senses, even if transmitting unusual messages, are in action, and fed from the environment. Of this, the juke-box may form an important part. An explorer who had spent weeks alone under frozen ground to make meteorological observations described to us his joyful social

* Cf. Edith Bone, *Seven Years' Solitary*, 1957, London, Hamish Hamilton.

experience of listening to famous London dance bands on the radio. But in a crew of two, 'familiarity can breed feelings even stronger than contempt', as Gontran de Poncius, a French trader-anthropologist, has described in *Kabloona*.

A first-priority problem for the solitary traveller in space would be the best way of using the time on his hands. His senses must be maximally stimulated. His time must be programmed: suggested work-making devices are study-courses, playing pin-ball, listening to records. Complications will arise, e.g. the relative attractions of such pastimes for different types of extravert and introvert, and the variability of intelligence among members even of a civilized, sophisticated community.

Anyone who has remained long in the silent room of a laboratory will know how disturbing the sounds made by his own body can be: an expert thinks that to some space-travellers their breathing might sound as loud as Niagara. The experience of being cut off from other humans can be so terrifying that even a psychiatrist, who volunteered to enter a silent room, in a matter of minutes was so disturbed that he had to be released, muttering that he had faced something in himself that he hadn't known about before. A predictable result of isolation and complete silence is irruption of hallucinations of vision and hearing. The psychologist's task may be to convince the space-man in advance that in such conditions his experiences will be normal. In the early stages of World War I, the misery of many soldiers would have been lessened had they, and some of their doctors, been briefed on this subject. Strong drugs to combat fatigue may, after temporary success, produce hallucinations.

Introspective evidence from subjects in space-ships tethered to the ground, or laboratory 'mock-ups', is of first-rate importance. And since it is believed that 'man's functional system cannot be fooled by gimmicks and gadgets', though numerous experiments are being carried out by biochemists, radio-biologists, sanitary engineers, astrobiologists and psychologists, it seems clear that wherever he is, man must have air, food and intellectual and physical activity. Psychologists 'tend to doubt whether a man can roam extraterritorially for years, months, or even weeks, without going batty'. Sociologists, too, suggest problems, e.g. how long would a separation in space justify divorce?

From experiments on sensory deprivation some psychologists

conclude that, contrary to a belief that a successful solitary traveller ought to be introverted, accepting temporarily the boundaries of his new little world, in these experiments, the introvert broke down soonest: the extravert, more strongly orientated to people and the external world, can tolerate the 'shut-off' feeling more readily. (Yet is not the hunting man who is confined to bed after an accident apt to be unusually restless?)

Must the space-traveller always be a man? Daniel Lang asserts (Peter Arno would scarcely contradict) that women have notoriously strong ties to reality, and could probably stand long periods of loneliness better; yet a brick follows this bouquet: 'they are content to while away the hours dwelling on trivia'.

Inspired by such thoughts, speculators have suggested that the ideal space-voyager would be a female midget reared in the Andes (14,000 feet above sea level) and educated in physics to Ph.D. level. It is urged that a knowledge of astronomy and medicine would be helpful, and that an anthropologist-linguist could communicate especially well with inhabitants of remote celestial bodies. So much the better, too, if he or she had powers of extra-sensory perception, or were an Eastern mystic.

(If this summary reads like an article in the old-style *Punch*, guying all new ideas on principle, one might remember that it was the *New Yorker* which suspended its regular issue to publish in detail John Hersey's uncomfortable facts about Hiroshima.)

If a large space-ship were to be built, what size of crew would prove most efficient and congenial? Factors making for harmony are not necessarily those promoting efficient action. Obviously an important question here is what the mission is trying to do: perhaps its several aims may be incompatible.

When a five-man crew was experimentally isolated for five days, as time wore on, the men, whose talk was recorded, revealed an almost obsessive preoccupation with food: 'It was on their minds three-quarters of the time they were awake.' The kind of suitable food—algae perhaps—is being discussed by scientists. Resultant action will have interesting psychological implications: diets favoured by Shaw and Chesterton are regarded by some as hints for a theory: Gandhi, Montgomery and Dr Barbara Moore are names fresh in memory. One hears speculations, based on the records of similar experiments, concerning the content of explorers' dreams, yet between home-based 'guinea pigs' and distant explorers there is a significant difference: the former know they will get home, and soon.

The effects of weightlessness are less open to speculation. Since the passenger, the air surrounding him, the warm carbon dioxide he exhales, will weigh nothing, he must learn to exhale deliberately and forcibly. All objects not fastened down—map, flashlight, pencil—will float freely, subjecting him to a haphazard crossfire. He must drink from a plastic squeeze-bottle, to prevent liquid from entering his nostrils, for 'a mere sneeze could propel the victim violently against the cabin wall and result in possible injury. . . . What would be a normal step on earth would . . . send the stepper sailing across the cabin or somersaulting wildly in the air'.

Human beings react to the experience of weightlessness in different ways, which it would be profitable to analyse, since reactions to ordinary sea-sickness are strikingly varied. Subjects who have seen things, even their own feet, float free without effort, are incredulous or slightly amused. Some jet-plane pilots, escaping gravity effects for as long as thirty seconds, find the experience extremely unpleasant, accompanied by nausea, sleepiness, weakness, sweating and/or vertigo. On different flights the reactions of the same individual have varied. Physical and mental results in long voyages can at present only be imagined. Without the task of resisting gravity, muscles will grow flabby. Lacking the pull of gravity, the fluid in the semi-circular canals of the ear would float freely: this would disturb, perhaps gravely, the sense of balance.

A man's body-image might be lost; indeed the architecture of his skeleton might change. As for his general orientation:

'In space, there is no air and no sea, so most of the pilot's old indicators won't mean a thing up there. He will have no horizon to look out on, he will be engulfed by blackness, for space has none of the air-particles that diffuse the sun's rays and give us our daylight. There will be no sound and no awareness of movement. So he will have a great deal of time on his hands. To tackle the question of human performance one has to deal with the whole spectrum of personality, from a genius to an African bushman, say; a simple fellow with a stomach that tells him he's hungry and eyes that tell him when the sun goes down.'

All this seems alarming, but some scientists think that if a man were given a small dose of the 'stress hormones', like adrenalin, the dangerous effects of anxiety might be brought more or less under control.

Some readers may find these assertions hard to believe. By the time this book appears, some of them may be surpassed in picturesqueness. The individual's perception and conception of the Self have never before been tampered with so extensively, or so often.

In some British regions 'I' is seldom heard. Erving Goffman[59a] notes that Shetlanders, who use it less than do Scots from the mainland, are shocked by its frequency in American visitors' speech. At one time, English schoolboys were warned against using 'I' in an essay. Some English autobiographies of the period were impersonal, as if the events described obeyed only the laws of physics. A college 'succeeded' prep school and public school: these institutions appear casually to have engulfed the narrator, who happened to be there. Later, a Fellowship and a Chair were offered and accepted. Such modesty has caused smiles in American and Continental critics.

Today, autobiographies are often criticized merely as 'literature', a term used arbitrarily to include and exclude so much. Freud has altered some critics' outlooks: his concepts help one to appreciate the littlenesses of the great, and the significance of childhood experience: Richard Church's *Over the Bridge* is an outstanding example. But the pendulum seems to be swinging back. A BBC critic recently praised a Life of Admiral Lord Nelson for its 'lack of psychological probing', yet his character was neither simple nor transparent.

The autobiography to be described has several unique features. In 1934, a young Englishwoman, 'Joanna Field', published her diary, concerned not with external events, but with her reactions to them. A *Life of One's Own*[50] has been republished in the USA as one of a select group of 'paper-backs' intended for students of psychology. No comparable book seems to have appeared, though there have been autobiographies influenced by psychoanalysis.

Joanna Field explored 'the no-man's land between the dark kingdom of the psychoanalyst and the cultivated domain of conscious thought'. She deliberately chose to introspect without supervision or help, and temporarily to keep her findings private.

At that time, the former activity was unfashionable. Behavourists implied that reports, even of practised introspectionists, would be dubious, since independent validation, in the nature of things, was impossible. Freudians dutifully ignored dream analyses not made under a true believer's supervision: Freud's auto-analysis was above the law. John B. Watson, in his time a valiant anti-introspectionist, once confessed to having, when young, used visual imagery to design apparatus, but possibly thought that about this early little mistake the less said the better: perhaps he knew his *Midshipman Easy*.

Now Joanna Field, wanting to discover and to describe standards of value truly her own, made this 'offbeat study in a minor key'. She had been impressed by the gap between knowing and living, between learning from the senses and from reason. Perhaps —in brackets—I may suggest illustrations. (An intelligent person needs no painful shock to teach him that electric apparatus, before it is repaired, should be disconnected from the mains, and the pamphlet supplied with it will usually remind him. But though he may understand handbooks, none can tell him what it feels like to make a clean swallow-dive.)

She distinguished two kinds of observation; 'narrow-focus', 'seeing life as if from blinkers, with the centre of awareness in my head'; and 'wide-focus', 'knowing with the whole of my body, which quite altered the perception of what I saw'. (The ski-runner's body appreciates the significance of snow-shadows.) Narrow focus is the way of reason, but wide focus makes for happiness. She remarks that the hardest task for objective reasoning is to understand its opposite: this may surprise nobody who has lived with an objective reasoner. Her warning 'Let no one undertake such an experiment who is not prepared to find himself more of a fool than he thought' is like Freud's: the man who relates his dreams to others must resign himself to being regarded as the biggest blackguard among them.

She notes that most dialogue is dull when you think of what is said as information, but entrancing when you try to follow the mind behind it. Under 'What comes into my head' she records common fears, seldom confessed to others, e.g, that important people to whom she bears an introduction may think she does not know how to behave properly ... of uncertainty about tips expected by porters, bell-boys, etc. She learns 'to let the senses

D

roam unfettered by purpose; to hold the interfering brain in leash'. (Light is cast here on Pierre Janet's psychasthenics, C. G. Jung's introverts, and David Katz's 'persons who try too hard'.*) The following sentences gain in force by not being expressed technically :

'Why had no one told me that the function of will might be to stand back, to wait, not to push?'

'I realize how dependent I may be on what people will think of me.'

'My wandering thoughts still contained childish distortions because they dealt with subjects that I had never really tried to put into words. What would happen to ideas which were never talked of, because I should feel too ashamed?'

'Rodin's Le Penseur well represented my first idea about thought, for he is making such a to-do about his thinking.'

For our present purposes, this series of introspections is more relevant than those in Aldous Huxley's The Doors of Perception since most of his references are to mescalin intoxication. Yet his comparison of mescalin experiences with those of his ordinary life casts new light on the nature of the self : this can be seen in the following passages :

'(For the moment, mescalin had delivered me from) . . . the world of selves, of time, of moral judgments and utilitarian considerations, the world (and it was this aspect of human life which I wished, above all else, to forget) of self-assertion, of cocksureness, of over-valued words and idolatrously worshipped notions.'

'In my present state, awareness was not referred to an ego; it was, so to speak, on its own. This meant that the physiological intelligence controlling the body was also on its own. For the moment that interfering neurotic who, in waking hours, tries to run the show was blessedly out of the way.'

'Mescalin, unlike alcohol, does not drive the taker into the kind of uninhibited action which results in brawls, crimes of violence and traffic accidents. A man under the influence of mescalin quietly minds his own business.'

* In a personal communication: the problem is implied in his presidential address to the International Congress of Psychology, 1951, Stockholm; 'The Limits of Safety'.

To summarize: the individual's awareness of his existence, and the relation of self to personality and to the body-image, have been discussed in the light of recent researches. The self's periphery and the gradient between self and the environment often change. The view that the self is especially important is characteristic of many forms of Western and Christian thought. Facts about self-awareness in unusual conditions are reported by airmen and subjects of experiments in 'space-ship' models. Introspective accounts of self from normal and drugged subjects are also available.

If psychological discussions of the self, e.g. William James's seventy-year-old chapter, are read today, it is evident that recently new problems have been formulated and old ones presented in new ways. An extreme extrovert, 'unselfconscious' in the popular sense, crashes through many social situations which would embarrass or distress ordinary people. Introverts may view his behaviour with resignation or amusement. An air pilot is usually more clearly aware of the physical environment, including his plane, than of himself, yet some describe 'cut-off' and quasi-mystical experiences. In these unearthly settings, problems of parapsychology cannot be ignored.

CHAPTER THREE

Psychological Approaches to Personality

When 'It's only human nature' is used to praise, blame or excuse actions, an individual may reasonably object that though his nature is human, he seldom behaves in certain ways popularly assumed to be 'natural'. Attribution to all human beings of 'instincts' of aggressiveness and acquisitiveness would be less widespread if the reports of anthropologists were better known. Today, commonly accepted criteria of abnormality or deviance are being closely scrutinized.

Mass methods of psychological research are convenient, but obscure knowledge of the nature of the individuals examined. There is considerable difference between current methods of studying the person. For selecting these, there may be psychological reasons, including the dictates of fashion and the researcher's idiosyncrasies, e.g, temperament, cultural, political and national orientations.

Non-psychologists occasionally ask 'Aren't all psychologists interested in persons?' An honest reply would be 'No'. The tendency of some psychologists to ignore, and not accidentally, the study of the individual, is significant. Yet nobody has forbidden any psychologist to introspect or to assess as important his own 'vivid irreducible stuff that to him constitutes immediately certain and trustworthy knowledge'. If he has not been scared in early life by the assertions of crude behaviourists, confident utterances of extraverts may suggest the question 'Does it seem like that to me?' After such reflection, he may revise his own values, but not always. When he hears important personalities declare gambling to be 'natural' or even 'instinctive', he may marvel at the heap of begged questions underlying this simple statement. His omission to learn bridge has protected him from many a dull card-party. It does not appear that any psychologist has obtained testimony from non-gamblers to discover how far their lack of enthusiasm may be due to religious teaching, parental example, or general boredom with the idea of unnecessary competition. Today, many English teachers are kind to a pupil who dislikes ball games, for the school doctor may have examined the boy's eyes. Many boys, if not urged that way, are not noticeably competitive. Anthropologists describe extant communities where competition seems to us, and even more to Americans, extremely lackadaisical.[92a]

I think it probable that many readers would be more interested in Helen Keller's *The Story of My Life*[90] than in a discussion of trends, tendencies and factors in the minds of a large population. A psychologist might find it difficult to discover and grade the significance of her mental 'factors'. In conversation with her, when one of us mentioned that a cartoonist had given a mediaeval figure Sir Winston Churchill's outsize cigar, she asked 'Isn't that called an anachronism?' That this highly intelligent, cultured, blind-deaf person could form such a concept offers many problems.

Personal documents of significance have been produced by leading psychologists. G. W. Allport writes:

'In a certain sense, nearly all of the classical productions in psychological science are but the personal records of their authors. Goethe's *Farbenlehre* is nothing more than an account by an intellectual giant of his private, personal experience. Helmholtz, in his incomparable *Physiologische Optik*, wrote little more than the autobiography of one pair of eyes: and even later in the laboratory era, Ebbinghaus's extraordinary experiments were almost exclusively a record of his own mnemonic abilities and of his enviable patience.

I do not presume to judge if examination of the world's psychological publications in the last decade would suggest a revision of Allport's views, published nearly twenty years ago, but when historians, anthropologists and political scientists, seeking deeper knowledge of the person, turn to Freud, is it not *faute de mieux*? Often he seemed concerned to demonstrate that John Smith is 'really' exemplifying laws governing the mutual activities of the Ego, Id and super-ego.

A human being can be interested in and attend to events in two ways: he may be concerned with a single happening, or classify his experiences, and contemplate emerging general principles. To these contrasted forms of knowledge W. Windelband gave the names *idiographic* and *nomothetic*.[182] Some historians favour the first; most scientists the second. Allport, holding that psychologists not only can but should use both these modes, has aroused a marked difference of opinion. Some psychologists maintain that unless their aim is nomothetic, they are not acting as scientists. This is one view, perhaps a little dated, of scientific method: yet neither affirming it three times, nor nailing it to the laboratory door over 'Here I stand' makes it true, or, in the human sciences, universally workable.

Fielding's Parson Thwackum, when he mentioned religion, meant the Christian religion, and not only the Christian religion, but the Protestant religion, and not only the Protestant religion but the Church of England. Psychologists who have no intention of being thwacked ask, 'What kinds of material does a psychologist who proceeds in a rigid "scientific" way select as data suitable for statistical treatment?' These are records of the experiences (of sight, sound, touch, smell, taste, etc; but usually of sight) of one person. Some of these records, not always the most characteristic, lend themselves, often after some pressure, to quantification. Others, less obliging, for years systematically neglected by experimenters and testers, may seem to young students irrelevant, even non-existent, for nobody has mentioned them in lectures or set an examination question on them. For example, a printed sentence may carry, for the reader, only one meaning, and framers of good questionnaires see to it that no *double entendre* appears. Various intonations of spoken English may convey deliberately several hints (nine have been recorded for one nine-word sentence) to a hearer born and brought up here. Would he discriminate as many nuances if the words were spoken by a middle-West American or an Australian? How many shades are appreciated by an erudite foreigner, just arrived, who has studied our printed language for years? This is written with no chauvinistic conceit. Occasionally when I hear a foreigner making a public speech in correct English, I wonder if he means to sound as he does to me sarcastic, ironical or bitter, and if the speech-melody he is now using, perhaps natural in his own language, would convey none of these unpleasing impressions to his compatriots.

Chemists and physicists, too, research with selected material but usually they know why some substances have been chosen and others rejected, and feel free to criticize proffered reasons. Are we sure that the psychologist always declares the reasons, other than convenience, for his selection? A reviewer, casting a baleful eye on an account of some claims to 'objective' approaches to personality, bluntly called the methods 'card-stacking'.

Allport writes: '. . . to the layman, the chief fault with psychological science seems to be its willingness to pile abstraction upon abstraction, with little regard for the concrete personal life. Unless concrete psychology progresses along with abstract psychology the discipline is likely to run wild. . . . Mass methods of research do little to engender understanding or respect for the individual person.'

Let us now consider the activities of 'personality psychologists'.

Some workers in general psychology regard psychologists who study personality as 'dissident rebels; grumblers at the existing state of affairs'. Personality theorists—to paraphrase Hall and Lindzey*—both in medicine and in experimental science, have rebelled against conventional ideas and practices, typical methods and restricted research-techniques, prematurely accepted theories and parochially conceived normative problems. The fact that personality theory has never been deeply embedded in the main stream of academic psychology has tended to free it from the grip of conventional preoccupations concerning human behaviour, but has not subjected it to some of the discipline and responsibility for systematic formulation which the well-socialized psychologist inherited.

'At a time when the experimental psychologist was concerned with such questions as the existence of imageless thought, the speed with which nervous impulses travelled, specifying the content of the normal-conscious-human mind, deciding whether there was localization of function within the brain, the personality-theorist was concerned with why certain individuals developed crippling neurotic symptoms in the absence of organic pathology, the role of childhood trauma in adult adjustment, the conditions under which mental health could be regained, and the

* In writing this chapter I have been greatly helped by G. S. Hall and Gardner Lindzey's *Theories of Personality*.[63a]

major motivations that underlay human behaviour. Thus, it was the personality theorist, and only the personality theorist, who in the early days of psychology dealt with questions which to the average person seem to lie at the core of a successful psychological science.'

These can be easily listed; some are popular enough to disturb many academic psychologists. Socially significant, for example, is the enormous success of Shaw's *Pygmalion* and the musical play, *My Fair Lady*, based on his fifty-year-old lay sermon. Equally important is the fact that in many parts of England a person is socially 'placed' as soon as he speaks: even 'branded on the tongue'. Class differences exist in American speech too: if this fact has impressed social psychologists in that country, the news does not seem to have travelled across the Atlantic.

Since some personality theorists rebel against what is called (perhaps only as a result of head-counting) orthodox psychology, it is not surprising to find marked differences of opinion among them. Some consider it legitimate to abstract and analyse, to examine only a small part or segment of the socially-behaving person; e.g. some problem of his hearing or vision: others regard him as a total individual. Of these latter, some emphasize that each act he performs; e.g. 'intelligently' or 'morally', can be properly understood only against the background provided by his simultaneous acts: others maintain that the organism is inextricable from the physical environment—the 'field'—in which it behaves.

Ordinarily, when we notice a person's behaviour, we comprehend the 'field' in which it happens. But such empathy is not always possible: a psychotic's meaningless gesture may be meaningful for him. A greeting like the military salute or the Continental male kiss, given at the 'wrong' time or in the 'wrong' place, may embarrass and puzzle a recipient ignorant of social anthropology.

Now we face a problem viewed differently by many psychologists and anthropologists; uniqueness. One need not be unduly introspective to realize that a sense of human uniqueness may depend on one's subjective frame of reference. A determinant of this feeling, or of its near-opposite, 'belonging', is membership of a culture or group. The possessor of a television set in Britain may realize that he has exiled himself from today's world of sound-radio, with its full-length presentation of symphonies, of new music, of foreign languages and of talks which viewers are apparently believed to be incapable of grasping. To consider self-consciousness as of minor importance seems unpsychological, in view of the fact that awareness of one's self in vivid contrast with the selves of others is common, for example, when the young regard the old, and vice versa.

Different students of personality vary considerably in their approaches, viewing with distaste the blinkers and ear-plugs with which, they think, some other psychologists study the 'same' subject. One psychologist may ask, 'Do short-focus mental testers never step back to admire, or ponder the fact that other people admire, a beautiful face or voice; never wonder if a certain person meant what he said, was teasing or flattering when he assumed (or pretended to) that his hearer had a sensitive ear and considerable knowledge of the language used?' If so, why does this personal sensitivity appear so seldom in their writings? Why this preoccupation with the average man? Can it lead to totalitarianism? The average man himself, who is often dull and knows it, seems to admire the un-average film-star or explorer, and avidly reads and hears about Napoleon, Byron and Queen Elizabeth I; not to mention Dick Turpin and Buffalo Bill.

Some psychologists, thus chidden, might reply that hard cases make bad law, that all human beings, however different, have a measurable height, weight and perhaps IQ; that the type of scientist with whom they wish to be classed is proud to ignore the single case, and may now even be losing interest in the planet on which he lives. If you know the world-outlook of a student of personality you may learn much about the reasons, conscious and unconscious, why he chooses certain data and methods and avoids others. Professor David C. McClelland writes[110] that different perspectives in personality theory seem to be in part, projections, e.g. the product of the author's personal and cultural orientations as well as of the data on which they are presumably based. . . .

R. A. Clark[63a] warns psychologists against borrowing hypothetical examples from novels. They may tempt one to

'a careful analysis of individuals' reactions to situations created in imagination. These may create problems which do not exist in nature. We human beings are subtle enough to populate the world with all kinds of personalities which do not exist in fact. Should we worry about devising a psychology of personality for the products of our imagination? We should perhaps have a psychology for their creators . . . but not for the fictional people they create.'

He remarks on American psychologists' strong interest in overt adjustment; because in a new country which demands from its immigrants major adjustment . . . there is perhaps less interest in the inner life: after all, scientists today are turned outwards towards the world. Our Western Christian tradition has laid such stress on the importance of the individual that we may tend to forget that such sharp focusing is a prominent characteristic of our culture pattern. Clark wonders if skilled phenomenological research by a monk at a Tibetan lamasery would yield the same basic themes as our own. He believes that the American psychologist 'abdicates his position as a source of categories' (there are exceptions) and deliberately chooses instead to work in terms of those chosen by the man in the street. Certainly it is difficult to name any other science which achieves clarity by decreasing the number of distinguishing terms already available in its own technical language.

The individual, as the name may imply, should be conceived as undivided, unitary, integrated. Some thinkers may regard a person not so describable as pathological or deviant. This standpoint was maintained by Alfred Adler, whose views have recently been presented by H. L. and R. R. Ansbacher.[9] Their book has been used in drawing up the following summary of respects in which Adler's theories are relevant to our main theme:

(1) Individual psychology regards the individual as socially embedded. 'We refuse to recognize and examine an isolated human being.'

(2) 'Objective factors' (i.e. objects and events in the subject's external environment) are 'used' by the individual in accordance with his 'style of life'.

(As an example, we may consider the various perceptions of a London '13' bus, by a country-bred child, a naturalistic and an abstract painter, an engineer, a tired clerk in the rush hour, and a professional guide who believes that this 'Golders Green to

London Bridge' bus passes through the maximum number of tourist 'sights'. Let us add, for good measure, a deeply superstitious person. Perception is always a social action: the ultimate determination comes from the inner nature of the self.)

(3) Adler's theory is opposed to dichotomizing; he did not accept the belief that the 'I' is made up of forces striving against each other, or that an individual's interests are intrinsically opposed to those of any other individual.

(4) By Adler, introspective explanations of behaviour are not devalued: a person's account, even if 'superficial', of why he did something, may be accepted as true.

(5) The individual's account of 'social interest' is distinguished from his 'socialization' (Freud and others).

(6) In the transformation of 'drives', all causal factors are relative to the individual's ultimate goal and 'style of life'. (We may take as an example the modern scientist, often actuated not only by what is popularly called the 'instinct' of curiosity, but by financial offers, social honours and the theoretical and practical attractions of power-politics. Would there be struggling Curies today, when the nuclear physics department of a university may receive more money than all the others?) In the process of confluence, one or several drives come to constitute the main axis . . . the 'style of life'.

(7) The three major problems of life are communal life, work and love.

(8) The social interest of an individual, an important 'nonintellective' factor in intelligence, determines whether his intellectual solution of a problem will have general validity (i.e. will be reasonable) or not.

(9) The first requisite for a science of psychology—recognition of the coherence of the personality and of the unity of the individual in all his expressions—is missing from psychoanalysis.

To summarize: though it may be widely assumed that all psychologists are concerned with personal experiences, the degree and direction of their interest in this aspect of their subject vary considerably. Personal documents should be studied oftener. The difference between the idiographic and the nomothetic approaches to knowledge is obvious in psychology today, though psychologists seldom explain why one of these aspects appeals to them, or why they have chosen a particular method of investigation. Abstract psychology progresses faster than concrete psychology: academic investigators even tend to leave the investigation of 'popular' subjects to others. The uniqueness of personality ought to be a troublesome fact for researchers who choose to examine only one segment of a person's behaviour, and to neglect the physical and social 'field 'in which he acts.

CHAPTER FOUR

The Individual in Society

The nature of a person's relations to the society in which, temporarily or permanently, he is 'embedded' is now considered. 'Socialization of the individual' is an ambiguous phrase. Not only behaviour which is ritual and prescribed, but also its more fluid forms called 'manners' vary interestingly even in adjacent cultures and sub-cultures. In civilized countries there are noticeable varieties of tact, *savoir faire* and diplomacy.

Study of the Chinese concepts of maintaining and saving 'face' suggests analogies nearer home. *The Organization Man, Life in the Crystal Palace* and *The Status Seekers* suggest questions relating to Great Britain as well as to America.

Can psychological studies add anything new to answer ancient questions of the individual's place in the world? To assess their value is a philosopher's business; to do this he would have to be unusually well-informed, not only of current events but about group relations today. In some English universities, Town and Gown still symbolize distinct areas: this week I heard visitors from Iceland and Denmark discussing, with the fascination of anthropologists on their first expedition, the institution of proctors in the Oxbridge they had just visited.

A psychologist need not be apologetic about breaking into this study: the mental constitution of powerful individuals is as significant as ever. About 1873, little notice was taken of an obscure foreigner who studied regularly in the British Museum's reading room, and in 1930, of an ordinary-looking man who, though neglected, brushed off or laughed at, gathered around him characters as unpleasant as himself, and, financially backed by some German gentlemen, mangled millions of bodies and seduced millions of minds.

It is of special interest to a psychologist that the significance of most individuals ceases on the day when their rulers inform them that they have declared war. When the returned soldier joins a trade union, how important does he feel? He may know by then that his estimation of the personalities and characters of some war-leaders was largely the result of publicity, public relations and propaganda. About ten years after a war, generals inform the public that some of X's staff always thought his intuitions crazy, or that colleagues agreed, affectionately or bitterly, about the brilliance of one-tenth of Y's suggestions and the foolishness of the rest.

The following questions are interesting: What are the commonly accepted social boundaries of a person? How are they prescribed by the customs and laws of different countries? When, in the eyes of the Law, does the Self and the non-Self begin? And where? Some years ago, a member of a theatre queue might have been stabbed in the face by the hatpin of a woman turning her head suddenly. Who, knowing the vagaries of fashion, would say that this accident will not happen next year? If so, what would be the probable result of an action for personal damages? Today, the last entrant to a crowded Underground lift may be injured by contact with another passenger's suitcase. Who is in the wrong: either of these persons, or the lift attendant who did not exclude the late-comer? In rush hours most London Tube passengers try to avoid bodily contact with strangers: this courtesy cannot be assumed in all lands. Anthropologists have studied the relative distances at which, in different countries, well-behaved persons stand when conversing. There are, too, legal definitions of 'offences against the person'.

Today there is much study of group behaviour.[cf. 78, 165] However, more notice might profitably be taken, not only of the ways in which an individual functions in an organized group, but also of his subjective account of his conduct. Consider a person who, in a 'leaderless group' test (with minimal explanations, a problem is assigned to be solved by the group) does not speak early in the preliminary discussion. What is he feeling and thinking? Would he have preferred to consider the problem, perhaps restated, alone? If he is an expert, the formula 'this is a case of ...' may indicate the recognized solution. Does he disapprove the suggestions of a confident aggressive rusher-in, suspect that a smooth manner hides guilty ignorance of the issues involved, or think it merely the habitual expression of a commanding social pattern? Does the perception of a group, with a prescribed goal to be reached in a stated time, stimulate or depress him? In the presence of these strangers, does he feel immature and inferior, or old and superior? Does he regard the exercise as an opportunity to test or exhibit his special abilities? Is his attitude regarded by the others as stand-offish or shy? An English scientist, now the leader in an exciting international enterprise, was, when younger, considered to be 'shy'; a word difficult to translate into other languages; especially American.[97a] He is now popular with scientists from foreign countries, who consider him an especially good mixer. Is this, perhaps, an appreciation of qualities which in England made him mix less well? The aggressive leader, nurtured by some English schools, is sometimes unpopular with the lower-middle and working classes, even if they respect his abilities.

Questions concerning the *persona*[cf. 131] arise here; for example, is the clipped speech of an ex-officer at times exaggerated, or assumed, to ward off questions or contradiction? Differences of sub-culture-pattern affect the readiness with which an individual, with or without an apology, sincere or affected, will interrupt a conversation, also the loudness and urgency of his speech, and the use of gesture. At international conferences, variations in importunacy of conduct thrust themselves on one's notice. There are, too, interesting differences in the exhibition of aggressiveness by aristocrats, gentlemen and others, at English committee meetings. The rarity of studies of class differences in the other British countries and the reluctance of some social scientists even to mention the subject are psychologically important.

An interesting question concerns the extent to which, in different social groups, lavish expression of the *persona* is encouraged, or permitted only in prescribed circumstances, e.g. ceremonial occasions. University dons have been known who, though dressing 'shabbily' ('crumpled collars but careful tweeds') for most of the year, thoroughly enjoyed robing for degree ceremonies and posing for painters and sculptors. In 1957, the Press reported that a London policeman's demonstration of his right to wear a beard when on duty had caused his employers to assert their rights. A little child who, finding clothes irksome, takes them off on a beach makes spectators smile and Press photographers swarm. In our culture, an adult may be naked only in restricted conditions, and stage presentation of scantily-clothed women becomes less and less profitable to promoters. In lands of the free, the extent of dress to be worn may be severely controlled, as an adult male wearing only shorts on Bondi beach may discover.

The individual's 'freedom' of choice in dress suggests interesting problems. To enjoy opera at privately-run Glyndebourne may necessitate four hours of travelling in evening dress; an opera-lover content with Royal Covent Garden can usually appear in day clothes. At Ascot, uncomfortable clothes unsubtly displayed are expected from many people. When the London temperature exceeds eighty degrees, judges occasionally take off their wigs. In the USA, in hot weather, some restaurant proprietors insist that male customers shall wear jackets, which, however, can be hired. Alistair Cooke has suggested that a succession of hot summers might result in jackets disappearing entirely from the American man's conventional summer suits. In August 1959, at Lord's cricket ground, an attendant asked several men spectators to replace their shirts: ladies had complained. The unchallenged basis of the ban was just 'Lord's is Lord's', yet a journal which prescribes correctness in men's wear gave another reason, based on class differences. Village greens, the cradles of cricket, may harbour grey trousers, braces and everyday caps, but the manners of cradle-occupants have always required some correction.

In Professor H. A. Murray's imaginary symposium on 'The Meaning and Content of Individuality in Contemporary America' (Daedalus, Spring 1958) a definition of an individual was offered. He is self-substantial; consults himself, waiting for the inner lift or fall of feeling, and consults others only when at the end of his own wits. An idea often ceases to interest him as soon as it has been generally accepted.*

Except for a few dissentients, like Professor Reuel Denney[39] American thinkers about social problems seem to agree that individuality in their country is declining. Whether Time, Life and Fortune merely reflect or actively increase this blunting cannot be decided 2,700 miles away, but we read constantly—not mur-

---

* Cf. the successive stages in the social acceptance of a new idea or theory. (1) It is opposed, often bitterly and scornfully, by representatives of vested interests: at this stage 'humour' is a useful weapon, especially if 'good-humoured'. (2) It is pooh-poohed for its long words, saying what anyone who 'knows' has always expressed simply. (3) It is just 'common-sense', like summer-time, derided for years by farmers, theatre and cinema proprietors, some religious persons and some scientists.

muring that it couldn't happen here—of social menaces, described by words ending in -ation: urbanization, mechanization, automation, structuralization, bureaucratization, departmentalization, specialization, systematization. All require frictionless co-operation. In such human machines 'the individual is sand in the ball-bearings'.

How did the Organization Man, he of the 'sincere tie and bribed wife', get that way? It began in infancy. His mother was assured that a solitary child is an unpromising child. When at school, he took his class-norms for granted, and may have used them to bully his parents into buying things or assenting to practices of which they disapprove ('Everybody else in my class has one, goes to the movies three times a week, watches TV till ten'). Such a person succumbs step by step, as John P. Marquand has portrayed, and wakes up one morning to the fact that he has reached the point of no-return—at least, the imaginary speaker implies, this is the conclusion of social scientists who go along with Riesman. There is an American hypertrophy of tolerance, loss of the ability to identify the meretricious, and a movement of all high and low values to a common level.

Yet in England we may ask 'How is one to act as an individual, whatever one may think privately, when faced by applications of science, obviously lethal or probably beneficial, e.g. injections against human diseases, spraying of fruit or wayside hedges? Which scientist is one to be guided by?' Of the Super Constellation airliner which crashed near Milan on June 20, 1959, killing sixty-nine, an expert said, 'Theoretically, airliners like this one are completely lightning-proof.' Can a military man who suddenly becomes a political leader really understand the intricacies of atomic energy? If he 'chooses' an adviser, how is this choice made, and does he listen to criticisms of his mentor's abilities? Inevitably one considers the value of, even the necessity for, any effective differentiation of thought, attitude, potential action, even of privacy.[cf. 64] It is hardly encouraged by the new American-type house, with its large living-room, 'picture window' and proportionately smaller bedrooms. The big room makes for matiness and rumpus-possibilities, but not for developing 'a heat and thought-retaining shell' of which one discusser speaks, of 'stoking one's own furnace in cycles of excitement and quiescence', of individuality and creativity. (As Richard Church puts it, 'what

E

is to be creative needs a tap-root deep and undisturbed'.) Not everyone can live in a beautiful country house, but another speaker asked can you imagine Freud in Pittsburgh or Jung in a suburb of St. Louis? Let us consider inter-personal relationships in detail.

It has been claimed by some teachers that the chief aim of education is not the child's intellectual development, but his 'socialization'. The nature of this process is seldom precisely stated: to some readers the term may suggest basic training by Nanny, who, London employment agencies testify, is still in demand; to others, the discipline of schools: nursery, 'prep', public and 'finishing'; or the types of indoctrination imposed by Nazis, almost yesterday, and by Russian and Chinese Communists today. But though psychologists—to name only a few: John Bowlby, Arnold Gesell, Ruth Griffiths, Susan Isaacs, George Lyward, Margaret Mead, Jean Piaget—have been interested in early socialization, few have compared the methods used in various types of English school, or different branches of the Forces in this and other countries.

Asked to name writers on manners, an average educated oldish man might reply 'Lord Chesterfield'; others, with a smile, 'Lady Grove, Emily Post, Amy Vanderbilt'. A sign of the times is that our forces offer printed hints about the manners expected of the newly-commissioned. The American Army gives advice to enlisted men and their wives, and to officers of both sexes.

The neglect of the study of manners by psychologists here and elsewhere is not entirely attributable to suspicion that the subject is socially important. One obstacle to closer examination of the phenomena may be the investigator's awareness of his own status: being serious about 'class' in a scientific way, as distinct from affecting amusement or condemnation, is middle-class behaviour. 'Why stir this up?' a cliché fashionable in reviewerland, serves to dissociate the writer, at least apparently, from the middle class.

Dr Erving Goffman, a social anthropologist, has worked in the USA, the Scottish mainland and the Shetland Isles. He has studied personal manners in small groups; in a large 'total' institution, e.g. a mental hospital, where relationships of the medical staff to non-medical colleagues and to patients are unusually complex and important; in prisons, battleships and camps for prisoners of war. He compares the behaviour in one group with that in another, similar in some respects but embedded in a different culture.

He has studied the Chinese idea of 'face', which one may 'have', 'maintain', be 'in' or 'out of'.[59a] In England, skills by which a person maintains poise or preserves his dignity, pride and honour, though esteemed, are seldom criticized and almost never studied. Sympathetically Goffman examines techniques which vary with a person's position in an acknowledged social hierarchy: tact, *savoir faire*, diplomacy, general social skill. He studies ritual roles, such as arrogance, and dissects situations which, in America and here, cause 'dropped bricks', snubs, 'digs', irony and banter.

Though most members of a civilized sub-culture pattern would admit to paying respect and deference to some differently patterned groups, Goffman is exceptional in examining these manifestations. Laments are heard today that respect has disappeared from English village life. Certainly fewer signs of deference are noticeable, but respect remains for unusual skill, expert knowledge and reliable character. Forelock-touching is 'out'; those which have reappeared on youthful farm-workers are frequently tossed out of the eyes, with a *tic* now shared with public schoolboys.

It is reasonable to choose a large State mental hospital in the USA when one is observing personal proprieties, since spectacular failure to maintain these is often the reason why the patient has been deprived of personal liberty. Hospital obligations and rules of conduct repay study, and societies in such institutions can be distinguished by certain criteria, e.g. whether a required ceremony is performed as an unpleasant duty, an enjoyed duty, or spontaneously, as a pleasure. The title of Goffman's article, 'On Face-Work; an analysis of Ritual Elements in Social Interaction', is self-explanatory.

In each social encounter, either face-to-face or mediated, a person tends to take a 'line'—a pattern of verbal and non-verbal actions, expressing his view of the situation and his evaluation of himself and other participants. A person is 'in wrong face' when communicated information about his social value cannot be integrated into the 'line' being sustained for him. He is 'out of face' when, in social contact, he has ready no 'line' of the kind expected from a participant in such situations.

Goffman continues:

'. . . the more power and prestige others have, the more a person is likely to show consideration for their feelings, as H. E. Dale suggests.[37] The doctrine of "feelings" was expounded to me many years ago by a very eminent civil servant with a pretty taste in cynicism. He explained that the importance of feelings varies in close correspondence with the importance of the person who feels. If the public interest requires that a junior clerk should be removed from his post, no regard need be paid to his feelings; if it is a case of an Assistant Secretary, they must be carefully considered, within reason; if it is a Permanent Secretary, his feelings are a principal element in the situation, and only imperative public interest can override their requirements.'

Military deference, impersonal bestowal of respect on the rank, regardless of its present holder's claims, is discussed. Even if the subordinate's verbal behaviour is 'correct', disregard can be insinuated by carefully modifying intonation, pronunciation and 'timing'. (One might comment that in articles on the psychology of face-to-face relationships, speech nuances are rarely mentioned. Perhaps they are less important in young countries, where many immigrants who arrived with 'foreign' language and gestures, remain all their lives insensitive to subtleties in their adopted language.*) He is interested in the deliberate avoidance of physical contact customary in some sub-cultures (though there seems to be a growing custom of public hand-holding).†

It is useful to discover the reasons, or rationalizations, offered for ceremonial behaviour. In England it is often regarded as courtesy, even common sense, if a person wishes for his own advantage to consult someone with whom he is unacquainted, to

---

* It is not surprising that J. P. Marquand notices speech-shades; e.g. Thomas Harrow observes that his son, an officer in the US Navy 'for the duration', has acquired the characteristic behaviour, but only approximates to the 'correct' way of speaking.

† Goffman does not make specific reference to sub-culture patterns; these are obviously important in England, e.g. when a 'gentleman from the Ministry' addresses farmers on their problems, and they, spotting his synthetic accent and well-cut suit, spoiled by the 'wrong' necktie, rag him good-humouredly by using technical terms current in their county, though knowing the usual ones.

write requesting an appointment. In some Continental countries, the visitor drops in without notice, taking his chance of seeing the desired person. He may have to wait a long time, or even to call again, but regards this as a normal risk, not a deserved frustration. A Continental acquaintance offered me an explanation : in his country, a stranger who wrote in advance, by so doing might suggest that he thought himself important enough to expect a formal appointment. (Still, had he made none, he would be free to call on someone more interesting, or more profitable, instead.)

A relatively novel pattern of social relationships is described in *The Organization Man*.

Most psychologists are resigned to the knowledge that a waiter, parent, doctor or other 'handler' of human beings may consider himself to be, *ipso facto*, a good psychologist. Yet probably few of these have tried, over a period of years, to account for their misjudgments. Some do not realize that different cases call for different methods, that a psychologist's task is to endeavour, with expert help, to find reasons for successful 'handling', and from these to derive and record tentative generalizations, for the guidance of others. Popular journalists' accounts and criticisms of psychology are limited by the necessity of being both interesting and comprehensible, not only to the intelligent reader, but to any reader. Consequently they are tempted to comment humorously upon 'fantastic' details of psychologists' procedures (recent pranks of the physical scientists are more fantastic and uglier) rather than sensible techniques.

A writer outside the brotherhood of literate clowns is William H. Whyte Junior, author of *Is Anybody Listening*[180] and *The Organization Man*.[181] The latter book describes the clash between the individualistic beliefs which the Organization Man is assumed to hold and follow, and the collective life he actually leads—and his search for a faith to bridge the gap.

Who is the Organization Man? The middle-class American who has left home, spiritually and bodily, to take the vows of organization life. He is found in corporations, in laboratories, in law-factories, in foundations in the hierarchies of churches. He not only works for, but belongs to, the Organization. He is at the centre of a deep conflict in American values . . . the Protestant ethic to which he gives lip-service, and the kind of group life which he has to live. To resolve his doubt he is constructing a new faith—to make morally legitimate society's increasing power over him. This book follows him from his pre-induction training in school and college to his moulding in the Organization. It describes the new standards of good and bad, as defined in the popular fiction he reads and in the 'personality' tests to which he is subjected. It follows him to the new suburbia, examining his social life in the 'packaged villages', which he accepts as natural; his religion, and the schools in which his children are growing up.

Whyte knows from first-hand experience about the conflict between individual and group desires: he was in the US Marine Corps at Guadalcanal and in business before and after World War II.

He is concerned with problems of the individual in society. Though the concepts of 'economic man' and 'industrial man' date nowadays, the USA is seeing the period of 'organization man', whose personality and character are being ironed out to fit the social pattern of some one great organization, and de-individualized with his (often with his wife's) consent.

I comment here only on paragraphs which seem particularly relevant. In a lively account of activities of students of 'Human Relations', he admits that vigorous criticism comes from social scientists themselves. He states that his country is training a generation of bureaucrats, whose interest in psychology is purely technological; in the 'how', not the 'what' or the 'why'. 'Social adjustment' is an overworked term, and its use leads to the most stringently anti-intellectual training in the country. Desire to adjust to a group may arise from approval of its aims and affection for its leaders (yet one remembers the advice in some political circles: 'If you can't beat 'em, join 'em').

He maintains that the great companies desire, at their upper levels, a man with a 'company character'. Their training programmes deliberately develop such a character. ('There may even be an ideal Union Carbide man or a W. R. Grace man.')

Let us now consider his views on some uses, by non-academic psychologists, of so-called 'personality tests'. (In England, non-psychologists, and those psychologists who still think in English, might term them tests of character, a word which the British use oftener than the Americans do. In England, to make imputations, even subtle, against a man's character, may result in heavy damages at law: to hint merely that he is introverted would be safer.)

A chapter 'How Good an Organization Man are You?' considers some stock 'personality' tests. The inventor of any one of these will probably think his brain-child has been dealt with too summarily by Whyte but he makes many references to original publications. He admits that in World War I many screening tests were much better than no tests at all, especially when they measured sensory acuity and discrimination, muscular aptitude and dexterity, verbal and arithmetical achievement and ability to grasp relationships, or even to educe them. (Most Britons above the age of sixty can remember tragic misfits in the army between 1914 and 1916.) The Americans extensively used tests for selection; so did we, on a small scale. By 1941, mental testing had improved so much that an officer who declared that he would ignore psychologists' findings might discover that he—and his sergeants—had been presented with an unusually dull bunch of recruits. It is said that one such officer—not in this country—received a specially chosen number of healthy borderline mental defectives.

After World War II personality tests were available for civilian use. Whyte, with others, asserts that their alleged objectivity is disputable. This seems reasonable, for can they be independent of the attitudes, sentiments, and world-outlook of their inventors and approvers? Since, for convenience of statistical handling, the answers allowed to any one question are few, there is no provision for a reply which, in the quiz-master's phrase, is not on the card. It seems improbable that Bertrand Russell, Samuel Butler or Bernard Shaw would have tamely ticked some of the expected replies.[cf. 13] What would the examiners do with an answer-paper bearing a denial that some of the words printed are antonyms of the one in question? (A university class of mine once declined to fill up a 'Synonyms-Antonyms' sheet. When assured that the test had been standardized in America, their comments might have amused Henry James.)

Even if erudite deviants in a selection test are neglected as statistically unimportant—though they might be useful in advertising or public relations—it can be objected that many 'personality' tests insufficiently respect individual mental differences. Moreover, in an interview, a candidate's assurance or lack of it, shown in his voice and speech, may be an important factor in a final judgment: perhaps the most important, if a potential leader is being looked for.

It is fair to mention that some tests, e.g. the Rorschach ink-blot, are not regarded by clinicans, for whom they were primarily devised, as objective.

What the corporations want is a battery of tests of loyalty to the firm. Whyte points to situations in Herman Wouk's *The Caine Mutiny*: reports of the Nuremberg war-guilt trials give food for thought.

In many attitude tests, 'don't know' answers are allowed, even if sceptical psychologists don't know what to do with them. We may wonder what would happen if an employee of several years' standing declined to submit to certain 'personality' (character) tests, or criticized a question worded by someone no more literate than himself. In schools, universities and the forces, tests are usually applied to beginners, or to entrants to a special depart-ment, but to use them to decide whether a man shall be promoted or dismissed is a very serious matter. *The Organization Man* sounds a note of warning.

In *Life in the Crystal Palace*,[67a] Alan Harrington makes scathing remarks about 'cunningly contrived spot-checks of your behaviour under stress', and reminds us that there exist poten-tially valuable employees who might not want to work for any-one who cheats in the first round. He deplores that 'more and more people are tending to accept, and worse, to seek, and worse still to conform to outside evaluation of themselves'.

To summarize: Between a person and his environment there are social and physical boundaries: their nature and permanence offer psychological problems. Many students of collective be-haviour neglect an individual's account of the ways in which his consciousness of the group, its individual members and its aims affect his general awareness. The extent to which in different social patterns the *persona* may be expressed was discussed. For an adult's mental development, privacy is assumed to be valuable: is it desired less today than fifty years ago, and by what types of person? Anthropological studies of ceremony, etiquette, manners, respect and deference reward the social psychologist.

PART II

CHAPTER FIVE

Intellectuals and Public Opinion

This chapter considers important issues constantly discussed but often ill-defined. Opinions are moulded, by whom? With what aims? Through what media? Who are resistant to various kinds of persuasion, and why?

The importance of such questions is obvious when the successful bludgeonings of opinion in the last thirty years are considered. Some powerful opinion-moulders are intellectuals: some are anti-intellectual, using the 'intellectuals' techniques.

Definitions of an intellectual are examined. Varieties have been named: e.g. functional and elected, conformist and individualist. A social problem is offered by the widening gap between intellectuals and scientists. Can it be bridged? What will happen if the social influence of the scientists overwhelms that of the 'Arts men'?

Recent views, in different countries, of the intellectual's virtues and defects are expounded and examined.

What is an intellectual? As a psychologist, I will not answer with quotations from a general dictionary; the concept is psychological. I have tried to discover what 'ordinary people' in England, perhaps middle-class, understand today by 'intellectual', and to compare formal descriptions with informal ones obtained in conversation.

For Lionel Trilling, 'intellectual' implies a certain intensity of commitment, the belief that the existence and conduct of the intellectual life are momentous in, and essential to, the life of the society, the acceptance of intellectual activity as a mandate, a status, a personal fate.

Marcus Cunliffe[36b] uses 'intellectual' to signify a person of unusual intelligence, who, as the possessor of such a gift, has formed the habit of generalizing (in words, paint, or merely in random movements not communicated to others through any medium) about mankind and his world. He adds, 'It may be objected that this definition does not deal adequately with the question of the artist, composer and creative writer. Such people are sometimes not highly "educated" nor articulate about what they are doing.' One might comment that this inarticulateness may debar them from being regarded as 'intellectuals' in some academic circles.

Norman G. Fisher[51] tells us what intellectuals actually do, 'assuming a uniformity of attitude among them which does not in fact exist'. This simplifies his task. 'Their training and disposition create a taste for order and a zeal for system not always suitable for the management of human affairs. . . . As the thinking and communicating part of society, they are leaders in thought and opinion, but not usually in action. Natural leaders, men of action, the heads of great power centres in industry, the services, trade unions and politics, are seldom intellectuals. Intellectuals are often bitterly opposed to such men, and struggle against them for leadership in society.'

Soon after the above article appeared, political columnists seriously warned Mr R. A. Butler and Mr Hugh Gaitskell that as intellectuals each would be regarded ambivalently by many members of his party. Mr Macmillan's intellectual status is not seriously threatened by occasional plunges into the quicksands of slang. His 'public image', recently projected, plays down intellectual qualities, and plays up simple, not to say simple-minded, characteristics. Note the stress of his family's peasant origin.

Mr Fisher, who concedes to the intellectual the belief that honesty and mental courage are most important and that evasion and superstition are despicable, views him as a disruptive critic. 'Intellectuals who have rightly criticized the inhumanity of industrialism have become wholesale critics of its fundamental processes, while nevertheless accepting the material and social benefits which it has brought.' The intellectual often severely criticizes the quality of culture disseminated by the mass-media, and Mr Fisher, who for years has used the mass-media, admits that today there is 'a flood of false verbal and aesthetic currency', but remarks severely, 'The intellectual has often imagined himself to be dedicated when he has been merely maladjusted. As a critic he should be both dedicated and normal.'

Mr Fisher has been an educator so long that 'normal' trips off his tongue more readily than it might off a doctor's, sociologist's, or anthropologist's. His article was written before the appearance of W. H. Whyte's *The Organization Man* or C. Wright Mills's *The Causes of World War III*, yet even at that time Denis W. Brogan and Edward Shils were gloomily regarding some English intellectuals' 'adjustment' and 'normality'. A *New Yorker* editorial, describing with apparent enthusiasm the normal rearing of some American leaders, commented, 'And they damn nearly did us in!'

C. Wright Mills[189], observing the trend of world events in his country and others, is profoundly disturbed by the dedication and normality of scientists.

'Both the drift and the thrust towards World War III depend on ideas':

Intellectuals deal with recollections of the past, definitions of the present, and images of possible futures. By intellectuals I mean scientists and artists, ministers and scholars . . . they are the organized memory of mankind, and such cultural apparatus as it has they create and they maintain. (Their work) justifies or criticizes ideas of authority. . . .

Intellectuals must reason and investigate, and with their passion to know they must confront the situations of all men everywhere. That the individual is alienated is another way of saying that he is capable of transcending drift, of being man on his own.

Are psychologists today dividing into intellectual and non-intellectual, and intermediate cases in danger of falling between two stools? Some physical scientists might be surprised to be called 'intellectuals'. C. P. Snow's view is that the literary intellectuals, while no one was looking, took to referring to themselves as 'intellectuals' as though there were no others. He writes[163]:

'I remember G. H. Hardy, one of the most distinguished pure mathematicians of his time, one remarking to me in mild puzzlement, some time in the 30's, "Have you noticed how the word 'intellectual' is used nowadays? There seems to be a new definition which certainly doesn't include Rutherford or Eddington or Dirac or Adrian or me. It does seem rather odd, don't y' know." '

If psychology's back-room boys are content to carry out routine observations or calculations, seldom thinking spontaneously or with any pleasure, about the general field of their subject, happy to express their results in esoteric terms, are they intellectuals?

Dr Herbert Hyman, who studied the relation of subjective status to social attitudes, writes in America: [81a]

'. . . among psychologists, a man's intellectual status may be a function of scientific achievement or theoretical ability, and whether he is cultured or not does not affect his intellectual status. In the eyes of the total population, the statuses may be linked. . . .'

(It is difficult to restrain oneself from leading at least two cheers for the total population.)
and

'In an investigation of American psychologists' interests, "interest in persons" ranks very low.'

Is it unfashionable for psychologists to be interested in culture or in human beings? This question is answered with vehemence and at length by Professor Pitrim Sorokin.[164]

Today some scientists deliberately ignore (others find it prudent to pretend to) the social significance of their work. A few ask why they are expected to do otherwise, and trot out the old argument that a box of safety matches may be used for dangerous purposes. I have heard an engineer maintain that if man were not allowed to fight with scientifically devised weapons he would throw stones, so why worry? At the beginning of any research it is difficult or impossible to foresee its social consequences; some mental testers today may wish that their predecessors had asserted more guardedly their beliefs in the comparative invariability of the IQ, the inheritance of intelligence and the possibility of devising culture-free mental tests. The general progress of psychology might be helped if more psychologists were concerned to report their results in ways which an educated public could understand.

Professor David Riesman, commenting on the style of some social science publications, writes:

'Terminological opacity will itself be taken as a judgment upon the world, perhaps a manipulative, frightened or unsympathetic one. Deadpan symbols may symbolize a deadly determinism in the researcher. Literate people are going to read what is said about them, no matter how many verbal formulae are set up as barriers; and what they cannot understand they may aggressively misunderstand.'

Professor Sorokin deplores the 'pedantic abstractness, the premature grey-hairedness of the hitherto young, fact-finding American sociology'.

In 1955 there appeared many dogmatic assertions about U and non-U speech and manners. These cannot be separated by a psychologist with the sharpness attained by some phoneticians. The statements often ignored social fringe-areas, and confused concepts of rank, stratum, class, status, élite, aristocrat and gentleman. Eventually it was remembered that the terms 'intellectual' and 'upper class' are not mutually exclusive. Speech, in any social class, may be consciously used to conceal thought. Some U's, when conversing, employ the narrow waveband of expressions customary in their circles, to avoid embarrassing any friends unable through defects of intelligence or of education to make delicate verbal discriminations. An erudite 'U' slips easily into high gear, to avoid being left behind in an intellectual exchange. Written contributions to a symposium usually contain few marks of social class, though listeners to radio discussions may sometimes note them in the introductory sentences.

Are there other kinds of intellectuals? A writer in the *Cambridge Review* suggested two, the civilized (conformists) and the intelligent (dissidents). Avoiding definitions, perhaps regrettably, he drew examples from senior members of his university: call them C's and I's. 'If the C spends a holiday in Spain, he attends bullfights: these are traditional, ritualistic, unsentimental about the brute creation, disapproved by I's. I's want the Church disestablished because in the past it has interfered with the State: C's, because the State now dictates to the Church.

Clifton Fadiman[48a] distinguishes three kinds of critics; presumably intellectuals. (A) the applier of a system, (B) the scientific, 'disinterested', (C) the literary journalist. In the USA, the A's and B's are increasing, the C's lessening, in number. There are ten brilliant A's and B's to one Edmund Wilson or Gilbert Highet or John Mason Brown. C is a character wistfully in search of an audience; A and B, along with King Science, scorn subjectivity.

Mr Fisher cites two current uses, 'functional or occupational intellectuals follow such occupations as teacher, writer, artist, scientific research worker, lawyer, cleric, civil servant, clerk or librarian. The elective intellectual is an intellectual by interest, ambition and personal identification. . . . To be an intellectual is to desire to enter into the full human inheritance of literature, music and the visual arts'.

Here is a psychological problem. 'Euphasic' intellectuals[131]; contributors to the literary weeklies and monthlies; many dons and other persons whom strong silent men regard as 'glib', could claim, with little risk of contradiction, to be intellectuals. But let us assume that the popular use of words has social importance: are persons who publicly express themselves non-verbally generally regarded as intellectuals: e.g. the painter, sculptor or musical composer who does not write or talk to the public about his work? When some of these try to explain themselves verbally they are fish out of water. Were Pachmann or Pavlova intellectuals? Is Chaplin?* Creators of mathematical formulae, or inventors of new drugs, may be known to the public as intellectuals, but only if they express themselves verbally. Then they may drift between Scylla and Charybdis. Expressing themselves elegantly in terms borrowed from other studies ('instinct', 'intuition', 'rhythm', 'character', 'refraction', 'polarization') may mystify and will repel experts in these special fields.

Professor C. Wright Mills states the intellectual's duties (the quotations are from different parts of his book).[189]

'What scientist can claim to be part of the legacy of science and yet remain a hired technician of the military machine? . . . What man of God can claim to partake of the Holy Spirit, to know the life of Jesus, to grasp the meaning of that Sunday phrase, "The brotherhood of man"—and yet sanction the insensibility, the immorality, the spiritual irresponsibility of the Caesars of our time? What Western scholar can claim to be part of the big discourse of reason, and yet retreat to formal trivialities and exact nonsense, in a world in which reason and freedom are being held in contempt,

---

* A friend comments: I think I and many others were prepared to regard him as an 'intellectual' so long as he kept his mouth shut, and didn't try to explain what he was trying to do. The social criticism and satire of his work inclined us, I feel, to give him the benefit of the doubt, to regard him as an intellectual artist, if not an artist-intellectual. The flood of platitudes in which he has indulged in recent years has given an excuse to doubt this.

being smashed, and being allowed to fade out of the human condition? . . .

'We must stop fighting the cold war of self-co-ordinated technicians and hired publicists, of self-appointed spokesmen, of pompous scientists who have given up the scientific ethos for the ethos of war technology. . . . It requires only sanity and getting on with our proper job.'

It is difficult to give a fair impression even of English intellectuals, but I will indicate a few matters of interest described in fairly recent writings on intellectuals here and abroad.

In *The Opium of the Intellectuals*[10] Professor Raymond Aron comments caustically on the activities of numerous intellectuals in France, and more kindly, if obliquely, on American and English intellectuals. Though at times he writes of the 'intelligentsia', the book's title permits the assumption that he means people usually called intellectuals.

In his view, the term, in its widest sense, comprises all non-manual workers; I do not know if he uses the Metro or the Subway, but the reading matter of non-manual workers travelling on London's Underground suggests that many would be even more surprised than physicists to be termed intellectuals. In his second sense the only intellectuals are experts and men of letters. Yet would a skilled detective in a fingerprint department, a tea-taster, a director of defence against coast erosion, for those excellencies alone, call themselves intellectuals?

Attempting classification, Aron starts from actual, and works outward to peripheral, examples. The 'inner circle' contains poets, philosophers, novelists, painters and sculptors: all live by and for the exercise of the intellect.

Having lived my working life in universities containing few painters and sculptors, my own demarcation may be—though I doubt this— unusual. I feel that if a painter or sculptor is known to write or speak effectively about the activities, aims and ideals of people in his vocation, or in others, he will be regarded as an intellectual; but not unless he has expressed himself verbally. Perhaps indeed it is to praise him if we say that he chose his medium because he felt words to be inadequate vehicles of expression: it may be that the more effectively he paints, sculpts or composes music, the less able is he to express in words what he

F

is driving at. A cartoonist often makes witty personal comment which, expressed in words, would land him in our law courts.

Aron indicates an important function of the intellectual. 'The professor (of law) seems to us more of an intellectual (than the barrister or solicitor) because he has no other objective than the maintenance, the transmission or the extension of knowledge for its own sake. . . .' 'The intellectuals transform opinions or interests into theories; by definition, they are not merely content to live; they want to *think* their existence. . . . Every political régime offers opportunities to those who possess the ability to manipulate words and ideas. . . . Governments need experts in the art of speech. Theorists and propagandists meet in one man.'

Yet the 'tendency to criticize the established order is . . . the occupational disease of the intellectuals'; Wright Mills and Barzun might dissent. Many scientists, whether termed intellectual or unintellectual, do not trouble to criticize the established order: they can change it, silently and covertly. An Arts-trained minister, however high his intelligence, must often in the last resort depend on a picture of the scientific situation, painted for him by chosen advisers. Whether they too have had complex facts explained to them in semi-pidgin English is a delicate question, sometimes raised in common-rooms.

The opinion has been expressed that the nature of their approach renders scientists, as a class, less loyal than many other workers. Inside a scientific group, personal loyalties may exert a fatal braking power. Some survivors of the Passchendaele mud are convinced that it was not an important feature of maps used by those directing operations from afar: a scientist may believe that the mud-patch from which he and his researchers have not yet emerged is being ignored by the higher-ups, to whom they are expected to be loyal.

Aron trails his coat when he writes:

'If the Paris of the Left Bank is the writer's paradise, the USA might be regarded as the writer's hell. . . . France exalts her intellectuals, who reject and despise her: America makes no concessions to hers, who nevertheless adore her . . . 1953 witnessed the outbreak in the USA of the "egghead" controversy, and the appearance in *Partisan Review* of the enquiry "America and the Intellectuals". The latter revealed the conversion to "Greater

America" patriotism of the professional thinkers, the former the latent hostility of an important part of public opinion towards men of ideas. . . .'

Are English intellectuals today notable for individuality of expression? One hears of groups, schools, sections of learned societies, even of 'rackets', though this word is often applied to organizations of which the speaker disapproves. Enmity towards 'intellectuals', or any groups arbitrarily distinguished, can be easily expressed to an uncritical public by a label.

The existence of 'schools' of thought may suggest that they bring pressure upon, or frustrate, individual thinkers. It has been asserted, for example, that 'action painting' is defended because it expresses no one personality, but a trend of a group whose members are not 'inner-directed', but 'outer-directed'. A small circle of Freud's disciples ignored outside criticism and even wore a distinctive ring.

At the opening of the nineteenth century, the English intellectual aristrocats were mainly individual thinkers. Noel Annan's essay[6] refers to

'an aristocracy of intellect which began to form in England at the beginning of the nineteenth century. A particular type of middle-class family started then to intermarry, and produced children who became scholars and teachers. They joined those who at Oriel or Balliol in Oxford, or at Trinity and St John's in Cambridge, were setting up new standards in electing to fellowships; they led the movement for academic reform within the universities and sent representatives to the new civic academies; and their achievements as headmasters at Shrewsbury or Harrow or Rugby were watched by the professional classes eager to educate their sons well at schools where they mixed with those of the lesser aristocracy and gentry. When these sons came in turn to marry, what was more natural than to choose a wife from the families of their fathers' friends whose fortune and upbringing matched their own? Thus the same names recurred as professors and tutors and schoolmasters; and by virtue of their affiliations their views of academic preferment carried weight.'

These academically minded intellectuals tended to stand

shoulder to shoulder when academic preferments were in question. Today we might wonder if they ought to be regarded as predominantly individual thinkers, yet the subjects which interested them—Cambridge offered many scientific themes—were varied, and their breadth and depth rapidly increasing.

An important function of this aristocracy was 'criticizing the assumptions of the ruling class above them, and forming the opinions of the upper middle class to which they belonged'. They agreed upon the importance of philanthropy, and of recognizing the dignity of the individual conscience ('they worked tirelessly for intellectual freedom within the universities') and of scholarship, with its solid, not transient, results.

The men's dress was symbolic, combining conformity with independence : 'a don should be well dressed in the style-before-last'. Faithful to this convention, A. C. Benson wore shapeless flannels : this addiction formed a basis for true stories of philosophers who, as unconsciously as M. Jourdain talked prose, paved the way for 'Oxford bags'. Their inter-personal manners lacked polish, and charm of any kind they despised. Perhaps, as Mr Annan suggests, they saved their good manners for their prose; most of them wrote for the intelligent public, but they could be intimidating to meet.

However individual they might have been, at the end of the nineteenth century they closed their ranks—against the materialism of wealthy snobbery and aggressive philistinism which arose when the restraints of religion and thrift and accepted class-distinctions started to crumble. They suggested that if public life was to be inseparable from spiritual ignominy, another life, devoted to unravelling the mysteries of mind, matter and heart, was to be desired. Annan comments on :

'the paradox of an intelligentsia which appears to conform rather than rebel against the rest of society. . . . Here is an aristocracy, secure, established, and like the rest of English society, accustomed to responsible and judicious utterance and sceptical of iconoclastic speculation. As a corollary, it is often contended that they exert a stultifying effect upon English intellectual life by monopolizing important posts and thus excluding a new class who, unbeneficed and indignant, eat out their hearts in the wilderness. Certainly the charge of monopoly is far-fetched . . .

their members are spread very thin over the crust of English intellectual life. . . . Here at any rate seems to be an aristocracy that shows no sign of expiring'.

When we search for criticisms of contemporary intellectuals, an embarrassment of riches presents itself. Lionel Trilling, discussing 'George Orwell and the Politics of Truth', says hard things about the intellectuals of the last two generations. Orwell charged the liberal intelligentsia of his age with refusing to understand the conditioned nature of life. Trilling asserts that G. B. Shaw insisted on remaining sublimely unaware of the Russian actuality: H. G. Wells pooh-poohed the threat of Hitler, and wrote off as anachronistic the very forces that were shaping the world: racial pride, leader-worship, religious belief, patriotism, love of war. Trilling examines the attitudes of some intellectuals after the end of the Spanish Civil War: in the personal life, what was undertaken by many good people as a moral commitment of the most disinterested kind turned out to be an engagement to an ultimate immorality. He asserts that English intellectuals, in spite of their divisions and sects, are more entrenched socially, more adequately defended by tongue and pen, and have a higher status than their opposite numbers in America. These, of course, as much more widely scattered than here: any secretary of an intellectual English society soon realizes that most members, wherever they live, admit, enthusiastically or sulkily, that for any big meeting arranged at short notice the only possible venue is London, though Birmingham is at the centre of England and Leeds at the centre of the North. Our great provincial papers have Fleet Street offices. Though the *Guardian* is printed in Manchester, its southern editions, rush jobs peppered with misprints, are avidly read by intellectuals who, understanding, forgive.

(I believe that if Senator McCarthy had begun his campaign here, Fleet Street would have given him no peace; he would have received shoals of well-publicized invitations to answer questions, in public halls and on the radio and TV. The methods of his 'hearings' would have been anatomized daily by legal, dramatic and other critics.)

'There is,' says Trilling, 'something about the American character that does not take to the idea of the (literary) figure as the English character does. He sees the difficulty of classifying English intellectuals: 'Even E. M. Forster, who makes so much of privacy, acts out in public the role of the private man; becoming for us the very spirit of the private life. He is not merely a writer; he is a figure.' The snobbish intellectual is distinguished from the intellectual snob: 'One can still meet an English snob so thunderingly shameless in his worship of the aristocracy, so explicit and demonstrative in his adoration, that a careful, modest, ironic American snob would be quite bewildered by him.' Trilling wishes that for a few weeks (we intellectuals could pay) no attention to the little group with which we habitually exchange opinions; (take) our chance of being wrong or inadequate; (look) at things simply and directly, and not be shocked and dismayed when Orwell speaks in praise of such things as responsibility and orderliness in the personal life, and fair play, and physical courage; even of snobbery and hypocrisy, because they sometimes help to shore up the crumbling ramparts of the moral life.

There is ground for the belief that in this country intellectuals are better off, socially and politically, than in the USA. 'Long-haired' and 'egg-head' are seldom heard here; 'highbrow' conveys ambivalent praise; many people who seldom listen to the Third Programme approve, even if they would not defend to the death, the BBC's claim to retain it: perhaps in these days of mass culture, the 'Third's' low audience-figures add to its distinction, envied by some other European countries.

It is a sign of the times that in October 1958 many British intellectuals came together for three successive days, to take stock of themselves. These healthy soul-searchings took off from the Herman Ould Memorial Lecture, 'The Role of the Intellectuals in Society', given by Dr A. L. Rowse. Perhaps it was two hinged lectures: they might have been delivered by different persons. That this impression was shared by many hearers seems proved by the fact that the first part, dealing with intellectuals in general, was hardly criticized by many writers who spoke in the subsequent discussions. (I am indebted here to Mary Treadgold's summary in P.E.N. News, Autumn 1958, No. 197, pp. 16-31.)

Since the title of the lecture implied sociological, psychological and ethical considerations, it might seem that a working definition of 'intellectual' would have clarified it. Insisting that 'we' ought to be better instructed in modern science and more clearly aware of the ways in which its applications are transforming our lives, there seemed only faint perception of the wide and widening gap between the world-outlook of theoretical and practical scientists and of the 'intellectuals', recognized as such by their fellows and the literate public.

Society (a vague term today in both Britain and America) expects the intellectual to lead in matters involving responsibility and judgment. The lecturer flayed the lack of both displayed, in his opinion, by some outstanding intellectuals in the recent past and the immediate present. Yet one may ask since 'we need to go forward with the way of reason', 'Responsibility to whom? Judgment, guided by what criteria?' In studying, as personal thinkers, the problems of nuclear warfare, are we to be guided by a Government-spokesman or by expert physicists who challenge his views? The professional soldiers? The armament makers? The politicians? Mussolini, Grivas and Makarios all displayed 'responsibility and judgment'.

What is the 'right' relationship to 'Society'? Most hearers guessed the lecturer's answer, with which, probably, some agreed, though they were silent in the discussions. Yet I feel sure that the lecture was not meant to be a recitation of the creed of a right-wing historian, criticizing his colleagues.

In the symposium on 'Responsibility and Judgment in Historical Writing', well-known historians spoke freely. One maintained that before he tackles his task, the historian needs to know himself well; judgment is a very personal quality, and few historians are good assessors of their own. Another reminded us that even if a story comes straight from an eye-witness, another eye-witness may have seen the happenings differently. What people 'see' depends on their receptive mechanisms and their degree and kind of intelligence. Yet if the historian is dull, few will read his writings. 'Is it a healthy sign that professors cannot speak to one another, because of what they think, or perhaps only feel, happened in the time of George III or the Civil War?'

Official history was described by experts as a contradiction in terms, and military history as offering the worst examples of suppression and distortion. A historian, even of the recent past, merely balances probabilities. The responsibility the historian chiefly owes is a responsibility to himself.

An outstanding negative feature of the discussions was a lack of interest in the gulf between intellectuals and physical scientists. C. P. Snow's Rede Lecture[163]* had not been given, though he had already written on this subject.[162] There seemed to be a view that intellectuals—presumably under a certain age—ought to know much more science: yet, alas! few of them do.

Let us consider the political attitudes of intellectuals. What trends can be observed in British intellectuals today? Introspection and retrospection by an individual will admittedly not take us far, but in a pamphlet 'Socialism and the Individual' Kingsley Amis discusses the political views of British intellectuals whom he knows. He describes himself as an elderly young intellectual, with connections in the educational and literary worlds and with left-wing sympathies. He is lower middle class, London suburbanite, went to a large London day school and studied English at one of the less pretentious Oxford colleges:

'There I went through the callow Marxist phase that seemed almost compulsory for my generation. Next came the Army, which clears the mind wonderfully. In 1945 I voted Labour by proxy, and have voted Labour in all three general elections since, as well as in all local elections. I feel that unless something very unexpected happens, I shall vote Labour to the end of my days, however depraved the Labour candidate may be and however virtuous his opponent.'

The middle-class intellectuals he knows are

'teachers in universities, colleges and schools, the lower ranks of the Civil Service, journalists, industrial scientists, librarians, general practitioners, some clergymen (predominantly Nonconformist) and various brands of literary, artistic, or arty, intellectual'.

From intellectuals he separates out:

(1) Academics; a class with sub-classes, e.g. the sociological; realistic, not romantic, social scientists, statisticians and the like. Also persons on the fringe of, or just inside, a political party. They are unromantic and comparatively undeluded.

(2) Intellectuals pure and simple . . . the literary and arty men,

* An interesting symposium on this lecture appears in Encounter, 1959.

writers, in the widest sense, journalists, self-employed intelligentsia. 'It is often said that in the thirties we had a predominantly left-wing intelligentsia, but now it's right-wing, if it's anything —and often it isn't anything.' Of Orwell, Auden, Spender, Day Lewis, he says:

'The notion of political writing and other activity as a kind of self-administered therapy for personal difficulties rather than as a a contribution to the reform of society—this, I think, is an important key to the whole intellectual approach to politics, not just to that of the thirties.

'The argument that equal incomes, and/or the destruction of the class system, would turn everyone into replicas of everyone else is an interesting one, and though totally erroneous, as can be seen at once by noting the wide range of idiosyncrasy in even a homogeneous environment like a senior common-room, is nevertheless extremely widespread.'

The mental processes of the anti-intellectual who, in his writings, uses the intellectual's techniques are interesting. In a review (*Observer*, November 13, 1955) of Charles Carrington's *Rudyard Kipling*, Angus Wilson refers to

'the excitement with which, in 1890, the literary world greeted *Plain Tales from the Hills* . . . to anti-intellectuals like Henley, Kipling made immediate appeal. . . . By 1910 he was an embittered man, out of temper with the age. . . . He loathed and vilified the liberal rulers; he found the intellectualism and temporizing of Balfour, his own party leader, hardly more tolerable. When he died in 1936, he was . . . irrelevant in the world of Huxley, Mrs Woolf or Auden'.

Mr Wilson remarks on the solid core of anti-Liberal right-wing individualism in English intellectual opinion today that would find much to like in Kipling's politics, and on anti-intellectual intellectuals. Orwell may have been prophetic in his treatment of Kipling as a serious figure. If Kipling was a joke to the smart intelligentsia of 1925, his pro-Boer Liberal aunt, Lady Burne-Jones, is more typical of the Aunt Sallys of the new *Punch* and *Spectator*.*

* The editorial policies of both these journals have changed recently.

Do our scientists consider themselves to be intellectuals? Put in this way, the question asks for instant demolition by whiffs of semantic grapeshot: - it all depends on what you mean by 'science', and by 'intellectuals'. There seems to be extensive acceptance, even by intellectuals, of the postulate that some physicists, chemists and biologists should be exempted from informing the literate public of happenings in their laboratories. Some researchers like it that way: for them the Royal Society and the British Association for the Advancement of Science may be two convenient stools between which disturbing facts can be allowed to fall unobserved.

The convention may perhaps be verbalized in ways like these:

The average scientist has not the literary ability to tell the public what he is doing, for he lacks the necessary training. Many scientific terms and all mathematical formulae are hard to translate, even into a language familiar to cultured intellectuals. For such purposes, pidgin English would be difficult to invent. When a brave soul has tried to do this, avoiding Greek neologisms which shield him from brick-throwers, professional humorists pin down a paragraph which they assume, for their own purposes, the ordinary reader will understand in a popular sense. Sensing this menace, psychologists spoke among themselves of 'g', instead of general intelligence, risking the obvious comment that they seemed oblivious to the existence of gravitation. Concepts of 'intelligence' and 'class' offer no difficulty to writers of letters to the Press: they might be surprised were they to attend a conference of psychologists. A literary reviewer may be lyrical in praise of an anthropologist's fascinating observations described in the first half of his book, but may object to 'repellent' jargon in the second.

Even if scientists could express themselves in words comprehensible to the ordinary reader, it is claimed that they ought not to try, because (a) it is enough to explain themselves to fellow-specialists, and this becomes more difficult every day; (b) they have no time; discoveries follow each other so fast; (c) there is a race for prestige, inside the researcher's university and outside it, especially now that travel is quicker; (d) a scientist's claims to priority of a discovery must be guarded. Tricky questions of 'secrecy' arise. 'In the national interest', so often heard in wartime when the meaning of the phrase was patriotically unexamined, may still be used to justify completely secret research. Sometimes it blurs the differences between a researcher's interests in his academic status, his scientific reputation, position of power in a public institution or private firm, and in the nation's welfare, real, imagined or postulated.

Sometimes, as during the war, when there was some excuse for it, humour supports secrecy. A scientist was reported to have said at a congress that lethal radiation from fall-out—the phrase is conveniently vague—might help to solve problems of over-population. Was this a grim jest, to amuse other scientists? Its resemblance to Nazi jokes about gas-chambers is disturbing. Robert Jungkh[84] has expressed views about the queer sense of humour characterizing some scientists engaged in preparing definitely lethal products. It is not surprising that the few psychologists interested in the social functions of humour are seldom popular with anyone.

To summarize: popular concepts of an intellectual vary interestingly in different countries and different strata in the same country. There is evidence supporting the views that in England today intellectuals are usually known for proved ability in verbal expression, and that they often lead in thought and opinion, but seldom in action. Yet every modern political régime offers increased opportunities to manipulators of words and ideas: 'theorists and propagandists meet in one man'. There is lively difference of opinion concerning the social desirability of the 'dedicated and normal' individual. An account is given of a recent conference of writers who discussed the intellectual's position in English society. The non-intellectual and the active anti-intellectual are socially powerful. An interesting subject for study is the English intellectual aristocracy since the beginning of the nineteenth century.

CHAPTER SIX

Loyalties

Concepts of loyalty will be examined. The preceding chapter implicitly raised the social problem of the professional thinker's allegiances. The meanings of 'loyal' and 'legal' are connected, yet most group loyalties have no legal implications. Among scientists, adherence to an old concept or theory is often regarded as obstructive. Concerning their loyalties, an increasing number of conflicting opinions are expressed. Some may be puzzling merely because they are based on facts withheld from the public. Secrecy, disapproved by many scientists, is befouling both international relations and communications inside a nation.

Conflicts causing mental breakdown may result if loyalty to a leader, as in the Forces, or to a political party is enforced, with severe punishment as a sanction.

Today 'loyalty' has so many different, if related, meanings that some definitions offered, in a dictionary, may produce in a social psychologist a guilty sense of lazy conformism, in another, annoyance at their question-begging. It is interesting that an American professor, Horace B. English, responsible for a dictionary of psychological terms, has been reproved in his own country for leaning too heavily on H. W. Fowler's *Dictionary of Modern English Usage*; the last modifications to this famous work of reference appear to have been made twenty-two years ago. Many events in World War II and its aftermath have distorted any simple, even operative, meanings of loyalty: 'terrorists', declared Archbishop Makarios in November 1958, are 'patriots'.

To examine unemotionally contrasting concepts of loyalty is difficult. Consider the loyalty of writers. If an author, telling the truth about his experience, regards it as material for analytic consideration, he is likely to appear disloyal to parents, family, friends, school, college, regiment, profession, country or church. Lone-wolf thought is strongly disapproved by persons who aim at shepherding writers into politically labelled groups, to be disciplined by overt reward, punished by less overt criticism. Some writers find it socially useful to allow themselves temporarily to be labelled as 'angry' or 'committed': later on, a 'disloyal' disclaimer will attract attention from critics still loyal, so two free advertisements are obtained. To some authors, constantly avowed loyalty to a famous father-figure or influential group may appear necessary for sheer economic survival. Even in the scientific world, few researchers are now free to choose their subject: apparatus is increasingly expensive and may have to be shared; team-work is represented to them by their directors as necessary, even if at times it is really a weapon in the struggle of power-politics. A lone inventor's idea may be bought by a firm, only to be suppressed.

Though loyalty is closely connected with legality, it, like other abstractions in this increasingly garrulous world, has acquired queer fringes of meaning. A contributor to the BBC's 'Any Answers?', commenting on Arthur Miller's alleged contempt of Congress in refusing to name Communist-sympathizing friends, maintained that such persons could not 'really' be friends of any non-Communist. The gravest of current fringe-meanings is 'guilt by association'.

Loyalty charged with feeling, not always publicly expressed, deters many persons even from appreciating the significance of a new concept. The early reception of Freud's ideas illustrated this. Soon, however, he had 'disloyal' followers. Perhaps in some psychiatric circles 'eclectic' is a term of abuse, denoting a weakness from which, regrettably, English thinkers seem always to have suffered.

How free can a loyal person be? Worded thus, the question is ambiguous enough to merit a Mediaeval Disputation on the Third Programme. Fifty years ago, such a question would have caused less conflict in the average person's mind. Let us ask, instead, 'What is the psychological nature of certain distinguishable loyalties?'

Since the word is derived from loi, the nature of an imposed 'loyal oath' can be understood without difficulty by the simple-minded. Today in this country loyalties to spouse, family and school usually grow out of affection: loyalties to authorities need not have such roots. Though I may approve the social purpose for which I am taxed, I may not pay up lovingly. To refuse to pay a rate or tax on conscientious grounds is unusual today; for this change, wars are probably responsible.

Let us consider the kinds of loyalty which grow out of liking and loving. Complicating many of them is ambivalence, which enters even into family loyalties. In this sphere, loyal conduct must often be distinguished from loyal speech or writing: the difference is increasingly important now that as a result of mass communication and increased verbal facility, more people talk with and about more people, using more discriminative adjectives and nouns. In well-known books by American wives, George's quirks are a constant source of humour. The establishment of a *New Yorkeress* might usefully channel female spleen.

A child's loyalty to school or 'gang' is implanted early, yet one may infer, occasionally from verbal report, that mental conflicts concerning loyalty are not infrequent in the young. Some small boys, bored with screaming companions who rush about brandishing weapons, may prefer the company of older boys or adults. In America 'adjustment' to a group, 'integration', are highly praised, yet a publicized characteristic of 'being one of the boys' may have a boomerang effect if a country's leader has to face serious responsibilities.

Many English schools indoctrinate loyalty to a 'house'. Yet a boy, using the 'sizing-up' ability for the reputed possession of which he was elected a captain, may judge, even if he hesitates to express his view, that his own house does not deserve to be top. In later school years, traditional loyalty to the school can present problems more complex than would be inferred from behaviour, especially a prefect's. If a master impulsively punishes a group for the misdemeanour of one undetected member, a senior boy who reads and hears daily of the failures of mass punishment overseas may note a resemblance between the two situations. If he joins a regiment, he may perceive details in which its discipline resembles and differs from that of his old school, and the reasons, good or bad, offered for these. Ten years after a war, memoirs of generals, 'selling their lives dearly', contain retrospective criticisms which different readers consider to be public-spirited, courageous, disloyal, disgraceful, mean. A pleasing aspect of regimental loyalty is the maternal solicitude often shown by members of the hierarchy for the mental and physical comfort and moral support of its 'sons'.

In war, some kinds of unquestioning loyalty may be necessary and so widely praised that many persons are still actuated by it long after peace comes. During the last forty years, a scientist, historian, anthropologist, economist or psychologist, whose university training had encouraged him, by example and precept, to observe without bias, to report fully, and to evaluate his own and other people's findings neutrally, may have been so deeply enmeshed in morale-building, propaganda, public relations and 'psychological' warfare that he may now be unable to recapture completely the disinterest expected in scientific reporters. There are writers today who, having helped to compile an official history of a war, feel morally obliged to warn the public against believing that the final reports are trustworthy. An assumption for, say, five years of a war, that the right way of life is English, French, American, Roman Catholic or Communist affords a chance of living one's life in peace-time relatively untroubled by mental conflict. The phrase 'producing the ideal soldier-citizen' will raise the eyebrows of many students of religion, ethics, law, military history and sociology, yet it was part of a recent statement to a journalist by a responsible publicist-officer of the American Army, impressed by its official report on Communist China's methods of 'thought reform'.

Little can be said here about the complicated loyalties demanded by trade unions, of railwaymen, dockers or doctors, but the subject grows in importance.

An individual's loyalties to institutions often conflict. Lord Montgomery's declaration that officers who had criticized an Army Council's decision to amalgamate two Scottish regiments ought to have their heads knocked together raised many interesting questions for soldiers and civilians. Serious differences of opinion concerning the proper distribution of loyalties arise among readers of the reports of the Curragh 'mutiny' of 1914 and of the Nuremberg trials of war criminals.

Does loyalty to a religious sect or to a community necessitate preserving the appearance assumed to symbolize membership? The decision not to grow a beard of a specified shape, to have kinky hair straightened or a facial feature altered, may offend relatives and be preceded by much personal worry.

Loyalty to a political party may involve serious trouble to an MP if the local committee in his constituency sits in judgment on him. In 1956, several young Conservative MPs, including some with creditable war records, 'rebelled' against their party, considering that the British Government, in attacking Egypt, had been disloyal to the United Nations. (Their view was shared by the US Government, India and Canada.) Problems concerning the relations of an individual to his community—he can have several —become increasingly complex. An English villager may consider himself 'part of the parish', since, like his ancestors, he pays rates, discusses his neighbours' behaviour, and can further or hinder local changes. Yet daily the mass-media remind him that he belongs to larger groups, and may suggest the fading importance of the local ones. He need not attend meetings of the local political candidates, because on TV he has heard and seen their leaders and speakers, specially chosen and rehearsed and made-up, who deal with the main questions. And today when, in certain respects of policy, our two chief parties are almost indistinguishable, he may not regard himself as owing loyalty to either.

Until 1914, our Governments made little use of available scientific knowledge. Englishmen went 'over the top', protected from a hail of bullets by soft caps. But by 1919, many important people in the fighting services respected, even feared, the opinions of scientists. It was now realized that the enemy would not oblige by indicating truthfully where he proposed to be in the next few hours. Service departments began to make demands flattering and embarrassing to some scientists: a distinguished mathematician resigned an important post under a Government because he considered that the Forces' increasing demands for immediate, narrowly useful results unduly limited the scope of what was classified as a civilian department. There were others who held that the Forces should pay for their own research, believing that they had not always been asked to do so.

This example of a clash of loyalties of kinds which Nelson and Wellington never foresaw points to the beginning of a new era. Speakers and writers, not all 'Arts' men, began to ask 'Advancements of Science—for what?' As early as 1931 Professor William McDougall described the danger threatening us if we had a topheavy, lopsided accumulation of practical knowledge, due to physical science, without a corresponding development of wisdom concerning the nature of Man. The theme was new enough then to enrage some scientists; it is now a pulpit platitude, none the less important for that.

By now, a love of secrecy for secrecy's sake had greatly increased. A psychiatrist described war (about 1939) as a game invented and played by boys, and Professor John Cohen has discussed the parts played in war by women,[36a] but in most countries men still hold the highest military posts. Children delight in secret games but, unlike scientists, expect no support for them from adults. At one time, the making of secret weapons and their alleged antidotes and anti-antidotes, which might be sold to the highest bidder, was not supported as enthusiastically as it is today by huge supra-national financial interests. Who can deny that when a war activity, or a preparation for one, appears to be slackening, panic on Stock Exchanges and mutterings about unemployment follow?

Some scientists who, after 1945, remained in, or half in, the forces, liked the 'hush-hush' atmosphere, acquiescing in official attempts to impose secrecy on civilians' independent research. In our nervy times, some kinds of concealment are necessary, but as Professor Edward Shils showed in The Torment of Secrecy,[156] before the facts were emphasized in the Press, for a long time the USA and Great Britain had been carrying out similar researches in wilful mutual ignorance. It is childish to believe that no scientist gains personally, in prestige and income, from such a wasteful overlapping of effort: consideration of the economics of advertising would dispel any such delusion, and Parkinson's Law operates here. Newspaper editors and weekend speakers warn us that one or other of our Allies—to say nothing of our enemies—is drawing ahead in the race for prestige . . . but of what kind, and in whose eyes?

'. . . when the Russians sent up the first, and still more when they sent up the second, satellite . . . the American reaction was described by the BBC as one of "shock, bewilderment and hysteria". We suspect that the shock, bewilderment and hysteria were mostly Press-manufactured.'[36b]

Those who urge the claims of national and other prestige possibly avoid thinking about the early meaning of this flashy word: 'sleight-of-hand mystification of an audience'. Many prestige-

G

mongers care as little for facts as their forebears did. Patter was regarded by early audiences as merely amusing: today it includes the phrase 'national tragedy', unconvincing in the mouth of a representative of an internationally-ramified armaments firm. Not a few scientists are ashamed at the mutual contradictions in some of their colleagues' replies to specific questions about the degree, extent and nature of the effects of the H-bomb; whether 'clean' or 'dirty' (odd terms in an 'objective' science). It is disturbing to note the extent to which scientists disbelieve in, even if they do not publicly contradict, each other's statements. 'Anyone in Fleet Street who believes that Truth is great and will prevail is plain daft,' said a journalist to me.

'On September 6, 1959, Mr Ritchie Calder told a public meeting that the findings of a World Health Organization Commission, of which he had been a member, to study the mental effects of atomic energy, were profoundly disturbing.

'We found that the crust of civilization was no thicker than an eggshell. Confronted with the release of atomic energy and radioactivity, people everywhere were huddling back in the dark days of their own emotions, cowering like our primitive ancestors from the menace of elemental forces. Science, which existed to destroy magic, had itself become a magic. Science, which existed to refute superstition, had acquired a supernatural import. The commission found that "public apathy" about hazards was the fear of being afraid. What concerned him was the manifest truth, revealed in their inquiries, that people no longer trusted the scientist. On the great issues which involved the whole future of mankind, the scientist contradicted himself. The explanation was simple. The scientists in the last few years had been invoked, not only as expert witnesses but as judges and juries. They had made social judgments at the behest of their political masters.

'It was the scientist's duty to give the facts, which only he knew at any given stage, and alert us as to their possible misuses. The scientist had the right, as a person, to his own viewpoint, but he was two people in one, and must make the distinction clear.

'The citizen left science to "the brainy blokes" and, by abdicating his responsibilities, betrayed them, because he left them as the instruments of politics. In an age dominated by science, the ultimate direction of science, with its incalculable powers for good and evil, was in the hands of people—statesmen, politicians, civil servants and, indeed, boards of directors in industry—whose education had been designed to deprive them of knowledge of science. We were not producing the educated who should exercise judgments about science. Ignorance of science was no excuse. Everyone should be aware of its implications.' (*Guardian*, Sept. 1959.)

Between the last two wars, some industrial firms offered grants, not always unconditional, to university departments. In the early stages of considering such advances, some universities on principle declined gifts to which strings were attached. At that time, few professors foresaw that after World War II they would complain that too much term-time was demanded by recruiting officers from large firms, interviewing and offering high salaries to students, the brightest of whom was, up to then, aspiring to join a university teaching staff and to do research neither secret nor anonymous.

Today, few university departments can attain prestige (in today's sense of that word) if their directors do not court the dispensers of benefactions. H. G. Wells once suggested that a university might be wise to appoint, for each subject, three professors. Let us bring his hint up to date. A socially presentable professor would expound or plead his department's urgent needs, real or imaginary, to the right people. A second, perhaps shaggier, would direct research, not all of it communicable, while a third might like to profess the subject.

With the threat of World War II, it was certain that our enemies would be States in which the individual was considered negligible. Consequently, when the war came, most Britons readily accepted temporary curtailment of many valued personal liberties. When the atom-bomb 'finished' the war, many tired minds ceased self-questionings about loyalties, yet soon, for scientists, came new worries: loyalty oaths, security risks, intrusions on private life, telephone-tapping, smear-campaigns and charges of 'guilt by association'.

The problems 'To whom and to what do I owe loyalty, in theory and in practice, in public and in private?' trouble the sensitive rather than the resistive mind, to use Wilfred Trotter's distinction.[171a] About 1910 many students of science were encouraged by their elders to believe that their professional activities were actuated by a simple, 'pure' desire to find Truth; their Grail. Had these teachers been asked Jowett's question 'And what did they propose to do with the Grail when they found it?' anger at such blasphemy would have been natural. Discussions of the nature of truth were sometimes guyed as 'hot air'. Truth, it seemed, was hidden from us by more than seven veils. To uncover her was the scientist's prerogative or sacred duty.

Upon 'real' facts, in the physical world outside or inside one's body, human values could be laid; seldom bolted down. They were, indeed, often regarded as irrelevant, interfering with the tidiness of a scientific statement. An old-style meteorologist, forecasting rain or fog, would seldom have considered the usefulness of such 'impersonal' information to a possible invader, but when physics became increasingly applied to devising new methods of attack, such problems multiplied alarmingly. When, about 1920, some persons forecast that any large-scale atomic research, involving enormous expenditure of manpower and money, the shanghai-ing of shy researchers from their favourite laboratories, and co-operation between groups of nations, could be practicable only in the prosecution of a very great war, some scientists regarded such thoughts as dangerous, characteristic only of do-gooders, and in the worst taste. At that time the public credited scientists with good taste. To most of them their duty seemed clear; to get on with their jobs, ignoring idle questions from ignorant bystanders: 'the dogs bark; the caravan moves on'. In those days some leading scientists thought of themselves as steersmen: often they were. Before August 1945, some realized that they were helpless passengers.

Even then, students of social behaviour saw clouds on the horizon. Human values were being arrogantly disregarded by many scientists, though at times some physiologist would assert that no human being anywhere ought to die of starvation, deficiency diseases; or effects of that romantic, honourable means of controlling population: war. A famous anatomist asserted that war was Nature's pruning hook; the polite, tepid reception of this idea ought to have been rude and hot. To consider the actual or possible social effects of a scientific discovery was described by some as 'monkeying about with politics'; perhaps an unconscious smear on simian behaviour.

At this time, there were warnings against the dangers of importing 'values' into scientific thinking (scientific values excepted). Some philosophers suspected the presence of the stowaway implication that Science is supremely important. Yet some scientists were already studying and comparing values. Social anthropologists were offering comparative data disturbing to ethnocentric thinkers. Some intelligent Eskimos were unable to grasp our civilized reasons for warfare. That two men should fight for a visible and tangible prize, food or a woman, they comprehended, but how, they would ask, can sensible men and women willingly suffer year-long pain and privation in order to destroy and mutilate millions of persons whom they have never met, and never can meet?

In this mood, inquiries into attitudes towards property were being made : [92a] there are social reasons why this line of research has seldom been continued; e.g. such investigations are unlikely to be supported by grants from governments or industry. In contrast, the study of attitudes towards competing varieties of branded goods is heavily endowed, and for similar reason, the use of mass observation and opinion polls has spread.

Since 1945, concepts of loyalty have become no simpler. In the inter-war period, a civilian's primary loyalty was assumed to be to his wife and family. To his employers? If, when he was conscripted, a small firm had supplemented his army pay, loyalty would indicate a return to his pre-war job. But if this had been in the service of a vast organization, he might discover that his mates expect union loyalty, which in a strike should preclude even worries about his dependants.

One may focus different loyalties (a Galsworthyian plural) to parents, husband or wife, children, 'house' in an English school, church, religion and ideology. Any reader who thinks these differentiations too finicky has probably never planned a description of English social life. For breaches of each of these loyalties there are approved ways of expressing resentment. Only a few involve legally prescribed sanctions: these may involve infliction of bodily damage; even capital punishment. Attacks by London bus drivers' pickets on 'disloyal' strike-breakers in 1957 provoked anger in many citizens. 'Sending to Coventry', a punishment one used to read about in books written for schoolchildren, has been solemnly used by factory workers.

To summarize: today, with the rapid spread of information about other nations, social classes, professional and other groups, many personal loyalties become less simple, and new ones are formed. As a result, ambivalence increasingly complicates important allegiances. Increase in popular literacy implies that loyal conduct must often be distinguished from loyal speech or writing; at least in a country at peace. In war, many loyalties become easier to maintain: some, though unnecessary or inimical to social welfare, are often adhered to in peace: this complicates any reformer's task, especially in the political and military spheres. The last fifty years have seen the growth of powerful groups of persons to whose existence some secrecy is indispensable, but in whom a love of secrecy for its own sake has grown. Since 1945, concepts of personal loyalty have become no simpler, as we note in war memoirs and controversies inside groups, such as those of trade unionists, scientists and religious leaders.

CHAPTER SEVEN

Treachery and Treason

Disloyalty is always a pejorative term, though often applied to a person who has transferred his loyalty. Some forms of disloyalty are treachery; of these a few are treason. In war-time, the ordinary citizen seldom has access to data with which to distinguish between these.

In early life, loyalties are directed towards persons: later they may be attached to abstractions—concepts, ideals or ideologies. Educators and propagandists, often helped by pictorial artists, usually personalize such high-level thought patterns. Causes of loyalty are frequently unconscious as well as conscious, e.g. to many people a father-figure or other personal symbol implying security seems indispensable.

Towards collaboration with a national enemy, opinions have changed considerably since the time of the Seven Years' War. Perhaps for some time to come the word 'collaboration' will seldom be used in its 'innocent' sense.

The crime of treason, especially grave and reprehensible in war-time, offers many legal and psychological problems. These are not always clearly distinguishable: in any particular case, it may be asked, what or whom was betrayed? To this subject, Dr E. B. Strauss's contribution[167] is unique in the English language: in this one article the legal, psychological and psychiatric aspects of treachery are discussed with exceptional clarity and in a variety of contexts.

The case of Italy in World War II is examined: 'At the outset, half the country was secretly anti-Fascist; against the War, in opposition to the existing Government. Italy's own Allies, the Germans, invaded and occupied it before the British and Americans arrived. The picture was further complicated by bands of pro-Ally Resistance fighters, followed by pro-Mussolini partisans. Innumerable Private Angelos must have been taken out and shot for treachery—against whom, or what, they could have had no idea.'

Dr Strauss, reminding us that our ideas of treachery, more and more important today, become increasingly obscure, asks, 'Does treachery, as beauty is said to do, exist in the mind of the beholder, or the mind of the traitor? Was Nagy a traitor, or Kádár? The victims of Senator McCarthy's committees? If so, traitors to what?'

Treason is always treachery, but not all treacherous acts are treasonable. Treason is a legal concept; of a crime. In Strauss's view, treachery is a sin. (Since his article was written, the distinction between sin and crime has been extensively discussed in connection with homosexuality, adultery, prostitution, artificial insemination, betting and gambling, and civil marriage in Italy.) That William Joyce was guilty of treason had to be decided by a court of law. According to the Oxford English Dictionary the legal definition of treason is 'violation by a subject of his allegiance to his sovereign or to the State'.

Dr Strauss traces historically the legal development of the idea of treason. Throughout the Middle Ages and right up to the breaking up of the feudal system the crime of treason and the sin of treachery were identical: 'The stability of society depended primarily on the idea of loyalty or allegiance, which, as often as not, involved the taking of an oath. The villein was bound in loyalty to his baron; the baron was frequently the liegeman of an overlord . . . (who) owed . . . allegiance . . . to his reigning duke or king, who . . . regarded himself as directly responsible to God alone.'

Loyalty to an individual is relatively easy to understand: when one tries to analyse loyalty to an idea, of the Motherland, Fatherland or State, psychoanalysts intervene, not surprisingly. The ordinary man today, vis-à-vis the State, is not a Kurvenal. He usually knows something about the views of the Opposition party, even if he does not share them. Sometimes, in educated minds, psychological thinking about the State has been obscured by a philosophical view. But when, as in war, the country's safety is threatened, national leaders encourage writers, orators, artists, poets and song-composers to supply symbols for allied and enemy nations. Influenced by a cartoonist, millions may share his dreams (cartoons are like dreams) of victory or revenge. Abstract thoughts are now replaced, even in persons capable of thinking at a much higher level, by images of animals, lions, eagles, butcher-birds, jackals, chickens, bears, dogs, faithful or mad, according to the propagandist's nation, or not uncommonly, ex-nation.

Loyalty, not to a person or an institution, but to an ideology, adds to the possibilities of a charge of treachery. A contributory factor to the complexity of social conditions is the enormous in-crease of 'rootless' people—refugees, persons 'displaced', with or without families. To these may be added male homosexuals, who under our laws are liable to constant blackmail. Important un-conscious motives for treachery are unsatisfied desires to enjoy the experience of 'belonging', or the individual's conviction that he ought to belong to a 'different' group.

Discussing collaboration, which, during the last war was re-garded as treachery, Strauss remarks that public opinion has changed considerably towards collaboration with the enemy, in its more innocent aspects: 'During the Seven Years' War, the Goethe family were hosts to the Military Governor, the French Count Thorane. At their house he met all the most famous Frank-furt and Düsseldorf artists and writers. When he departed, there was genuine regret on all sides.'

Strauss compares this 'natural acceptance' with the situation in Vercor's *Silence de la Mer*; a sympathetic description of the emotions aroused on both sides when, as a firm gesture of non-collaboration, the French family sent the civilized young Ger-man officer to Coventry:

'For Pétain, non-collaborators and members of the Resistance movement were traitors. From our point of view, the situation was reversed. To cross the Rhine; after the German capitulation, the Allies claimed to be entering and occupying German territory as liberators rather than as conquerors; and we expected the Ger-man and Austrian peoples to co-operate (i.e. collaborate) with the occupying powers. . . . How does the concept of treachery work out in South America, the sub-continent *par excellence* for poli-tical revolutions?'

Or, we might ask, in Cuba, Algeria or South Africa?

Here I venture to compare, with Dr Strauss's view of one aspect of loyalty, my own. He seems to attach undue weight to the assumption that a loyal person, uninterested in psychology, analyses out reasons for his sentiments, or—if he is a naturalized immigrant with reason to hate the once-loved fatherland—complexes. Does a simple-minded person, often among the most loyal, often link his love for family or country with an estimate of its importance for the stability of society? Is his country or region always clearly conceived? Lancastrians usually stick up for the 'North'; asked whether this description includes Yorkshire, some have hesitated before replying.

I believe that, when considering the ways in which an individual's political allegiances have developed, the inevitable quotation from *Iolanthe* 'dates'. It rang truer fifty years ago. At one school which I attended, the boys, and most of the masters, assumed you to be a Conservative unless your father was known to have other leanings, e.g. as a Nonconformist minister or owner of a local Liberal weekly. In that case deviant ideas were condoned: this was too harsh a term for long-declared pacifist views of famous Quakers living nearby in gracious houses. Eventually I realized that a Liberal might be rich; even a rich Churchman. Not until I had lived in Manchester did I reflect on the fact that few of my friends and acquaintances there were Churchmen, and that in the various circles to which I belonged Tory views were unusual and regarded as lovable eccentricities, or accounted for by birth or inherited wealth. But attitudes towards political parties have changed. We accept the idea that gratitude for the services of a beloved father-figure may co-exist with decreasing enthusiasm for his political ideas, and may even remember that his party affiliations have not always been constant. Edmund Wilson, in *Europe Without Baedeker*,[181a] relates that during the last war he was in Greece. Only when he came to talk with British 'other ranks' did he realize that while most officers intended to vote for Churchill's re-election as leader, many privates and NCOs declared they would vote Labour. When they did so, many Americans were surprised. Reading this, an ex-service psychologist writes:

'Many of the younger troops were compelled to suppress the natural hostility that everyone feels to the most benovolent father-figures. The Press-stimulated adulation of Churchill during the critical war years, and the taboo on any serious public criticism of him inevitably created a strong reaction when the hostile activity of not voting for him once more became possible. He had helped to save the free world, but by that very token had been responsible for hardship, danger and misery; the personal experience of many soldiers and resentment for this had been banked up. Paradoxically, had the public image of Churchill as the good, omniscient, omnipotent father not been presented so strongly he might have won the election. There were many other factors, social and political, at work, but this seems to me to have been an important one.' Assuming that father-figure worship may influence party political leanings, we wonder if it can determine loyalty to an ideology whose leaders are successively removed.

In what respects does 'ideology' mean more than a system of ideas? Is intense emotional loyalty to a 'mere' system of ideas commonly experienced? It seems improbable that many scientists ever felt a burning loyalty to the wave theory of light; on the other hand, belief in the inheritance of acquired characteristics still raises complicated political issues. The leader of a school of thought or a laboratory sometimes exploits his juniors' loyalties, but that is nearly another matter. Ought Kapitza, who left Cambridge for Russia, to have been loyal to Rutherford, the Cavendish Laboratory, to physics-in-general, to the USSR, or to himself, if he knew himself? To some scientists, at the time, such a question was novel: Polonius too was untroubled by developments in physics and psychology.

There seem to be available few psychological studies of loyalty; records of what it feels like to be loyal and to act loyally under strain, but some sociological writings on this subject have psychological implications. An example is Professor Harold Guetzkow's *Multiple Loyalties*.[62] Developing a fundamental theory of loyalty and its implications for the problem of simultaneous multiple loyalties, he defines the general concept as 'an attitude predisposing its holder to respond toward an idea, person or group with actions perceived by the holder to be supportive of, and/or with feelings which value the continued existence of, the object toward which the attitude is directed'; and national loyalty: 'loyalty directed toward a nation-state, in actual existence or still-to-be realized'.

Webster's *New English Dictionary* gives a political definition: 'the state, quality or instance of being faithful and true to the lawful government, to the prince or sovereign of whom one is subject' . . . 'Loyalty, in modern usage, oftener connotes the feeling or sentiment (often strong and even enthusiastic) accompanying a sense of allegiance.'

Here one notes with interest the term 'sentiment', which most American psychologists avoid. Is this because they fear that its use may make scientists regard them as sentimental? Their preference for 'attitude' exemplifies a significant difference between American and British psychological terms. Some immigrant psychologists from the Continent, in this country, have adopted an American terminology. Yet in England, educated non-psychologists whom I have consulted use the two words differently. An attitude may be temporary, even transient, as when we are annoyed or pleased by the appearance or behaviour of a person casually encountered, or of an actor who tries to produce such feelings in us. At one time, advertisers aim at creating a long-standing sentiment for some object. At another, to implant a belief that an article is made to last a short time, is part of a deliberate policy—to induce 'psychological obsolescence'. Towards one's parents, home, birthplace, school and a beloved leader, one usually has sentiments, but an old-established sentiment can coexist with impermanent attitudes. One may work for years with a loved colleague, who often arouses short-lived attitudes of exasperation. The average mother can distinguish between sentiments and attitudes towards her children—the ranks of psychologists are not thickly populated by average mothers. Attitude 'measurers' usually aim to cause verbal 'here and now' behaviour; their questionnaires seldom ask for information concerning the origin of a personal attitude. It may stem from a complex, the result of divided loyalties, or from ambivalence, which characterizes non-reflective persons more than they would acknowledge.

Light is thrown on this and related problems by Alan Moorehead in The Traitors,[115] Rebecca West[178] and Robert Jungkh.[84] Moorehead examines the treasonable actions of certain scientists in this country. One may doubt, however, if his eloquence does much to dispel the obscurity which surrounded world-events in the years when the USSR, our ally, was officially regarded with extreme suspicion. Some of Moorehead's passages help the reader to understand, as no official history will, monstrous muddles which have brought about the present 'torments of secrecy'.

Defending Alan Nunn May at the Old Bailey on May 1, 1946, Mr Gerald Gardiner said:

'Doctors take the view, rightly or wrongly, that if they have discovered something of benefit to mankind, they are under an obligation to see that it is used for mankind, and not kept for any particular group of people; and there are scientists who take substantially the same view.' (Moorehead, p. 44.)

(One may doubt if the number of non-medical scientists who take that view is as great as in 1946.)

Moorehead remarks: 'Politics themselves have changed drastically in those six years, many new issues have come forward, and there is a cast of unreality and puniness over all the things that Nunn May and his friends may have hoped for in 1945.

'Loyalty . . . can only be guaranteed by tradition, by fixed habits, by a long period of freedom from fear, and by affection. And all this must be backed by a philosophy or a religion or . . . some kind of faith which is rather stronger than the democracies have yet been able to engender.'

Let us consider the motives of research scientists today. It would be too easy to record amusement, real or pretended, at activities—some bizarre—termed 'motivation research'. Perhaps non-specialist readers, if English and no longer young, smile at ideas which disturb them, more than at those which they used to take for granted. Some members of the British Association for the Advancement of Science think that the titles of many papers in sections other than theirs might start the *Observer's* Paul Jennings on another 'Oddly Enough'. But since the law takes cognisance of imputation of motive, and many public personages, especially those who cannot answer back, find that motives are freely attributed to them, this question inevitably forms part of a psychological consideration of loyalty. Today the social psychologist is compelled to consider the motives of leading men in politics, war and business. Since scientists are now the high priests of civilization, their motives are not exempt from examination, though this statement may surprise some of them.

During the last war, especially in this country, which conscripted women as well as men, it seemed natural to most citizens to obey authority: many had enough personal worries to discourage them from conflicting with people who, they believed, were doing their best to win the war. In some persons, even in peace-time, a desire to be ordered about is intense. For many citizens the war ended a few days after Hiroshima; not for numerous research scientists, who do not differ mentally from their fellow-creatures as much as the public is led to suppose, though a few, it is said, have in their veins not blood but high-tension currents. A psychologist cannot nod obediently at pontifications about the scientist's sacred, or dominant, 'instincts' of curiosity. Where have those uncurbed drives led the world today? *Si monumentum requiris, circumspice!* Whether the rich amateur ever had more right than anyone else to indulge his 'instincts' is a question belonging to the ethics of aristocracy, but today nearly all scientists are full-time professionals. About 1912 the son of an American biologist who told me that his father had sent him to England to seize rapidly-diminishing chances to meet amateur scientists was working with a perfect example of the complete professional, Rutherford.

Most scientists today marry and acquire financial responsibilities similar to the ordinary citizen's. Many war-time scientists faced a dilemma—whether to enter or re-enter academic life, offering freedom of thought and speech, a wide circle of cultured friends, chances for travel, a social status less prescribed than that attaching to most trades and professions, and unusual security . . . or to be employed at three times an academic salary, with curtailed freedom and the constant possibility of being 'fired' for reasons which need not be made public.

Much of the last paragraph might have been written about England in 1946. In America situations were even more complicated. Why, some time after 1945, did many American scientists leave universities to carry out research for the Government? Was it only because, as General Groves is alleged to have declared, the promised researches were 'just too exciting'? For centuries, less intellectual and less intelligent men in most countries had fought in foreigners' wars for that very reason, but from 1946 onwards the driving force was not only excitement:

'military men had cleverly turned the scientists' flank by infiltration into the strongholds of the scientists themselves. . . . The universities had found a new and extremely wealthy patron in the armed forces of the State . . . (they had) greatly expanded departments of physics, chemistry, technology and biology, in consequence of military support. . . . In the universities, once the home of free speech throughout the world, the spirit of secrecy came to prevail. . . . Professors began to have "secrets", and could only talk to each other like priests of some peculiar religion, in a special language'.[84]

In the University of Chicago a parody of this jargon was circulated. Every word looked as if it might make sense to some (other) scientist: actually it was contrived nonsense. Examination of articles on hearing and speech by some experimental psychologists suggests that their authors were concerned with problems of war, rather than with fundamental issues of these eminently social activities.

The taboo against speculating about scientists' motives is now being defied, chiefly by non-psychologists: most motivation research has other aims. But in this connection Professor G. W. Allport's hypotheses of the transformation and functional autonomy of motives[3] are suggestive. He assumes that human 'drives' are seldom if ever excited singly, and that the result of several drives acting simultaneously is a fusion and transformation. Imagine a scientist who early in life showed unusual curiosity in a certain direction, and was encouraged at school by an attractive father-figure to follow his bent. At the university he attained local fame. After graduation he acquired in succession public acclaim, money and power to influence the distributors of research grants. By this time the relevant drives have combined and functional autonomy set in. The administrative activities at which he is now most successful may have acquired a stranglehold and he may now find it harder to stop a research project than to let it proceed. He began as an amateur, in the best sense of that word: he ends as a full-time professional. Perhaps at times he wonders if he has become yet another sorcerer's apprentice, with little hope of his master's return to tidy up the social mess.

To summarize: the same writer seldom discusses legal, psychological and psychiatrical aspects of treachery. Concepts of it become increasingly obscure and important. Treachery is seldom, but treason is always, crime. Behaviour loyal to an ideology involves possible charges of treachery. An intelligent person's loyalty to a father-figure is usually ambivalent. There seems to be a widespread tacit agreement to exempt scientists from the category of persons whose motives may be properly examined, yet they may determine the future of civilization.

Loyalties and disloyalties of scientists have been publicly discussed much less than defections of war-prisoners and the pressures which led to them. To these we turn in the next chapter.

CHAPTER EIGHT

'Brainwashing' and 'Thought Reform'

In the last few years, new invasions of individuality have been contrived. Some were camouflaged: this chapter deals chiefly with overt assaults. Its data come, not from novels, but from medical experts' reports. Defects of popular expositions of brainwashing are demonstrated, and an account given of the uses made of evidence obtained under the influence of 'truth drugs' and 'lie detectors'. There follow descriptions of Chinese Communists' attempts to control a prisoner's mental and physical environment for long periods ('thought reform') and of recently published revelations about brainwashing. These techniques are compared, and comments from the public cited.

The Chinese Communists in the Korean war made a concerted attempt to control not only the physical but the mental environment of an adult, whether simple and uneducated or cultured and sophisticated. In this type of 'thought reform' the results of experiments on lower animals are scarcely relevant: the subjects were subjected to millions of words, spoken, written and read. In these 'experiments' (I use the word loosely, for there were no controls, and factors could seldom be singly varied) deep-lying beliefs were undermined and new ones built; whether with lasting success is unknown. That we shall strongly disapprove them and the methods of their implantation is highly probable, but I describe them as objectively as seemed possible.

The facts have been obtained from official reports and medical articles.[7, 52, 53, 95, 98, 99, 100, 150, 151, 152] These, in contrast with many descriptions offered to the public, give masses of detail described unambiguously.

In countries whose citizens daily fear bodily assaults, intrusions on mental privacy are expected. Examination of their nature illuminates old problems; e.g. suggestion, persuasion, morale, loyalty, leadership, rational and irrational thinking; even the nature of the Self and its relation to society.

H

What concepts—if they can be dignified by this name—can we accept from popular writers on 'mind-moulding'? We may scrutinize their ideas, to reshape them for scientific purposes. In the use of an apparently simple term like 'brainwashing'—a perfect example of the misleading use of plain words—any reference to the brain is speculative and misleading. Though the superficial meaning of the word is fantastically incorrect, it has become the centre of a journalistic myth; used as a missile by highly-placed soldiers, priests and politicians, some of whom forget that they live in glass houses. 'Any man who believes that has been brainwashed!' begs many questions. Here, novelists' ways of using psychological theories seldom make matters easier for the psychologist himself.

What is the derivation of 'brainwashing'? Dr John C. Lilly[100] says 'it has come apparently to have a meaning created by the national press. In this meaning, the term is more or less defined by an indoctrinator, talking to his victim: We make the brain perfect before we blow it up. No one whom we bring to this place ever stands out against us. Everyone is washed clean. There is nothing left in them except sorrow for what they have done, and love of the party. It is touching to see how they can love the party. They beg to be shot quickly so that they can die while their minds are still clean'.

At times a psychologist seeking concepts to aid his thinking and to expound its results to others is torn between desires; to cite a definition from a standard (soi-disant) dictionary, or, emulating Lewis Carroll, to declare what he means by a word here, now and in a context prescribed by him. From comfortable shielding behind authority he may be deterred by a publisher's warning that his new dictionary is a 'must'. But when a psychologist reads of attacks on the mind by 'brainwashing', 'depth interviews' and 'subception' he may wonder what is a modern physicist's view of 'thunderbolts', a physiologist's of 'thinking with one's blood', or an anthropologist's of 'lesser breeds'. Edward Hunter's book[78a] is disappointing for several reasons, including the absence of factual reports of interviews. Concerning Chinese Communists' attempts to implant in captured American soldiers the belief that their nation had practised germ warfare, one may comment, in 1960, that few Ministers in any country have been happy when questioned on this matter: for many years most nations have had 'bacteriological' and 'biological' 'defence' departments. Official denial, or assurance that a charge is 'grossly exaggerated' forms part of the technique of modern warfare; hot or cold. In war-time or during an uneasy peace, many people believe stories which are sometimes officially contradicted, but not at once. In World War I, little was done at the top to destroy the rumour in Britain that the Germans were boiling down human corpses for fat. Presumably, even then, *Kadaververwertung* was not beyond the ken of our translators. In the last war, with Belsen in mind, we could have believed this. Even as late as July 5, 1945, most Americans might have disbelieved rumours of Hiroshima's impending fate. In the autumn of 1930, in a train between Vienna and Graz, a stranger, uninvited, told me of Hitler's plans for torturing Jews if (to me it seemed most unlikely) he came to power. I had seen nothing about this in any English newspaper. Had I, on return to England, repeated this 'tall' story, many English friends, including those who thought a bit of Hitler discipline would do us good, would have furiously rejected such a smear on the man who was restoring Germany's self-respect, and on his simple slogan 'Ein Volk, ein Reich, ein Führer'.

It is easy and often unfair to criticize from the side-lines: I have not experienced the pain, degradation and invasion of privacy which 'thought reform' involves. Yet in any search for understanding, criticism of theory is indispensable. Reports of expert psychiatrists and psychologists now offer the facts.

Methods of torture used in the USSR, Hungary, East Germany, Communist China and Algeria, though they share common factors, must be distinguished if their special techniques are to be understood. Physical interference will have gradations, from torture deliberately thought out by medical men, as in the German 'horror camps',* to harsh treatment which the American army considers its soldiers should be prepared to undergo, since on war service they may experience exposure to cold and immersion in freezing water.

It might be remembered that many current school systems involve invasions of personal privacy and thought reform. Some educationists assert that both are necessary and beneficial. As one travels from Western to Eastern civilization, or reflects on our changing social patterns during the last fifty years, the indivi-

* Cf. *Guardian*, Feb. 8, 1959.

dual's right to privacy seems to be less and less recognized or claimed.[64, 131] In this connection, the popularity in Britain of holiday camps and the increasing distaste for old-style seaside lodgings is worth considering. That every year it becomes easier to influence an individual's belief and action is one of the principal themes of the present book. Exhortations to 'strengthen our defences against irresponsible suggestion', 'to remain aloof', in order to win 'the battle for the Mind' presuppose in the average person exceptional detachment usually associated with certain types of non-worldly thinker. And not all professional suggesters are boors, bores or dolts.

Individual differences in suggestibility are considerable: a person's scepticism towards some subjects or persons may coexist with, even cause, gullibility towards others. This characteristic has been observed in some physical scientists easily spoofed by fraudulent mediums. Inanimate objects play the game: mediums do so—with their own rules. That a 'couldn't care less' attitude may accompany high suggestibility is known to students of juvenile delinquency.

Experiments by Professor D. O. Hebb and others show that healthy adults, cut off from messages from the outside world even for a few days—not months—become unusually pervious to suggestions. A special torture of solitary confinement is to tell the prisoner, as if with authority, that bad news has been received concerning his nearest and dearest, with a hint that more details will be forthcoming only if he consents to do what he is asked.

Was the actual number of Americans—twenty-one—who chose to stay with the Communists astonishing?* The American Army staff was astonished; *c'est son métier*. Still it seems unlikely that mercenaries used by the British against the Americans in their war of independence could have been well briefed concerning the pros and cons of their cause. Ex-officers of many armies, faced with the prospect of a greatly reduced income, have fought in wars of foreign 'liberation', or helped to train fighters for them, without intensive studies of moral reasons for their enthusiasm.

---

* An American correspondent comments, in a personal communication: 'The twenty-one Americans who stayed did so only because of great pressure on the part of the Chinese. As far as I know, there has been extensive collaboration and defection in virtually every war that the US has participated in, except perhaps in World Wars I and II. *Andersonville* certainly paints a similar picture for the Civil War.'

The Chinese Communists treated civilian prisoners worse than combatants. Any handling of the latter is almost always restrained by thoughts of retaliation. Why were intensive studies of the minds of a few educated civilians prosecuted for so long? Were immediate useful conclusions the only results hoped for? Perhaps not; one remembers traditional Chinese patience and contempt of the passage of time. Today, concentrated exploration in many directions—operational research—characterizes scientific activities. Might the Chinese have been seeking purely theoretical knowledge? Before examining their techniques further, it is useful to compare them with others currently used to influence minds forcibly.

It would be surprising if spectacular assaults on individual minds did not receive widespread notice in the Press. Reports of 'truth drugs', 'lie detectors' and 'mesmerism' are usually sensational, but the task of verifying alleged facts leads to a harder one: to determine in a single instance which verified fact is important or even relevant.

Professor H. J. Eysenck, in *Sense and Nonsense in Psychology*,[48] gives an account of hypnosis, 'lie-detection' and criminal investigation. The subject of witnesses, testimony and trials is extensively discussed by several writers in the *Journal of Social Issues* (vol. 13, 1957). Though the early work of William Stern and G. M. Whipple was well known to psychologists, since then there have been few investigations of testimony. This is surprising, since two wars and civil dissensions during and between them caused many trials in which a witness's veracity was all-important. An account of some of these is given in *The Psychology of Rumor*, by G. W. Allport and L. Postman.[3a]

Early psychological investigations of testimony concentrated on the witness's mental processes, not on his examiners' motives and techniques. We need a social psychology and sociology of testimony. Questions of urgent importance are: What criteria of veracity and validity are accepted by the public in a democracy which defers to judges and lawyers, but is their employer? What criteria, beside legal ones, of testimony, are assumed by investigators in totalitarian states?

As an Englishman, I say little about the procedures of the McCarthy committees. When, however, a former witness before legislative committees, Corliss Lamont, alleges that a witness deemed to be 'unco-operative' might for this reason alone be dismissed from his regular job, I wonder if the investigators expected him to help them to prove his guilt.

Discovering and assessing the importance of another person's motives is a difficult task which the public expects someone to attempt. That he is often a psychiatrist may help to explain ambivalence towards him. Most people feel safer in approving 'simpler' techniques to ascertain if a person committed the action of which he is accused. These, described below, can give only objective data, and their interpretation is not easy.

The 'lie detector'—many operators prudently avoid this question-begging label—depends for its success on objectively observable, measurable bodily events, e.g. changes in blood pressure, respiration and the skin's electrical resistance; 'psycho-galvanic reflex' or 'galvanic skin resistance' ('PGR' and 'GSR'). These data are interpreted more enthusiastically by some operators than by others.

To facilitate narco-analysis, drugs popularly called 'truth serums', e.g. scopolamine, sodium amytal and pentothal, are used. There is no reason to believe, a priori, that a drugged person's utterances are, or are not, true. Some famous self-accusations in totalitarian States may have been precipitated by the action of such drugs. This is not surprising: at times, in public-houses one hears, unwillingly, 'confessions' by persons who, when sober, would not have made them; naturally, their truth is questionable. The possibility of induced amnesia is important if it is suspected that a witness has been tampered with; for example, sodium amytal, even in light dosages, can produce amnesia for events occurring in the period of narcosis. Narco-analysis is of value in true, especially psychogenic, amnesias, resulting from repression rather than suppression. Dr J. F. Kubis writes: [95] 'Those who confess in the drug-interview would most likely confess under normal circumstances to a skilled interpreter. It is the criminal who stands to benefit from the technique: he may so contaminate the interview with conflicting information that the physician may become genuinely puzzled as to the validity of his story. And the creation of a doubt as to his guilt is all in favour of the guilty.'

Apart from problems arising out of the possible drugging or bullying of a witness, a question which, in the present writer's opinion, should always be asked in court procedure is 'What were the actual words used?' Why should it be assumed that a witness can remember these correctly, and honestly swear to them? Individual differences in recalling experience in visual and verbal terms are soft-pedalled here. The defiant reply that only the gist matters may be prompted by fear of psychologists'—to say nothing of Freudian psychoanalysts'—criticisms. By what mental processes, unconscious and conscious, is any gist arrived at? If even a twenty-minutes' conversation, at an average of 150 words a minute, is 'summarized' by one only of the speakers, who has his self-respect to maintain, how were his memories recalled, sorted, and their meaning boiled down? 'Did they ever say it?'— an 'Emperor's Clothes' question—ought to embarrass lawyers: it occasionally annoys historians. Even in 1959 I read in a reputable newspaper that whenever Goebbels (this time, for a change) heard the word 'culture', he would reach for his revolver. If alive, how would Wolsey, Pitt, Wellington, Galileo, Queen Victoria, address those who attribute certain famous phrases to them? 'Verbal encoding,' writes a psychiatrist, 'doth make liars of us all.'

Witnesses notoriously differ in ability to verbalize their thoughts, but now, seeing that quiz-programmes, tests of intelligence and information, and debates are everyday experiences of the younger generation, we may expect them to do it better than their elders. It is relevant, however, to remark that in England 'glib' is an epithet often applied to others by persons whose IQ is low and vocabulary sparse. A witness's world-outlook depends in great part on the number of things, people and ideas which he has discriminated and named. One's 'verbal map' is not the same as the 'factual territory', as Korzybski has said, and even the scholar's words approximate only roughly to his data of experience, particularly if he despises technical terms hammered out by scientists. Literary people have made a word-world which imprisons them oftener than they know. Not a few students of law now believe that the McNaghten rules of forensic psychiatry 'force psychologists and psychiatrists to limit their testimony and to cast it in terms of obsolete and meaningless criteria'.*

The stress-interview, whether its operators' intentions are 'good' or 'bad', demonstrates the extent to which inter-personal tension can disorganize or impair a subject's verbal behaviour.

* Barbara Wootton criticizes this attitude.[186]

By telling the exact truth, as it appears to him, a witness in a law court might embarrass himself and others. A demand that an expert in a subject, perhaps the only expert present, shall answer in 'plain' language may subject him to exceptional stress. He may bite back the retort that he cannot do this, and would like to hear anyone who can, but if he tries to make his meaning easy for others, he can flounder badly. The plain man may sail through a cross-examination, delighting everyone by his honesty,* though an expert might judge that his replies blunted the scientific terms hinted at. Some of these, indeed, are seldom translated for the benefit even of other scientists working in a different field. F. L. Rourke, writing in America, says 'The law is demanding of other disciplines a unanimity that is rare even in the supreme councils of its own profession.'

We return to consider detailed accounts of 'thought reform' ('soul-surgery', 'brainwashing').

Edward Hunter's *Brainwashing: The Story of Men Who Defied It*, exciting as it may be to the general reader, is unsatisfactory to a psychologist. This book is not made easier to understand by frequent gushes of indignation, often justified, though an Englishman notes censorious remarks about 'tousled Bevan' and our Royal family, and that the name of MacArthur is given much more prominence than those of McCarthy and MacCarran. The Chinese knew much about refinements of torture before any of them were inspired (this is doubtful) by Pavlov's experiments. Hunter seems ignorant of psychiatry, even of hypnotism. His frequent references to 'Reds', with no suggestion of differences between the Communism of Russia and China, discourage a reader seeking to be instructed and not merely thrilled or shocked.

Contrasting with the commitment of this book is the scientific detachment achieved by Professor Robert J. Lifton, whose long articles are full of facts, comment and valuable references to the work of others.†

'The Chinese Communists have developed a peculiar brand of soul-surgery which they practise with impressive skill—the pro-

---

* A magistrate asked a fun-fair proprietor to estimate the proportions of skill and chance involved in operating a certain type of machine: he cheerfully replied, in simple English, 'Chawnce, sir? Not a bloody earthly!'
† His book, *Thought Reform: A Psychiatric Study of 'Brainwashing' in China*, was published in 1961 by W. W. Norton in the USA and Victor Gollancz in England.

cess of "thought reform". They first demonstrated this to the American public during the Korean conflict, when they obtained the fantastic germ-warfare confessions from Air Force officers and various types of collaboration from some other United Nations personnel. And more recently we have seen even more remarkable results of its full impact: Western civilians released from Chinese prisons, repeating their false confessions, insisting upon their guilt, praising the "justice" and "leniency" which they have received, and expounding the "truth" and "righteous-ness" of all Communist doctrine.'

No scientific thinker could accept or use the 'concept' of 'brain-washing'. A brain, detached from the body, could be washed, but this could not remove 'traces'—even this term is metaphorical —as when a recording tape is demagnetized. If the analogy had not already broken down, it would do so at several other points. Memories causing important beliefs often result from condensa-tions of experiences recorded at long time-intervals, perhaps years. These 'similar' memories (often similar in one aspect only, apprehended by the dreamer, the poet, the wit and the crank) may be fused into a new whole, dramatized with regard for presenta-bility. It seems odd that Freud's great edifice, 'dream work', is often forgotten or ignored in this connection. All these processes probably take place too when memories of quite recent events are stored and recalled.[cf. 127]

In Communist China, says Lifton, 'the authorities have vigorously applied "reform" methods throughout all levels of their population; in universities, schools, special indoctrination centres, business and government offices, and even peasant groups. Their expressed justification is the conviction that all people retain "influence of the reactionaries" or "ideological poisons" from the former, pre-Communist society, and must be made over into "new men" in order to take their place in the "new society". But it is in a vindictive prison-setting that " reform" reaches its greatest intensity'.

In the British Crown Colony of Hong Kong, Dr Lifton for seventeen months conducted a psychiatric investigation of 'thought reform'. He interviewed Westerners and Chinese who had been exposed to its pressures. Work with repatriated Ameri-can prisoners-of-war in Korea had increased his interest in the subject. Among the interviewees' reasons for initial co-operation in this study was a strong need to resolve guilt-feelings and to be helped in their struggle for integration of personality. Lifton describes the so-called 'penal reform' scheme. In Communist China, all crime is attributed to residual harmful effects of the 'old society'. Penal institutions and 'therapeutic centres for reform' or 're-education', 'meditation houses' and 'hospitals for ideological reform' all co-ordinate punishment and control with ideological reform, and labour production with political education. Four types of institutions are detention houses, prisons, labour service for reform corps and juvenile delinquents' institutes.

Among 'reform' procedures devised for civilians is interrogation. 'The prisoner is taken to a room with two interrogators, an interpreter if necessary, and a secretary. A bright light may be shone in his eyes. The interpreter may open with the vague, damning accusation that the Government already knows about the prisoner's crimes; therefore, if he will confess them, he will soon be released. Should he protest that he is innocent, he is assured "the Government does not arrest innocent people". He is then asked to describe all his activities from the time that he first came to China, his professional interests, the groups with which he was associated, the political activities in which he has engaged, his social life and economic status.'

Few serious students of society would believe that in other countries anti-Communist interrogations would pose questions very different from these, but here the resemblance may end: 'The Communist interrogator assures the prisoner that his associates have already confessed everything, and that his case has been thoroughly studied. When near collapse from mental disturbance, he is returned to his cell, believing that the ordeal is over, but is allowed to sleep just long enough to enable him to undergo interrogation again. This "rest" period may be as brief as one hour. If he still declares his innocence, handcuffs, and later, foot-chains are fitted. In his eight by twelve feet cell, Chinese cell-mates led by their "chief" demand to know what took place in the interrogation', and they 'help' him to confess. Meanwhile their chief learns methods considered suitable to build up a guilt-complex in the prisoner. These include physical violence, degradation, insult and humiliation: e.g. being forced to look at an obscene picture of Christ.

The prisoner's food is vitamin-deficient and causes diarrhoea and dysentery. On top of these discomforts is the restriction of his visits to the latrines to two a day, and approximately forty-five seconds to attend to his needs there. In the cells, prisoners are so crowded that during the night they can turn only *en masse*.

'After two or three months of this treatment, the prisoner is greatly fatigued, under-nourished, physically ill, confused, perhaps unable to demarcate clearly truth from fiction, guilt-ridden, demoralized, depressed, often suicidal, and experiencing transient psychotic states, e.g. auditory hallucinations.'

Calculated kindness follows; cigarettes and tea are offered and good food, books and better hygienic conditions promised as a reward for co-operation. But the interrogator's attitude may change to anger if this seems likely to extract a confession. This may be the result of enforced silence for as long as three weeks. He is 'guided' towards 'adopting' the 'people's standpoint'.

'The degree to which reality has thus become blurred varies greatly with the prisoner's make-up. Some come to believe untrue elements of their confession, but many view the distortions and falsehoods as a necessary compromise.'

Study-group sessions follow, for ten to sixteen hours a day. The group must solve every problem, political, economic, ethical or psychological, by discussion and persuasion. Each prisoner must express and denounce 'bad' thoughts before the group. Interviewees told the psychiatrist, 'If we did not express any bad thoughts we were regarded as not telling the truth, since, as reactionaries, we must have had them.' The prisoner signs his confession before photographers and moving-picture camera men, and reads it for sound-recording. This 'proof' is widely disseminated as propaganda throughout China and other parts of the world.

One might comment that in this impressive catalogue of cruelties many are age-old, and some are practised by non-Communists. But specially relevant to the present book's theme is the subject of tortures selected to fit in with the victim's idiosyncrasies. Of psychological importance is the technique of 'emotional assault'; aimed at annihilating the prisoner's sense of identity, reducing his reactivity to a primitive, subhuman level. It is arranged that he shall be surrounded by persons—interrogators and cell-mates—who will teach him to feel guilty.

In English middle-class society at least, few healthy persons

who feel guilt about a misdemeanour are likely to confess it, except to a trusted confidant who they believe may help them.
Chinese Communist treatment applies a technique thought out
and practically planned to produce self-annihilation. The
prisoner's physical and mental environments are controlled as
strictly as possible. To break his spirit is made easier because he is
in continual conflict with an inflexible environment, completely
discordant with his natural milieu. Both in permitted behaviour
and in admitted standards of reality he is cut off from the 'related-
ness', without which he cannot survive. A 'divided self' results; it
is just this which, according to William James, is a prerequisite
for religious conversion. So the solution comes from within, and
the victim takes 'the people's standpoint'. His non-specific feelings of guilt-anxiety are channelled into a paranoid, pseudo-
logical system. He views past events as an outgrowth of personal
evil. His guilt becomes attached to specific actions, real or phan-
tasied, and broadens to include the major elements of his basic
identity. Eventually the prisoner experiences lessened dis-
harmony with his newly-acquired fellow-thinkers.

Dr Lifton describes the psychological 'rewards' of this integration in terms which express his disapproval, yet, since most of
the phrases which he sceptically fences inside 'quotes' are also
used of most religious conversions, I try here to recast them
neutrally.

The early period of imprisonment has been unbearably painful. But through 're-education' the prisoner has come to enjoy
the 'togetherness' of intimate group-living, of self-surrender, of
sharing the strength of an all-powerful force, of believing that
no problem need remain unsolved, of the catharsis of personal
confession and the satisfaction of frankness, the moral satisfaction
of participating in a great crusade of redeeming oneself and others,
and on a level of mass mysticism, of joining the struggle for peace
and the fight for equality.

The above passage paraphrases Lifton's account only slightly,
because it describes mental processes through which persons
whom the present writer knew were won over (some temporarily)
to the Moral Rearmament Movement,[30] and steps by which the
'Organization Man' achieves 'togetherness'. These techniques,
however, are chiefly based on overt reward, though to many persons disapproval or withdrawal of affection is punishment.

What is new in Chinese thought reform? Is it mysterious? Does it use techniques—e.g. hypnosis, drugs, the rationale of which is only guessed at by its users? Does it differ from Russian Communists' methods, and how? Are any of the Chinese methods borrowed from or suggested by Pavlov's investigations? To these questions American medical experts in technical publications give detailed answers. This thought reform is neither mysterious nor incomprehensible: it contains nothing for which Eastern or Western cultural history does not furnish a precedent. It induces 'confession' by utilizing anxiety accompanying guilt-feelings, and by moral exhortation; indeed, its 'therapeutic' approach is simpler than some which have been developed in Western psychiatry. The novelty lies in the fusion of its techniques into a powerful cohesive process; Milieu Control. The Chinese Communist prison is probably the most thoroughly controlled and manipulated group-environment that has ever existed. More and more the external milieu replaces the prisoner's internal milieu, bringing about reform from within. Orwell, in 1984, envisaged milieu-control through a two-way tele-screen, but the Chinese have accomplished it via the human mechanism, thereby extending their control even more deeply into the prisoner's innermost world.

Techniques borrowed from Russian Communist practices are summarized by Lifton, who contrasts them with those of the Chinese. In Russia, confessions are generally associated with the 'purge' part of the ritual of 'liquidation'. In China they are used in individual reform, as part of a programme of group-education. This 'thought reform' is at least twenty-five years old. It emphasizes the conduct of inter-personal relationships; an 'exquisite, superb art' in China, but used destructively in general thought reform. 'To abuse the mind and body, to turn man against himself, to dissolve his trust in others—whatever the justifying cause —can only result in the fragmentation of the human organism, where integration is so desperately needed.'

The articles containing the above extracts dealt with civilians. The treatment of soldiers will be described later: meanwhile it is important to read what Eugene Kinkead discovered to be US Army representatives' opinion concerning Chinese Communists' treatment of captured American army officers and men. On this the *Guardian* (November 25, 1957) commented:

'The US Army has enabled a journalist, Mr Eugene Kinkead, to publish in the New Yorker[91] a full and disturbing account of what happened in the camps beyond the Yalu. The account, based on elaborate investigations by the Army itself, can be summed up in one sentence: "Many appeared to lose all sense of allegiance, not only to their country but to their fellow-prisoners". . . . The Chinese are virtually absolved of using torture, though they did use harsh, capricious and unlawful treatment. The Army blames its failures rather on the breakdown of discipline. . . . It does not blame indiscipline alone. The Chinese, it finds, did do their utmost to win prisoners' minds and to break down the group into dependent individuals. . . . The Chinese, it seems, were as genuinely bent on rehabilitating what they took to be errant minds as we were on denazifying some Germans—though, of course, they used their own methods . . . The publication of this account is a sign of courage and health.'

My remarks below are based on the New Yorker article: at the time of writing I had not seen Kinkead's extension, in his book In Every War But One.*[92]

The Chinese Communists' treatment of army prisoners rarely included downright cruelty, but was a highly novel blend of leniency and pressure. The Korean war marked the first time in history that the American army had been confronted by an enemy who attempted to manipulate prisoners' minds, thus extending combat tactics into prison camps. Interrogation was used less to elicit military information than to produce a state of mind vulnerable to indoctrination. Physical torture was rarely used, but many forms of mental pressure and physical hardship were part of the treatment. Food, medicine, hospital care and mail were withheld: thus it was possible to assure the prisoner that his people no longer cared about him. A field-guide advised Chinese interrogators that prisoners most likely to be co-operative would be chiefly young enlisted men of higher quality, A Negro's allusion to racial discrimination in the USA, or a coal miner's son's account of family financial struggles were invariably used as bases for indoctrination.

Psychological techniques deliberately employed were repetition, harassment and humiliation. If a man failed to answer a

* English title Why They Collaborated, 1960, London.

question in class, he was given a long lecture on the necessity of paying attention to the instructor. He might receive another lecture at midnight, a third one at 2 a.m. and even a fourth later. If, in class, a man objected to some statement he considered serious enough to justify this action, the entire class was made to stand until he abandoned his objection. Next day he had to apologize both to the class and to the instructor, and for four or five days afterwards to repeat his self-criticism. The class, ordered to criticize him, obeyed: then he had to criticize his classmates. This was one of the principal methods of deliberately causing chaos in a group's relations.

Dr Edgar H. Schein's article 'The Chinese Indoctrination Process for Prisoners of War'[150] gives a generalized picture of what happened to the average soldier from capture to repatriation. Cruelty deliberately imposed on civilians was on the whole far less severe in the case of soldiers. In camp, prisoners were segregated by race, nationality and rank. No formal organization was permitted: some squad-leaders were appointed without consideration of rank, a method of 'getting at' the individual. Young or inept prisoners were put in charge of the squads, to remind everyone that former bases of organization had been destroyed. All friendships, emotional bonds and group activities were persistently undermined: all forms of religious expression prohibited. Chaplains or others who tried to organize or conduct religious services were ruthlessly persecuted. There is no evidence that the Chinese used drugs or hypnotic methods, or offered sexual objects to elicit information, confessions or collaboration. Some cases of severe physical torture were reported, but their incidence is difficult to estimate. Schein's conclusion is judicious:

'those who are attempting to understand "brainwashing" must look at the facts objectively, and not be carried away by hysteria when another country with a different ideology and with different ultimate ends succeeds in eliciting from a small group of Americans behaviour that is not consonant with the democratic ideology.'

In November 1956, the American Group for the Advancement of Psychiatry met 'to clarify the differences between Orwell's fantastic account and the real processes actually used in authentic cases'. Dr Lifton said: 'Brain-washing for our purpose no longer means anything specific, particularly in view of the manner in which it has been used in this country.' Among all the people he interviewed in Korea and Hong Kong no one who had been through the experience ever used the term, unless he had first heard it from a Western source. But the process of *szuhsiang-kai-tsao*, translated as 'ideological remoulding', 'ideological reform' or 'thought reform', is very much a reality.

There were three stages of 'thought reform':

(1) The *'Great Togetherness'*. The individual soldier was helped to identify himself with a group. To his astonishment the newcomer was often welcomed warmly, with proffered handshakes and cigarettes. The aim was to give the impression of a climate of *esprit de corps* and optimism. To 'mobilize' his thought, lectures, followed by discussions, were given.

(Since the lectures lasted from two to six hours, a non-Chinese university teacher, accustomed to a fifty-minutes' limit, may wonder how much the average listener absorbed. Sheer fatigue might increase suggestibility.) There was, in the Chinese manner, much repetition. Only about 5 per cent of the American army captives had received any college education, one aim of which is the formation and examination of concepts. At this stage, the prisoner was led to suppose that coercive manipulations of his thinking were morally uplifting and mentally harmonizing experiences.

(2) The *Closing-in of the Milieu* (particularly the mental milieu). In (1) the prisoner's intellectual processes have been worked upon; now comes the turn of the emotions. The object of study is now the learner, not the Communist doctrine. He is made increasingly aware that his chief activities must be criticism—of others and of himself—and 'confessions':

'Not only his ideas, but his underlying motivations, are carefully scrutinized. Failure to achieve the "correct" "materialistic" viewpoint, "proletarian standpoint" and "dialectical methodology" is pointed out, and the causes for this deficiency carefully analysed.'

In time, students are infected by the compulsion to confess, 'vie to outdo each other in the frankness, completeness and luridness of their individual confessions'.

An advisory *cadre* helps the emotionally-disturbed student, by talking over his 'thought problems'. The diagnosis of bodily troubles is apt to be 'reform-oriented' and 'psychosomatically sophisticated'; 'You will feel better when you have solved your problems and completed your reform.' And most students would need relief from inner tension and conflict.

(3) *'Submission and Rebirth'*. Group discussion produces a thought-summary or final confession. It is to be a life-history, including a detailed analysis of the personal effects of thought reform, and of the confessor's class origin. Nearly always the father is denounced, both as a symbol of the exploiting classes and as an individual.

With the fair-mindedness of a good psychiatrist, Lifton comments that in our own milieu-manipulations we should do well to retain a certain degree of humility and to keep in mind the dangers of imposing our own values and prejudices too forcibly.

In Britain and America, assertions are still made that the psychiatrist's aim is the patient's social adjustment; even sometimes that non-adjusters can be shown up, by tests, to be neurotic, or worse. A report by the Rockefeller Brothers' Fund (*News Chronicle*, June 25, 1958) arraigns 'the public lassitude that has accepted without question an educational system dedicated mainly to turning out good little conformist Americans who, as Stringfellow Barr puts it, even when they have graduated from college (famous institutions) are unfamiliar with the ideas that are the stock-in-trade of Western culture'. The report warns of 'the dangers of an age of conformity' and calls for the development of more creative individuals.

We have seen that an important aim of working on the prisoner's mind is to stir up guilt and shame, which help him to prepare a formal confession. Guilt-anxiety, says Lifton, consists of feelings of evil and sinfulness with expectation of punishment: of shame-anxiety, feelings of humiliation and failure to live up to the standards of one's peers or of one's internalized ego-ideal, with the expectation of abandonment.

He suggests that we too might profitably examine some of our

I

own concepts of guilt and shame. Examples come readily to mind. Diminution in the extent of clothing worn by both sexes in sports reduces the shame which fifty years ago would have been 'normal'. Since Hiroshima and the Nuremberg trials, 'war-guilt', which about 1922 weighed down many Germans too young to have fought in World War I, has now become the subject of cynical jokes.

In this connection Lifton discusses the relation between language theory and behaviour. Terms used in 'thought reform' are morally charged—either very good or very bad—and take on a mystic quality.

To psychologists attracted by the concept of 'patterns of culture' the above account of thought reform is impressive because it shows that in all social orders its elements are present in varying degrees.

At the conference, Professor Edgar H. Schein spoke on 'Patterns of Reactions to Severe Chronic Stress in American Army Prisoners of War of the Chinese'.[152] He selected observations throwing light on collaboration with the enemy. Typical experiences of an American army prisoner of war were:

'The first phase, lasting one to six months, was capture, an exhausting march to North Korea, and severe privation in inadequately equipped temporary camps. The second was imprisonment for two or more years in a permanent camp. Here, instead of the physical pressures in the first phase, chronic "persuasion" was applied to make the soldiers collaborate and to exchange existing group loyalties for new ones.

'The men reacted with the feeling that for these experiences of capture they had been inadequately prepared, both physically and mentally. They were not clearly aware of the kind of enemy up against them or, indeed, what they were fighting for. Expecting death, torture or non-patriation, they were taken completely by surprise and felt that inadequate leadership of the UN command was to blame. Understandably, therefore, a prisoner was inclined to listen without much scepticism to the Communist "explanation" that, since the UN was an aggressor, having entered the war illegally, all UN military personnel were in fact criminals and could be summarily shot. The Chinese, however, considered the prisoner to be a student, capable of learning the "truth". Yet if he did not co-operate he could just be reverted to war-criminal status and shot. So a chronic cycle of fear-relief-new-fear was set in motion.

'The one-two week marches caused increasing apathy, facilitating systematical destruction of the prisoner's formal and informal group-structure. Knowing that his own ranks contained spies and actual or potential informers, a man might eventually feel that he could trust nobody.'

Dr Schein considers that very few actual conversions to Communism occurred, but that success in producing collaboration was greater. Some collaborators perhaps believed—subsequent affirmation of this belief may have been rationalization—that they were infiltrating the Chinese ranks and obtaining information which, if they were released, would be useful to the US Army.

It is interesting and valuable to compare with the above accounts of army prisoners-of-war, a report by Professor Louis West on prisoners from the US Air Force. These were even less prepared for captivity, and their literal descent from the heavens into enemy hands must have given unusual possibilities of shock and astonishment. Often they were injured before capture. The Chinese considered these as a distinct group, to be handled in ways differing from those regarded as suitable for soldiers; e.g. after February 21, 1952, responsibility for germ warfare was placed on airmen.

It is important to note that of the Air Force 'returnees', 53 per cent had received some college education, compared with 5 per cent of army captives .As with the latter, the techniques employed produced 'debility, despondency and dread'. But many airmen tried to incorporate in their 'confessions' implausible material : details of weapons, speeds, altitudes, etc, which the interrogator, whose ignorance of technicalities they had estimated, would not detect but which, to any informed person, would appear palpably false.

Many people are inclined to speak of all 'public relations' as ballyhoo or propaganda, perhaps overlooking the early meaning of the latter word; even the significance, in England, of the second initial in 'S.P.G.'. They are invited to consider the facts that when a prisoner's 'confession', or even his letter home, contained

'Commies', it was 'suggested' that 'Chinese People's Volunteers' should be substituted, and the only address to which any prisoner's relatives could send letters was 'c/o the Chinese People's Committee for World Peace'.

Dr Lawrence E. Hinkle, in this symposium, suggests on the basis of extensive study that these conclusions can be accepted: 'The methods of the Russian and satellite State-Police are derived from age-old police methods, many of which were known to the Czarist Okhrana, and to its sister organizations in other countries. Communist techniques, when their background is studied, remain police methods. They are not dependent on drugs, hypnotism, or any other special procedure designed by scientists. No scientist took part in their design, nor do scientists participate in their operation. The goal of the KGB—the present designation for the Russian State police—is a satisfactory protocol on which a so-called "trial" may be based. The Chinese have an additional goal; the production of long-lasting changes in the prisoner's basic attitudes and behaviour.'

How could a prisoner-of-war resist such pressures? Hinkle offers the following hints. Since an important factor of indoctrination is the pupil's belief that his captors' control is omnipotent, he should try to maintain a secret private sense of psychological superiority. Inside his group, he should develop communication methods excluding the captors and demonstrating their fallibility, e.g. by using code-words which appear complimentary —only to the guards; by teaching them Western games—with absurd twists of the rules and methods of play, and by inventing petty annoyances to guards forbidden to inflict physical punishment. (It seems fair comment that for complete success this assumes high intelligence in the prisoner and obliging dimness in the guard.)

With reference to a prisoner's wish to mislead by giving inexact information, the US Military Service Code of Conduct for Prisoners of War instructs him to give only his name, rank and serial number, so long as he is able to resist. In the conditions of captivity imposed in Korea, this rule is almost impossible to obey for any length of time. In the symposium it was suggested that in view of the facts of modern warfare (nuclear warfare did not appear to have been discussed) this section of the code needed reviewing. One comment was 'The report written to the Secretary of Defence was a highly literate and informed document which made obeisance to the view (that every man has his breaking-point) and completely contradicted it in the final decision, accepting rather the traditional views held by Marine generals; that moral strength can enable servicemen to resist any sort of brainwashing, and similar views advocated by religious persons who testified before the Committee.'

Kinkead's apparently uncritical acceptance of the exposition of the American way of life by US Army officials, and his failure to demonstrate much insight into the prisoners' minds, have not escaped criticism in this country and, almost certainly, one would suppose, in America. His worry, said G. F. Seddon (*Guardian*, April 22, 1960) 'is not why men ceased to be men, but why Americans, unforgivably, ceased to be Americans'. . . . While Kinkead urges rethinking by government, educational and religious leaders into the American way of life, he avoids it himself, giving only the narrow interpretation that the Army had worked out. This was that the new generation of American soldiers had grown up undisciplined and soft. . . . As for the future, there was very little that could not be put right by old-fashioned Army discipline and new-fangled immunization against indoctrination. The Army officers whom Kinkead quotes also talk a lot about 'moral values, ethical intangibles, social responsibility, strength of character, making them all sound like regulation Army issue for ideal American soldiers'. This Seddon describes as the kind of romantic view that afflicts professional fighting men. . . .

In the *Spectator*, April 15, 1960, Professor Leopold Kohr tossed a bomb into the US Army Code of Conduct. He severely examined its basic assumptions, not as a system of morals, but as a technique of resistance. This will scarcely make him popular with the people who on religious, moral and patriotic grounds advised the code's formulators. His view is that to defeat Chinese brainwashing, wits as well as stamina are indispensable. Wits will be sharpened not by learning old-fashioned Codes of Conduct, but by realistic empathetic familiarity with the antagonist's moves. Sherlock Holmes caught criminals not by hating them, but by using his ability to put himself into their shoes, which honest Dr Watson never could.

In his article, Kohr refers to the Chinese techniques, and

presumably not to others. The code's formulators, he asserts, assume that any soldier likely to undergo attempted 'thought reform' will be fortified not only by saying to himself (do all soldiers think in words?) 'I am an American fighting man. . . . I will make no oral or written statements disloyal to my country', but by remembering a film of terrifying torture, and by preliminary submission to bodily hardships. However, the chief weapon of 'thought reform' is the induction of sympathy and 'understanding'. 'Its aim is to produce agreement, which can hardly be achieved by pummelling your naked stomach.'

So far as the US Army technique of indoctrination makes the soldier expect horrifying experiences when taken prisoner, it may help the 'reformer', since stage I of his 'therapy' bewilders the prisoner by demonstrating the incorrectness of the image of his captors which was suggested by his elders and betters. 'No horror, no threats; just a warmish apparent friendliness.'

At stage II, a drink is offered and a toast to the people of the USA proposed. This is intended to enlarge the beach-head in the prisoner's mind, by praising enthusiastically his nation's constitution, its form of government, its freedoms. Points of similarity are emphasized between the institution with which he is familiar and the enemy's. To his consternation, and perhaps eventual relief, the prisoner may begin to believe that 'his' highly publicized egalitarian ideas, their emphasis on community rather than personal pursuits, their subordination of conduct to the dictates of public rather than private opinion; their collectivist enthusiasm for government for the people rather than for the individual; the talk of a new form of people's capitalism : instead of constituting the antithesis of Communism, permit him to agree with it, say, 90 per cent. This reduces the area of difference to a mere 10 per cent. : the vital area, but to the prisoner, taught to think in terms of 100 per cent. opposition, 10 per cent. may seem hardly anything. So in the brief terminal stage III, blank docility (at least for the time) may be induced.

Personally I doubt whether today the average member of any army can be relied upon to despise or to oppose his wits to those of an apparently friendly interviewer. The psychology of this relationship is an advanced stage. Like an experienced class teacher, the interviewer knows most of the tricks which a bright but inexperienced leg-puller may try on. Most schoolboys who refer ribaldly to their form master respect, in their fashion, his intelligence and special knowledge. Will a farm worker, recently put into the army, expect to outwit the interviewer?

Even high intelligence may be an insufficient defence against the Chinese techniques. Assurance that one knows facts contradicting the 'reformer's' suggestions, possession of a pattern of sentiments opposed to his, and a stubborn woodenness are often necessary. These advantages are not always found in one person.

Though the term 'brainwashing' is still popular here, in America enthusiasm for it is said to be waning. Professor Schein suggests possible reasons for its early use:

(1) the need to find new terms for new ideological systems: a system without a name cannot be fought;

(2) 'scapegoating'; the desire to find someone, or something, to blame for the Chinese Communists' success in stalemating the Korean conflict;

(3) the impressively growing 'technology of influence', which in certain quarters inspires the belief that some agents of society can overwhelm the human mind;

(4) the changing international position, leading many Americans to doubt their capacity to deal with international problems.

He considers that books by Aldous Huxley[79, 80] and Dr J. A. M. Meerlo[112a] do not 'tell us where in our society we are to seek the positive motivating force and the institutions to which to attach such programmes as Huxley and Meerlo propose; e.g. improvement of education, rearing children to become more mature adults, legislation to prevent mental intrusion, improvement of methods of conservation and birth control, rehumanization of urban life'. 'In the rash of books and articles which, in the last few years, have condemned American society and character lies perhaps the most interesting phenomenon of all. Many of these works have posed difficult problems for some of our educators, e.g. for the military training officer who is attempting to instil pride and group spirit in recruits who have been publicly condemned as morally poor material to start with. It is perhaps time for the social scientist to shift his focus from the weakness in our society to the reasons why self-criticism is currently so popular in certain segments of our society.'

It is now possible to compare the 'thought reform' described above with another technique, not disclosed in this country until March 1960. The Chinese aims were unsubtle, even crude. They were fairly successful in controlling a human being's mental and physical environment. They relied on mere repetition as a feature of instruction; an old-fashioned idea, though attempts were made to fit treatment to the prisoner's mental characteristics. In this 'experiment' time was an unimportant consideration. Did the 'reformers' succeed? Not very well, if the large numbers treated and the small proportion of these 'permanently' converted are considered. About this last point it is impossible to argue satisfactorily: the view that anyone who 'fell for' this propaganda was seriously abnormal seems insecurely rooted when we remember the present eagerness of some prominent British publicists to assert that anyone who differs from them on political or religious lines must have been 'brainwashed'.

The pattern of techniques now to be described is much more complicated than that used by the Chinese, and its devisers have learned more from recent advances in knowledge of the workings of the human body and mind. The main part of the present chapter was written before March 1960, when brainwashing hit the headlines for several days. Since this book deals not only with facts but with popular reactions to them, and to speculations which they suggest, it is impossible to present only a coldly scientific view of this technique, or at the time of writing (late March 1960) of the ambiguity of governmental statements in reply to questions in the House. Answering a question about psychological and physical methods designed to disintegrate a prisoner's character, the Prime Minister asserted that brainwashing had never been used 'by any organization responsible to Her Majesty's Government'. He left open the question of what, if anything, our Government would do, or have done, if assured that 'practices of this kind' (another vague phrase used in a reply) were carried out by an organization not so responsible, or by individuals acting independently under cover of a responsible organization. On this the *Observer* commented on March 20, 1960:

'The Official Secrets Act makes it unlikely that the full truth will ever be learned. Individuals charged with the conduct of wartime interrogation often acted very much on their own, and the "organizations" which employed them did not inquire too closely into the methods they used to get results.'

We will pick our way through a thicket of statements and speculations which shot up after the delivery of Professor Alexander Kennedy's discourse to the Royal Institution: 'Scientific Lessons of Brain Washing'.* He described techniques designed to extract information from prisoners: in many respects they differed from those used by the Chinese Communists. An important part of this lecture (it might be called 'swords into ploughshares') explained how the noxious exploitation of personal relations in the case of men who had been 'softened up' by isolation from human contacts and by cunningly induced disorientation, spatial and temporal, could be used beneficially to restore to lonely old persons self-respect and a sense of the nature of their personalities. This socially important part of the discourse was overshadowed in the excitement of the Press and the public over the destructive methods: swords are more glamorous than ploughshares. Naturally, public interest was focused specifically on the question whether the British had ever used such methods on any prisoners, even spies. One cause of public disquiet was an account by a *Daily Mail* observer, in the issue of March 9, of his visit to the Intelligence Corps depôt at Maresfield, Sussex. He described physical discomforts and degradations inflicted on selected volunteers undergoing a course designed to acquaint them with attempts which, in a war, might be made to break their spirits and to extract information.

Since this article described chiefly bodily 'interferences', a psychologist's interest in it might have been indirect, had a photograph not headed the columns: it featured the Royal Arms on a signpost pointing to a 'Psychological Warfare Centre'. (Perhaps in this context 'psychology' includes physiology.)

It should be emphasized that the accuracy of Professor Kennedy's statements has not been questioned. Whether brainwashing was, or is, used by, or in, Britain; whether psychological methods were 'helped' by physical ill-treatment; whether in the 'inescapably dark corners' of all wars, sadists might privily

* I thank Professor Kennedy for kindly lending me his typescript so that the present account could be prepared before the printed discourse (*Proceedings of the Royal Institution*, April Number, 1960) was available.

improve these methods; whether spies received special treatment: all these questions are important in their places, but to ask them here would muddle a theoretical description of 'mind-moulding'. We are concerned here with the nature of the methods, the ways in which they were combined to achieve particular aims, and the borrowing of concepts from pioneers like Pavlov and Freud.

Professor Kennedy's description is scientific, uninterrupted by ethical comments. The main features of the technique, evolved after considerable trial and error, were derived from (here I quote his condensed statement):

(1) Knowledge of the physiology of consciousness, of changes in perception induced by fatigue and drugs, and the psychological effects of sensory deprivation.
(2) The (Pavlovian) theory and technique of the conditioned response as applied to the conditioning of the physical concomitants of emotion in man and the induction of artificial neurosis.
(3) Psychological study of the mental mechanisms seen in human beings under acute stress and of the interpersonal relations and transferences encountered in the course of psychotherapy and religious conversion.
(4) The empirical and largely personal methods of experienced interrogators who had realized the importance of eliminating factors of guilt and responsibility and of creating uncertainty as to the aims of the interrogation.

In its turn the method, with its unique opportunities, has pointed the way to further observations in each of these disciplines.

The division (below) of the method into stages is artificial, since the management of each person is a continuous process. (The following paragraphs are taken from both Professor Kennedy's lecture and Dr Anthony Storr's article 'Torture Without Violence' (New Statesman and Nation, March 12, 1960).)

(1) *Disorientation and Disillusion*
The prisoner is completely isolated: all ties with the outer world severed. He is left alone with his fears, knowing that he is entirely at his captors' mercy. Since his sense of personal identity depends upon communication with others, he ceases to behave

as 'himself'. He is deliberately deprived of many sensory messages which he would normally receive, and is subjected to confusing stimuli: this disorients him in time and place. After about four weeks of complete isolation, most prisoners become severely depressed, cease all spontaneous activity and allow themselves to become dishevelled and dirty. They may sit all day, muttering to themselves. This is the clinical picture seen in chronic schizophrenia and, in some old persons, of emotional isolation due to lack of social contacts. Now it is known that normal persons can be reduced to a similar condition.

(2) The Interrogation

This is often welcomed by the prisoner, as affording him an opportunity for human relations of a kind. By this time he may have become uncertain of his contacts with the environment, of his personal identity, of the very existence of right and wrong. The interrogator contributes to this bewilderment by pretending complete indifference to questions asked and answered, even to the prisoner himself. All this increases his confusion and loss of identity. He is now uncertain of the dividing line between his thoughts and the interrogator's. By systematic conditioning, psychological tension, with its distressing physical concomitants, is produced, yet the feeling is unattached to any particular system of ideas. Later, when mental conflicts have been artificially synthetized, based on circumstances carefully chosen from the subject's life history, 'free-floating anxiety' is attached to them by conditioning.

The object of this technique is to increase anxiety to the point of crisis, when the subject cannot guide his attitudes or solve his conflict by any system of reference. When a breaking point is judged to be near, the interrogator suddenly changes into a kindly father-figure, intimating that the subject can be helped to find his bearings again. It is indicated, largely by implication, that a way of life and thought exists which can provide a stable basis for existence, and produce peace of mind by acceptance of an idealized, dogmatic frame of reference.

The prisoner is now induced to believe that the contents of his thoughts, which by now he may not be able to distinguish from the interrogator's, and even of his dreams, are known to the interrogator. Since he has conditioned the subject by stimuli given in light sleep, this seems less uncanny to the unsuspecting victim.

As soon as a 'confession' has been obtained, the interrogator jumps in to cut off the subject's line of retreat. He is induced to make a token act of treachery to his previous beliefs and sentiments, denouncing former colleagues in a broadcast or recorded speech. He is now irrevocably committed.

The interrogator, in a kindly manner, proceeds to explain to the prisoner his past errors. He is now given better food and quarters, and made to feel convalescent, which indeed he is. Experiencing this sudden exhibition of 'friendship' causes him to pour out his emotions and often, too, whatever information is required from him at this point. A conversion is now occurring, with emotional catharsis following states of doubt and conflict. A sense of quiet supervenes, and the desire to atone for 'bad thoughts': this is no longer ignored by the interrogator.

(3) *Rationalization and Exploitation*

An introspective search is now carried out for ways in which the subject's knowledge of the enemy's activities can be used to further the aims of the new system, now invested in the prisoner's mind with qualities of reasonableness and justice. He is integrated into a limited community already loyal (i.e. brainwashed) to the induced credo, with ceremonial and symbolic acts of acceptance which stir him deeply. His re-education and training are carried out in a group of similar subjects who voluntarily police each other, so far as their new-found loyalty is concerned.

The *Observer* commented:

'(This technique) involves a profound invasion of the subject's personality by the interrogator. . . .

'The end does not justify the means. . . .

'Human beings should not be treated by the State as a collection of reflexes to be manipulated at will. . . .

'We ought to know more about its long-term effects. Do the police in this country ever use it? A detailed statement on the whole subject should be made by the Government.'

Dr Anthony Storr, in the article cited, wrote:

'These statements are bound to cause anxiety throughout the medical profession. Are these methods still being used in our public service, either at home or overseas? We are no longer at war, but doctors are employed by the British Government both in the armed forces and in the prisons. Are they ever asked, in the course of their duties, to advise upon, or to take part in, interrogation procedures? If so, it is appropriate to recall part of the Hippocratic oath: "I will use treatment to help the sick according to my ability and judgment, but never with a view to injury and wrongdoing".'

It has been stated that, in training special types of our soldiers, these methods have been used on volunteer 'prisoners', with the help of mock 'informers' and 'double agents', to ascertain how such soldiers would be likely to react to pressures. The RAF has officially denied using such methods (*News Chronicle*, March 18, 1960).

Diverse views, relevant and irrelevant to this 'limited' question of training, were expressed in the Press and on the air. The samples quoted below all came from public figures regarded as serious and responsible. They should interest any social psychologist, as they were made in good faith and given the widest currency, even if some of them are based on no special knowledge.

(1) Ethical considerations apart, are such methods likely to achieve their presumed aims? Could mentally tough persons, of high or low intelligence, resist successfully, but for different reasons? What are these? If they are known, can a special type of mental resistance be taught, and how?

(2) What kinds of interviewee, normal under all ordinary strains, is likely to crack under this unpredictable mental torture?

(3) Where does the legitimate art of interviewing end and the horror of brainwashing begin?

(4) Does the increasing use of interrogation, in the Press, on sound radio, and especially on television, lead to a revived public tolerance (to put it mildly) of trial by ordeal? An ordinary citizen being 'needled', or presented with questions deliberately loaded, under glaring lights to which he is unaccustomed, is interrogated by an expert who has prepared his questions. One may speculate that the popularity of such staged dramas might at least not diminish if the interviewee had at his elbow an

adviser who knew some law, psychology and logic. Perhaps, too, the candidate might be allowed, as he would be in the civilized atmosphere of a university oral examination, to ask an occasional question to clarify the issue.

(5) One aim of brainwashing was said to be 'to make the subject realize that there is more to be said for the other side than he has realized before'. This statement would be unpopular with morale-boosters, but extensive brainwashing carried out by both the opposing sides might have surprising effects on wars of the non-nuclear kind.

(6) Successful resisters of 'reasoned' propaganda may be simple people with little background knowledge, who will simply disbelieve all that the interrogator says, though the disorientating treatment might have shaken them badly. Effortless resisters would not be educated persons with no great faith in any political system, who feel that they have been let down by being offered a caricature of the other side's beliefs.

(7) Brainwashing, said a distinguished student of past wars, is based on a technique successful with dogs, but disgusting as applied to men. (Yet much military drill is rough-and-ready conditioning. Arguments in favour of it, e.g. that in danger or stress a well-drilled soldier will 'instinctively' do the right thing, can be supported by much evidence from the study of habit formation—exact repetition, absence of exceptions, frequency and, as sergeants know well, intensity.)

(8) An ex-prisoner-of-war remarked on the radio: 'I can't say how much the Japs knew about brainwashing, but we never knew what was to come next.' (In some cases, this might have been a help to morale, since a premonition of the nature of the 'punishment' to come might unsettle minds.)

(9) On being interviewed, a doctor who 'spent the war studying Army morale for our War Office' replied that a training which disclosed to the men the nature of brainwashing is completely misconceived: the driving force behind our troops ought to be, not hatred, but love and comradeship. 'If the War Office is planning for their possible capture—well, what sort of an outfit will they think they are in? This is an ideal way of creating disloyalty to one's own army.' (This reply confuses loyalty to comrades with loyalty to ideas. As a result of its failures in Korea, the US Army intends to tell its troops what they may expect if captured. In the

war, our civilian air-raid drills, describing the dangers that might be expected—the German experiment on Grimsby gave us information, passed on to the civilians, about anti-personnel bombs —did not create disloyalty, and probably decreased fear in many persons.)

Another variant of mental torture, not even exercised in the privacy of a prison, is reported by Sebastian Haffner in the *Observer* of April 3, 1960. He writes (Berlin, April 2) that during the spring of 1960 there has been a high-pressure drive for collectivization of farms in East Germany. The victims are independent peasant farmers in eight of the fifteen districts of East Germany. The collectivization is enforced by individual blackmail, in which the whole pressure that party, State and political police are capable of is brought to bear relentlessly on each individual farmer until he breaks down.

'The operation starts with the "occupation" of a village by a group of trained party agitators, usually about fifty strong. They call on the peasants to surrender both their possessions and their personal services to a local collective.

'Sometimes a village meeting is held, sometimes not. The real work of "patient persuasion" which provides the results is always done in subsequent home visits to the individual peasants, and enforced marathon talks, which are never relaxed till the victim has given in.

'The peasants often bolt their gates, loose their dogs, try to flee to the fields, all in vain.

'In the ensuing discussion the farmer is often trapped into making anti-Communist remarks, and thereupon threatened with arrest and trial unless he signs on the dotted line. Sometimes arrests are actually carried out, and some farmers have been given widely-publicized deterrent sentences—of up to fourteen years' hard labour—for exactly this offence.

'Always the chief means by which resistance is finally overcome is sheer wearing down through relentless insistence; the "Darkness at Noon" technique. . . . While a village is under this treatment, the local police are often reinforced from outside and extra precautions are taken against the flight of the inhabitants.

'This novel method of collectivization by individual blackmail is being carried out like a prepared military operation, directed by the State against its own rural population.'

This chapter discussed methods of 'thought reform' practised by Chinese Communists in Korea. It concentrated on psychological rather than physical aspects of these techniques, not all of which were applied to both civilian and combatant prisoners. Official advice for resisting such pressures was discussed. A social psychology and sociology of testimony are needed. Early investigations of testimony concentrated on the mental processes of the witness, not of his examiners: these may be at least as important. The use, in court trials, of 'confessions' obtained by 'lie detectors' and 'truth serums' raises many legal and psychological questions. The 'stress interview' shows the extent to which inter-personal tensions can disorganize a subject's verbal testimony. A psychological re-examination is needed of the relations between speaking, thinking and general behaviour, and the formation of concepts of guilt and shame.

In a more recent account of a different kind of brainwashing the manipulations of the personal relations between prisoner and interrogator are described. Considerable difference of opinion exists concerning the wisdom of experimenting on volunteer soldiers to acquaint them with the kinds of ill-treatment they might expect if captured.

The techniques of social isolation and disorientation can be used in reverse, as curative treatment for old persons whose loneliness has caused a degree of mental disintegration.

A newspaper account of another variant being used in East Germany reports that repetition of argument combined with the instilling of fear of imprisonment is being imposed on the rural population to force the acceptance of collectivization.

CHAPTER NINE

Advertising and Publicity

Writers with conflicting outlooks, philosophical, political and financial, are discussing publicity, public relations and advertising. Though these activities influence the individual and the community, a single author seldom considers both these effects. Unemotional assessment of their social desirability is rare, and humour often distracts attention from disquieting facts. These are not always adequately described, since in this competitive field secrecy is imposed.

Of theoretical and practical interest is the use by advertisers of symbols of status and sex, motivation research, 'depth interviews' and 'group reveries' to discover subsurface motives.

There has been much popular interest in the 'threat' of subliminal persuasion. 'Subception' has significant psychological and ethical implications.

The relation, in advertising, between information and persuasion, and the general nature of persuasion are discussed.

This chapter describes certain methods of influencing minds. No attempt is made to suggest to the reader his helplessness in the face of attempts, morally justified or not, to mould his thoughts and beliefs. It does not support or condemn 'advertising' as if it were a single activity.

A difficulty arises for a psychologist who studies certain branches of advertising: to many critics these seem to be, and sometimes are, fantastic or funny. This destructive approach gives tempting opportunities to humorists, satirists and parodists. For well-understood reasons, replies to such attacks are usually serious, even when the defender may be known to be capable of humour. An observer with no axe to grind, or wield, may be regarded as childishly credulous. These assessments must be cheerfully accepted as a few of the psychologist's burdens.

Nobody observing daily events is likely to doubt that his freedom to think and act as an individual is seriously affected by the

K

myriad forms of advertising, managed 'publicity' and 'public relations' which have grown up recently. Most of them limit such freedom; yet, if a psychologist tries to fit the subjects of the present chapter into a social picture, he is impeded by the lack of seriousness with which the public, the aim of the exercise, regards them. It might be tedious to speculate here concerning the reasons why, in England, important social forces are considered as suitable matters for jokes, wit and humour. Perhaps this attribute keeps us all—on a short-range view—sane, though Hitler and the atom bomb were once popular subjects for music-hall humour, and our late enemies remember a singularly unfunny song about the Siegfried Line. Some forms of advertising seem a blessing, some a menace; the choice of descriptions depends upon the classifier. Ringing church bells is obviously advertising, yet even to the same person there is a difference between hearing them across a mile of country fields and a hundred yards away in a town. Few people, except the perpetrators, are enthusiastic about sky-writing, or posters which flash past interminably on the *autostrada*.

Simple, quotable arguments for and against advertising are hard to find. This is not surprising, on the assumption that many arguers are not trying to be objective and neutral. The 'aesthetics' of visual and auditory advertising seems to be a string of assertions about personal tastes: in the late nineteenth century many a home was gladdened by Millais's 'Bubbles'; today, children are delighted by pictorial hoardings which 'decorate' breakfast tables, shouting the virtues of rival cereals, and by TV 'jingles'; yet all these may distress minds far from super-sensitive. Many women's magazines are bought chiefly for their coloured advertisements, and until a few years ago advertising panels in Underground trains were often more amusing than the newspaper. We seem reduced to the platitude that without advertising, people would never know of the good things of life as well as the bad; the bland assertion that nobody can continue to advertise a 'bad buy' was probably thought up on Madison Avenue.

To discuss detachedly the psychological aspects of modern developments in large-scale competitive advertising is not easy. A psychologist writing about it is embarrassed by the available data, for they hint at the quality and quantity of those unavailable. Since these are usually sold privately, and if generally known would be financially valueless to any agency, they are guarded as efficiently as, if less spectacularly than, some military secrets. A psychologist may be forgiven for suspecting that some of his readers will wish for a fiery polemic, others for soothing syrup; few will be satisfied with the results of an attempt at impartiality. It has been suggested that if advertising is attended by evils, they are slight and necessary, and since not all its activities are overt no scientist should allow himself to guess at the nature of covert ones. Indeed, in this business there are more security-implications than appear at first glance. Loyalty to the agency is insisted upon: one critic considers that most agencies 'have sold themselves too thoroughly' on this idea.

Most results of psychological research are probably published, communicated orally to societies or communicable to colleagues working on similar subjects. As long as a generation ago, the necessity of secrecy, to establish priority of discovery, worried many chemical and physical researchers, but most psychologists would have felt insulted if they were called secretive. Two wars, an uneasy 'peace', and the development in technically advanced countries of 'psychological' warfare (itself, like 'biological', a convenient camouflaging term) have made psychologists realize that the most effective way of learning the truth may not be to attend conferences.

A discouraging fact is that most 'discussions' of the social aspects of advertising are attacks on or apologies for the activity. A hidden snag consists in the ease with which popular language can be used to conceal puzzling facts. This is not always the writer's fault; few editors of newspapers would print attempts to attach precise psychological meanings to 'subception', 'subliminal persuasion', or 'perceptual defence'. Such terms, because the ordinary reader half understands them, are sitting birds for the predatory humorist. In contrast, the quantum theory has never been easy to caricature, and a famous scientist's recommendation of brown paper as a protection against the results of the H-bomb was not meant as a joke. Humorous articles about advertising often succeed in their aim of distracting attention from the facts.*

We may consider a few statements on advertising in general. Discussions between representatives of advertising agencies and

* Deadly serious, however, is S. J. Perelman's 'La Plume de Mon Ami est dans le Flapdoodle'; New Yorker, October 11, 1958.

their critics are usually conducted in apparently simple terms. As almost invariably these relate to psychological, sociological or economic matters, it is not surprising that issues become confused. A little muzziness is not always displeasing to some of the discussers, since it makes it harder to pin them down. Yet advertisers, like politicians, might profitably reflect on the tendency of popular phrases used defensively, or vulgar ones used condescendingly, to backfire. The assertion in our Press that the public are, by and large, a mighty smart bunch of guys preceded reports of the American television quiz scandals, 'Payola' (the alleged bribery of disc-jockeys by gramophone companies) and widespread criticism of the FCC, the Government agency which polices the American ether. More than one concern has instituted inquiries into the American public's attitude towards television and radio after these exposures. Some investigators declared that the revelations were no more than a nine days' wonder. An English visitor with special knowledge of radio and television here and in America met a number of thoughtful Americans who admitted ruefully that this was probably true and they felt it to be disturbing.

People who carry out consumer research have been described in a book on advertising as 'dangerous characters who want to tell us what is good for us'. It is good for us to be protected against the dangers of drip-feed oil heaters and some alleged flame-proof garments, and the instructions issued with some potentially dangerous machines would be all the better for criticism from literate, even if dangerous, characters. Another resentment is of 'a superior group which wishes to stunt individuality and the diversification of tastes and choice'. Persons intimately acquainted with a commodity offered for sale are often shocked by an advertiser's over-simplification of the facts concerning its action. In a newspaper discussion, a dental surgeon reported that a tiresome duty is to disabuse his patients of the notion that certain proprietary drugs possess magical properties. 'The effectiveness of simple analgesic tablets bears little if any relation to price: here is one field at least where not only is the will for a better life not served by advertisement, but where sickness is exploited for financial gain.'

Another correspondent asserted that the whole point of advertisers' increasing reliance on applied psychology, aided by motivation research, is to by-pass the level of conscious argument and rational choice in order to mobilize unconscious impulses in the service of mass production and commercial enterprise. A 'reply' was that individuals, whether as tax-payers or as philanthropists, will contribute more or with greater conviction to the financially starved sections of the community if needs are adequately explained: what better instrument for this purpose than display advertising, which so many social institutions already employ? Still, secretaries of most social institutions for helping the financially starved sections of the community find display advertising expensive.

Advertisers use pictorial symbols extensively: since some act at unconscious as well as at conscious levels, the customer's freedom to choose is constantly being affirmed and denied, at the level of popular speech. Attempts to think rationally about irrational beliefs and behaviour are often greeted with sceptical amusement, but how does one think rationally about sudden changes in styles of hats or shoes, except to attribute the usual motive forces to the fashion dictators?

I have found no discussion of advertising in which psychological problems are formulated separately. Most of the 'psychological' terms carry such vague meanings, as deduced from the examples quoted, that one longs for definitions. In debating one important issue, for example, it was confidently stated (1) that information differs from persuasion, (2) that they are never distinguishable, even in theory, (3) that in practice they always overlap. Statement (1) seems justifiable. 'Big Ben', striking midday, informs millions of hearers, and may persuade some to knock off for lunch. 'Bradshaw' gives information unpersuasively, in contrast with the travel agency's brochure which prints the departure times of the Paris Night Ferry in large print in an attractive frame. It may add facts about comfort or flattering exhortations to Top People to arrive fresh for important work. Private advertisers seldom pay much for non-persuasive communication.

To support the assertion that information and persuasion often shade into each other, the *Guardian* of January 25, 1960, reports that Professor Ralph Ober, former member of the *New York Times* staff, and now at the new School of Social Research in New York, has declared that American newspapers use 'a substantial amount of "Payola" '. He refers to the practice of under-cover payment for mentions, in news stories or other features, of certain products or personalities. 'A typical column frequently contains eighty per cent of partially or wholly inaccurate material from public relations sources, and eighty per cent of all newspaper material emanates from public relations sources. . . . The Press it-self should not have the right to practise payola and at the same time criticize other media for doing the same thing.'

In the *Observer* (October 26, 1958) Pendennis asserts that people in the advertising agencies are always half-expecting some-one to be rude about them. Yet the business is too prosperous for agency men to worry much, except about matters like 'brand image', 'motivation research' and the conventions of their pro-fession. These are strict. Agents must not ask an advertiser to let them handle his lucrative 'account' if he is already doing business with another agency which is a member of the Institute of Prac-titioners in Advertising. They must be very careful with medical advertising (yet sailing close to the wind is a challenging sport). The organizers of market research, trying to establish who buys what, when and why, offer high salaries to statisticians, socio-logists and psychologists. Motivational research, despite, and occasionally aided by, jokes about it (the delvers have heard the names of Ford and Goldwyn) continues. Few practitioners will talk freely about its applications, for fear that their expensive analysis of the reasons why people *really* choose this soap or that chocolate will be used by rivals. To judge from some criticisms of 'motivation researchers' one might infer that no civilized human being ever does anything for a reason which is not economic. Yet some economists fall in love, and go so far as to have wives and children.

Inevitably, agencies use special techniques to advertise them-selves. Some win friends among simple down-to-earth thinkers by asserting that they are 'not interested in bright young men straight from the universities'; others, with that modesty which endears the English to the English, murmur, 'There are very few clever people in the industry.' The good, we note, are still hard on the clever. Agencies which 'rib' motivational research are diplomatically described by some rivals as 'possibly not very scientific'.

Some observers regard 'public relations' as a cousin of advertising. Though Martin Mayer[109] states that today their aims are not identical and their methods differ, at times these near-cousins co-operate to build up a political personage. The public relations man seeks to 'project' his client's reputation, character or 'image' in such a way that the public is influenced.

On November 4, 1958, a commentator in the BBC's *Today* stated that Mr Harriman and Mr Rockefeller were employing advertising agencies to further the aims of their candidature. One agency urged more tactile approaches; hand-shaking, arms thrown round the shoulders of a stranger, baby-tickling; perhaps the harbingers of Aldous Huxley's 'feelies'. The statement that advertising agencies help in similar build-ups here was made in Parliament in the same month, and in January 1959 a *Guardian* editorial was significantly entitled 'Crawfie in Politics'. In July 1959 the visit to this country of Japan's Prime Minister was handled by 'public relations'.

An example of semi-hidden persuasion, creeping into respected newspapers, is the column' slanted' towards a commercial product, yet phrased so that the 'secondary' theme is not apparent until the reader nears the end. Journalists have protested against its use.

There seems no conclusive simple answer to the question 'Does large-scale advertising of an article decrease its price to the consumer?' If only one firm is advertising the product, this might be so, yet today much money is spent in merely trying to get ahead of competitors. The assertion that the formula of a product has been modified several times in the customer's interest may invite questions of several kinds.

A *New Yorker* drawing depicts startled faces around a directors' table; a member has asked, 'What if some day they all decided it didn't pay to advertise?' What, indeed, would happen to the *New Yorker*?

The usefulness, in advertising, of psychological and sociological knowledge cannot be judged only by its fruits. An agency may not wish to wait for fruits; still less to pay for their careful nurture and scientific examination. One practitioner asked Mayer 'Who the hell wants to be *safe*? Persuasion is an art.' If a new idea of a picture, slogan or jingle seems good, yet so topical that it might occur to a competitor, why not get in first? Yet an individualist's bright idea might dazzle few other people and nowadays most agencies carry out pilot surveys. But in the early days of World War II a splendid, dark red, expensive poster, widely distributed, assured passers-by 'Your Courage, Resolution' (etc) 'will win Us the victory'. Suggestions were not wanting that the slip was Freudian.

Advertisers deal in symbols, and find symbols of status useful: Any symbol may be 'over-determined', the cross and swastika being examples. Whatever may be a person's estimate of the importance, in England, of social differences, he sees, hears, smells, tastes, touches, and, if he rides, sails, dances or skis, he feels in his muscles, many status-symbols. Ascending the social scale, aided by a pony or horse (never a motorcycle or greyhound) is an activity noticeable in this country. There are obvious psychological reasons why, for this purpose, very expensive cars are less useful, and, in some parts of America, a social handicap. Yet in most places the car and the telephone are status symbols. A well-known actor who drives regularly from London to the country described to me the change in his reception at filling-stations when he appeared in an ancient Rolls instead of his small car. Eyebrows were raised when he insisted on buying his usual brand of petrol.

An account of the way in which status-symbols vary in different social contexts is 'almost pure sociology', yet since sex symbolism is important and its discussion excites protests, smoking-concert jokes and 'common-sense' criticism, the psychological researcher's lot is not a happy one. Finding himself an Ishmael, he is tempted to react by over-statement. Yet consider the popularity of the expensive cigarette lighter, a symbol of financial status. We wonder how many are given to persons of the presenter's own sex.

A status symbol may become a sex symbol, and vice-versa, as the publicity agents of film stars know. Yet the subject is tricky; Mayer says that social aspiration may conflict with social status: either or both may disagree with social origins. Forces which dictate individual patterns of buying will operate very differently in the parvenu oil areas of Texas and in the disintegrating enclave of Tuxedo Park, in the open working-class suburbs of Los Angeles and the nasty slums of Chicago. Emphasizing the social symbolism of a product may influence the market for the brand in a way which the advertiser did not desire. The social plunge of the neo-Edwardian suit caused young men who could ill afford it to send theirs unworn to the second-hand dealer. To advertise effectively, the manufacturer must know his present 'brand image', the community it selects, and opportunities for increasing the market offered by the facts of social stratification.

The treatment of this subject is simpler in younger countries. In ours, the wording of some advertisements may hold off newly-rich, shy people, but a current publication depicts young people with horses, suggesting that a tailoring firm is prepared to sell them correct riding clothes.

'Motivation research' ought to designate studies by psychologists (non-advertisers) who for years have been asking relevant questions and attempting to answer them by techniques available for general purposes. 'Brand loyalties', however, is part of the advertiser's professional vocabulary. Do such narrow sentiments exist in enough potential customers to be worth intensification? No reliable answer can be expected from one person's introspections, but if my attitudes are not atypical I would suggest that towards articles bought frequently—shaving soap or razor blades—I experience only faint brand-loyalty, and am ready to try a novelty; often returning to a trusted brand. I am loyal to what advertisers call a 'magic circle'; e.g. of teas and coffees sold by an old, famous company. Towards an expensive mechanism, the structure of which is beyond my comprehension, I play for safety, choosing a firm with a good reputation, though seldom inquiring if it has been maintained, or if the original proprietors have been 'taken over'.

Is it sacrilegious to wonder if certain public schools build up a 'brand-image', to last for generations? A famous school proudly exhibits to visitors a family name cut into its panels repeatedly for centuries: prize-day speeches often suggest that a 'brand-image' guided their preparation. German university students used to liken Oxbridge undergraduates to cats, faithful to a building, and themselves to dogs, attached to an admired leader, ready to move with him if he is 'called' to another post. It seems unlikely that the loyalties of earnest students of the physical sciences will be attached to laboratory buildings of the new type to be found in Oxbridge, Redbrick, or remote parts of the country, favoured by industrial firms.

It is important that the investigator of an advertisement's

efficacy shall see the goods with the eyes of an average consumer.
This will not come easily to the science-trained man, accustomed
to admire and to write cagey, critic-proof sentences, regardless
of non-scientific readers. The effectiveness of print-advertising is
hard to determine. What, for example, is the relation between the
number of persons who can be proved to have 'read' (an ambiguous word) an advertisement, and those who, as the sole result of
reading it, buy the article recommended? Problems of individual
psychology arise here. A recognition test ('Did you see this advertisement?') is easily administered: but 'see' is vague. On one
side of the display title of a national newspaper, my favourite for
many years, an advertisement appears. I cannot remember what
it is: some years ago I ascertained that the current one referred
to the branded cigarettes of a shop which I often passed: I had
never entered it. Nor did I after that discovery, though to any
cigarettes I was faithful only in my fashion. Tests of 'aided recall'
can discover if a part of the advertisement was remembered, yet
an insertion so pretty, witty or bizarre that the reader recalls it
may not tempt him to buy: he may distrust funny men.

A negative assertion, implying that all rival brands have a
defect from which the product advertised is happily free, may
help to build up a brand-image. In the early days of radio, one
firm admitted that its sets could not get twenty-five Continental
stations, even simultaneously. 'Xs are not injurious' may suggest
to readers untrained in logic that rival brands are.

Researchers into the effectiveness of advertising use 'attitude
measurement'; a question-begging term. This gives useful data
about attitudes to a brand, but, as Mayer says, 'product advertising seeks to influence people's behaviour, not their attitudes, and
the relation of attitude to behaviour on any fixed basis is a fact
beyond even the claims of the social scientists'.

It is interesting to consider the extent to which, half a century
ago, social conditions affected a person's freedom to buy whatever he could afford. In this context the meaning of 'freedom'
could be examined: in 1910 a middle-class Londoner would often
patronize a large general store, a specialist firm, and a corner
shop. From emporia in Victoria Street or Westbourne Grove he
would confidently expect delivery, on credit, of goods ordered on
a postcard; specialist retailers could be trusted for superlative
quality; from the corner shop he cheerfully accepted what they

had in stock. Though many firms were advertising specialities, he often preferred non-advertised goods from the famous store, assuming that its buyers knew where to get good hams, sausages and pork pies, and being uninterested in makers' names. He believed that the customer eventually paid for all advertising. Early stunts were interesting: free samples of powders to make jelly or ink, or to cure drunkenness without the sufferer's knowledge, came through the post. Self-conscious atypical 'Quakers' walked the streets, bullock wagons were led by sheepish men, there were jokes about soap, not yet an object of romance and veneration; a funny poster of a fisherman, but fully clothed, advertised Skegness. 'Oracles', touched with the glowing head of a match, spelt out a name now famous both in pharmacies and opera-houses. Articles were recommended for their relevant qualities: breakfast foods were to eat, not, as an old-fashioned customer growled, to snap, crackle, pop or make any damn silly noises.

Now, some say, we are much freer to choose our purchases. This simple statement is unconvincing. Many more, and more different, articles are available, though one's favourite brand may have been called in; 'reconstructed' under the same name, or ruthlessly liquidated. In practice, freedom of choice is psychologically narrowed by reiterated insistence, to our eyes and ears, that So and So's brand is the best. 'Best for what?' is a pertinent question, applying to bread, beer and bombs.

It is unnecessary to emphasize the economic and social significance of modern advertising. In 1957, Unilever spent on advertising alone eighty-three million pounds, spread over nearly 200 companies in more than 100 countries. North America alone accounted for nearly half this total. These figures are obtained from Lord Heyworth's speech on April 24, 1958, reported in *Advertising* (Unilever Ltd). 'The advertiser's target,' he said, 'is claimed to be the whole population of the free world; i.e. 1,800 million possible consumers.'

The morality of advertising might be a much-discussed subject. Under the heading 'The Challenge to the Individual', Lord Heyworth expresses his belief that 'people' are a good deal tougher than those who wish to protect them have realized. This seems a broad generalization about 1,800 millions. Of 'people' he observes confidently:

'Naturally, they will sometimes make mistakes, but they learn from those mistakes, and build up a resistance which one might compare to that which the human body develops from measles and other childish ailments. . . . As a result, they are not all that easily misled.'

Unilever's medical researchers might raise their eyebrows at this confident leap from facts of epidemiology to speculations in psychology. The establishment, here and in America, of Consumer Research and periodic reports to subscribers (*Which?* and *Shoppers' Guide*) suggests that a significant number of people are building up a willed resistance by employing scientists to protect them from 'educative' mistakes.

Vance Packard's *The Hidden Persuaders* is extensively documented. He refers to professionally recognized psychologists and sociologists. This fact might suggest that, in view of the book's wide circulation in several countries and the numerous reviews it received on both sides of the Atlantic, some comment could be expected from those who do not believe 'never explain' to be a good principle in the conduct of science.

Since for certain degrees of some American universities the study of psychology is compulsory, speculation is permissible concerning the motives of graduates free to choose further work on this subject. Mr Packard was told that some 'psychologists' employed by the advertising agencies were out-of-work actors. Probably some members of this profession have had academic psychological training, yet ability to speak, with varieties of emotional expression, lines written by others, and to behave as a director wishes, with the special kind of extraversion characterizing many actors, would not equip them, without curative training, to conduct research into people's motives. Concerning the 'graduate in psychology', one would like to know how many had an honours degree in this subject, and how many had taken it as one in a group. Professional sociologists might ask similar questions.

Having read few criticisms by psychologists of *The Hidden Persuaders*, I venture to record my impressions of it, explaining, for the general reader, the meaning of the persuaders' concepts and methods. Their chief tools are signs and symbols : these can be distinguished. Since jokes directed against the investigators often depend for success on smudging this difference, everyday illustrations may be admissible here.

A signpost's message usually suggests nothing about the nature or functions of the destination towards which it points. Until recently, to classically educated British motorists—so much the worse for any others—a torch symbolized a school. This symbol is now wisely replaced by a sign, of scholars about to cross a road. Ambiguity of a word or a symbol may be welcomed by an advertiser. Certain common objects suggest to more people than would admit it biologically important thoughts: anyone who believes that some hills 'ought' not to suggest female breasts, might be reminded of the Paps of Jura. Here, the psychoanalysts nearly have it both ways: they may assume the vehement denial of the existence of a certain sexual thought to indicate repression; especially if the speaker laughs at a 'naughty' reference wittily wrapped up.

In the motivation-researcher's conversation or his 'depth' interview, the subject's associations of ideas are likely to be studied. Any doubter of the value of this old-established technique should honestly 'free-associate' before a tape-recorder for ten minutes on each of ten days and then note not only the nature of the associations but also the blockages. The launching point of the stream of ideas may be either to one of a set of words prescribed by the interrogator, or the choice of the first word may be 'free', the inverted commas acknowledging some philosophers' belief that a mind never works freely.

Concerning such reactions, two facts are not always appreciated; in mathematical theory, probable associations to words like 'red' or 'pierce' may be infinite: in practice, most replies— except from the leg-puller, whose reaction times, facial expression, and associations may leave him naked to his analyst—fall within a fairly narrow range. The person who reports an unusual association may be unable or unwilling to explain it, and embarrassed or angry at the invitation.

When associating freely, most subjects soon give a reply which might surprise a non-psychologist. Queer mental happenings cause such answers. How they arise; what use the mind makes of them in poetry, painting and literature; to what extent a person's phantasies are characteristic of his sex or social group: such questions are shrugged off by 'objective' psychologists who dream at times, but seldom write about this weakness.

It is often alleged that the persuaders can influence, even manipulate, our thoughts and behaviour more than we realize, because some of their suggestions act below our threshold of awareness. It would be possible to recommend in this way goods, attitudes, ideas, aims, even the possible leader of a political party or a nation.

In America, public relations experts, using techniques borrowed from psychology and the social sciences, and possibly modified, claim to 'engineer' (a grimly ambiguous word in this connection) behaviour. Professional politicians use, and at times are used by, persuaders, who can get tough if their directions are unheeded.

These trawls into the mind bring up queer, even frightening catches. 'We seem,' says Packard, 'to be revealed as comic actors in a Thurberian world.' From this we move into the chilling realm of George Orwell, as we explore some of the extreme attempts at probing and manipulating now going on.

'Certain of the probers . . . are systematically feeling out our more hidden weaknesses and frailties in the hope that they can more efficiently influence our behaviour. At one of the largest advertising agencies in America, psychologists on the staff are probing sample humans in an attempt to find how to identify and beam messages to people of high anxiety, body consciousness, hostility, passiveness, and so on.'

Some persons may consider that a life-long education makes them immune to most irrational appeals. This belief not only ignores fifty years of work on the relation between general and specific training, but is based on an over-sharp distinction between rational and non-rational thinking. Is it rational to place implicit trust in a salesman, tempted by a large commission if he can sell us a particular object? When political party agents use techniques of persuasion, they ought to interest any rational person. Packard asserts that the national chairman of a political party indicated his merchandizing approach to the 1956 election by talking of his candidates as 'products to sell'. A trade school in California boasted that it 'socially-engineers' its graduates so that they are, to use the phrase of an admiring trade journal, 'custom-built men', guaranteed to have the right attitudes from the employer's standpoint. Packard adds, thoughtfully, that trade journals of the persuaders occasionally publish soul-searching commentaries on some of the manipulative practices of colleagues.

An attempt will now be made to discuss, in untechnical terms, some methods used in advertising research.

The 'Depth' Interview

Any assumption that the mind can be described in spatial terms, upper, lower, inner, outer, can be challenged. Acceptance of such postulates makes it difficult to resist a false extension, that 'higher' and 'lower' imply ethical and aesthetic values. (Freud's use of 'sublimation', borrowed from chemistry, has been similarly criticized.) If 'lower' means 'instinctive', few people would term 'lower' an impulse which causes a mother to risk personal danger in saving her child's life.

Having registered these protests, and suspicion of the concept of mental 'depth', I use the term to examine psychologically some aims of the 'depth interview'. One is to implant in consumers a belief that they 'must' often 'trade-in' their cars or refrigerators, or buy the latest nonsense in dress. For such an attitude, the necessity, real or imagined, of 'keeping up with the Joneses' is often a conscious reason, but there may be others, e.g. awareness of economic stratum, or of class—in England these are usually distinguishable.* In some American suburbs, however, *not* getting ahead of the neighbours may be an important 'outer-directed' aim.

Among sub-surface motives, not disavowed by anyone capable of simple introspection, are:

(1) *The Drive for Conformity*, which most English people feel, but in different ways. The English aristocrat (distinguishable from the gentleman) may exhibit marked independence of public opinion, yet he is apt to dress 'properly' at weddings, balls and 'meets', and, in speech and manners, to conform to patterns recognized in his class. Today in England, among the middle to upper-middles, such motives seem less powerful; Ascot is not what it was. Modes of Sunday observance are increasingly unpredictable, yet some upper-middle Londoners who wear old clothes only on Sunday mornings visit the right pubs and read the right paper

* Less easily in America; cf. Vance Packard's *The Status Seekers*.

in them, over the right drink.

(2) *The Need for Oral Stimuli.* Nutrition, sceptics may say, is biologically necessary; why analyse? Were they to be quizzed about the rituals of smoking and drinking in public they might emerge less sure of their motives. Some sherry drinkers really prefer a less 'correct' drink. Some smokers admit that when working they would rather suck an empty pipe than not suck at all. If middle-priced chocolates did not taste similarly, advertisers would not press other alleged advantages.

(3) *The Yearning for Security.* Public objections to National Health Insurance and 'free' education (both contributory) often come from persons who enjoy spreading the news—sometimes for pay—that they can afford the cost. This exhibitionism is not pure: it may be fused with pleas for the sanctity of the family, for religious freedom, for income tax exemption. 'Security' is a much battered word.

In attempts to discover a possible purchaser's motives, hidden or not, he is persuaded to recall freely every thought, pleasant, unpleasant, silly or puzzling, that an advertised product or its brand-image suggests. Group reveries are encouraged: improbable as it may seem to introvert intellectuals, many people enjoy reminiscing before a small audience. Differences of age, sex and culture are influential here: one remembers the effect of alcohol on inhibited Scots. If a member of such a temporary group makes an egotistical, intolerant or risky assertion, it may encourage others to agree or disagree at length vehemently. This is what the investigator desires. He may be even glad when the discussion gets off its original point, for the relevance he seeks is affective rather than logical. A free discussion of whisky drinking by a group containing heavy and moderate drinkers, some who like most alcoholic drinks except whisky, and total abstainers for physiological, aesthetic or moral reasons, might be illuminating. What happens if a 'whisky of distinction' is increasingly bought by the obviously undistinguished?

Depth probings are not always carried out with the subject's clear awareness of their aims. Asked to complete an unfinished drawing or story, to say immediately what a complicated inkblot reminds him of, and then to find more 'pictures' in it, he may project on these objects personal desires, anxieties, conflicts and feelings of inadequacy. What, if suspecting that this is a mantrap, he bluffs intelligently? Though Mr W. H. Whyte offers helpful hints for hoaxers, not all interviewees, especially those suggestible to advertisements, possess his IQ and educational background. Instantaneous covering up of one's tracks requires rapid mobilization of memories intended to mislead, combined with ability to verbalize them in convincingly commonplace language. Many 'revealing' memories cannot be recognized as such, and censored quickly enough to spoof a trained investigator, who probably has played the accused person in this game much oftener than the layman, besides having read of many relevant experiments.

Researchers have made interesting discoveries about the fashionable creation of an appealing, dominating or bizarre 'personality' to increase the sale of goods. Whiskies are usually undistinctive in appearance; often, a distiller told me, in quality, so that without strong, repeated suggestion, many persons would hardly care which brand they bought. For reasons which may not be obvious to Englishmen who have not seen a certain American advertisement, an expensive shirt sells well because a moustached, black-eye-patched man is always depicted wearing it. In one advertisement, the man, with eyeshade and moustache—neither of them a *proprium* of shirt-wearing—was presented, but no names were vouchsafed.

The decision, when advertising motor-boats, to offer their owners a 'sense of power' was suggested by the discovery that many men who had bought several in succession chose faster ones each time. 'Giving the extra margin of safety in an emergency', was intended to produce a semblance of rationality to these goings-on.

Depth-charges are not always needed to disclose sex factors in visual advertisements. A Chinese philosopher-poet, praising (in *Punch*) pictures glimpsed from London Underground escalators, expressed surprise at seeing no gentlemen in their underclothes.

Today, few observant people wonder why a psychologist should take serious notice of ballyhoo, for in this age of mass communication and the fusion—and confusion—of scientific information with political propaganda, the line between sincere and insincere declaration becomes ever harder to draw. The study of fashion, fads, crazes and rumours is not only interesting, but may be socially useful. When we read, in an evening paper, an exciting 'story', many of us may resolve to hear what the BBC will re-

L

port on the matter at 10 p.m. Yet many people neither resent nor resist being manipulated, in certain directions by advertisers. Women's journals owe much of their popularity to the coloured advertisements, more varied and less predictable than the pictures illustrating the love-story. Many readers now tolerate interruption of an article with the insolent command 'Turn to page 79'. The advertisers, without whom the paper could not appear, insist upon it. Interruptions of ITV programmes however cause a few uneasy worms to turn.

Though advertising can sell you a machine, to be tested in your house, it can sell to a nation a leader whose conduct is unpredictable and who cannot be quickly exchanged, under guarantee, for a more satisfactory model. As Professor Kenneth Boulding writes, 'A world of unseen dictatorship is conceivable, still using the form of democratic government'.

The practically-minded psychologist may 'lay on the table' any dossiers about subliminal communication, feeling that it can't happen here—at least, not yet. Claims for or protests against its use are common and it is salutary to remember that in the last thirty years some famous scientists' assertions and denials about the social uses and the material developments of their discoveries have been tragically wide of the mark. We cannot steer our way lightheartedly through the complexity of 'motivation research'.

Predecessors of the 'advertising MRs' sometimes claimed to know 'instinctively' (carping psychologists had not moved in) what their customers wanted. The new adviser to an advertising firm urges that armchair (or grill-room-chair) diagnosis of the public's desires is unscientific. Most English people eat bread and butter, but if the chief suppliers of bread read the correspondence columns of the newspapers, they will find many acid remarks about tasteless steamed pulp pushed at customers who have no time for baking. On the other hand, conscious desires for various kinds of butter and margarine are studied. Most people in this country use soap to wash themselves; whether the chief underlying motive is to look and feel clean, to remove body odour, to destroy bacteria, or to attract the opposite sex, is a matter of interest to the manufacturer, since his agents can exert considerable influence on the buyer by suggesting motives which he or she had not experienced before. The advertised reasons for using an expensive 'skin-food' are sometimes 'derived' from history, chemistry and physiology in ways which might surprise specialist scholars.

Though it is possible to believe that one way to discover why a person performs certain actions is to ask him, it is naïve to expect him always to know, or to be able to frame a muddled thought in clear words. To paraphrase one of Professor G. W. Allport's examples, a man who, entering his house late at night, raids the pantry, may be unconsciously revolting against the idea that his ménage is being run with oppressive efficiency, may be regressing to childish naughtiness, or just feeling hungry. The person who resists such temptation may be obsessively timid, fearing censure or loss of love, may think it unsporting to swipe a delicacy, or may not like the food he finds. But casual introspection suggests that our motives for choosing a particular brand of article among a number of competitors are often not entirely conscious. The drives most easily touched off are graded by the advertising planners' insights. They know that the intensity of any motive attached to an object will vary with a person's age, sex, social class, and with the winds of fashion, their direction controlled by planners.

Let us consider efforts to discover the most effective ways of establishing in the potential buyer's mind a 'brand-image' of an object or a word. It has been defined as 'a characteristic set of feelings, ideas and beliefs associated with a brand through its advertising and product performance'. (This use of 'image' is not unambiguous.) The advertiser hopes that this image and its concomitants will be evoked 'automatically' when a possible purchaser thinks of an object, like a razor, shirt, pen or cigarette. Establishing a new brand-image for an object in common use may be difficult but 'jingles' in TV 'commercials' can be so effective that customers have been heard to hum the tune connected with the name they have forgotten.

When a picture is exhibited in a magazine, on a poster or vehicle, controversy sometimes arises concerning its alleged sex-appeal. Because of taboos governing the free mention of sex, it is easier to preserve a reputation for good sense and politeness by denying an advertisement's sex appeal than by agreeing that it might stimulate sexual thoughts. A portable typewriter is none the better if a pretty secretary carries it when boarding an expensive plane. Many a mass-produced suit is probably sold because a girl is depicted congratulating a glamorous youth with the taste to buy one. And since youths seldom drive cars slower because a girl is beside them, who can doubt that the choice of a fast car, even by older men, may be influenced by thoughts of display before a woman passenger?

The above examples may seem obvious, but in this region the unconscious works hard. The advertiser who began his pictorial appeals with the sentence 'I dreamt that . . .' probably knew that he would be laughed at by intellectuals.

Researchers using methods inspired by psychoanalysis often come up with findings which for obvious reasons are opposed to common sense. But a significant difference between interpretation of their results and the psychoanalyst's is that he suggests validity for his inferences as they relate to a single person, while if the advertising researcher were so modest, his suggestions would stand little chance of acceptance.

Researchers have been frank about their difficulties: a sales policy may be altered on their advice just before a competitor's tactics are altered. People in different social classes may react very differently to the same question: 'What do you take for a hang-over?' may be regarded as impudent by some 'contacts'. An advertiser assures me that the psychology of directors, both of companies and of some agencies which compete for their 'accounts', is as important as that of the millions who buy branded goods.

To anyone imperfectly acquainted with ramifications in the advertising world, as I was until, at conferences, I heard discussions between practitioners (many statements in this chapter are based on communications by experts) it might seem that a firm wishing to increase its sales had 'only' to employ an advertising agency, with research sections the heads of which would pass recommendations upwards. Their journey, however, may be far from smooth. At the top of most large administrations there is presumably a board, which is likely to be dominated on many occasions by one or two members. Decisions to approve, reject or modify an agency's suggestions, to allocate money for their proper implementation, to determine the time allowable for the research and the aspects of it which deserve support, may be made after discussion of pilot results, by board members who grasp the relative merits of methods proposed for use in a lengthy, expensive investigation. Yet, if a pilot survey suggests a policy consonant with an influential member's personal hunch, he may get the project approved even if its suggesters might have liked to have more evidence of its validity. For any psychologist who has tackled an advertising problem a special difficulty may arise. Should he explain his findings technically, he may encounter a stifled yawn or a misleading nod : if he uses simple terms he may be misunderstood by his agency's potential employers.

Consider, for example, the terms 'guilt', 'sex' and 'status'. If an invention frees a housewife from chores which once she regarded as inevitable in the day's duties, it may increase the guilt she feels at having finished housework by mid-morning. (Many professional soldiers and leisured persons feel happier when seen to be working.) The unnecessary supplement to a 'cake-mix' was once 'justified' by the assertion that this addition would reduce guilt feelings. Whether we think this funny may depend on our concept of guilt. There may still be some North-country matriarchs, famous for outspoken common sense, who kneel to redden their front doorsteps. Their mothers slaved for hours to iron white petticoats for their little girls. Both these types of women would have felt guilty had their duties not been carried out. The Americans and us are continually discussing the meanings, and fringe-meanings, of those 'plain' terms—sexual desire and status consciousness.

Perplexity may await any researcher dissatisfied with casual chat as an answer if he tries to discover whether a certain article or idea can be recommended more effectively by suggesting the good it may do or the harm it may prevent. Ought a cough-cure picture to suggest the sufferer's distress, or his relief? Should a road-safety poster depict an accident, causing some drivers to become over-cautious or fidgety, and others to avoid looking at such a reminder? Was the 'Black Widow' poster withdrawn as the result of an opinion poll of a representative sample of the public, including pedestrians, or of motorists' pressures?

Today, in appraising any application of theoretical knowledge, the increasing difficulty of obtaining relevant facts must be kept in mind. Secrecy of a degree unknown thirty years ago now afflicts even scientists. But one can study effective ways of improving 'secrecy', which for obvious reasons tends to be termed 'security'.

The almost world-wide lust for secrecy, a development to which society is unfortunately becoming accustomed, makes it hard for many scholars to get information, not only about facts, but about concepts. The 'hard news' behind a theory may be hidden, reported only in part, or deliberately distorted.

What are the facts reported by Vance Packard in *The Hidden Persuaders*? It is impossible to brush them off, and irrelevant to gloat, as one reviewer did, that the hidden persuaders are hoisting themselves with their own petard. In the advertising field, there is plenty of scope for a fringe of irresponsibles, occasionally calling themselves sociologists or psychologists. Some are not members of a professional society; perhaps for cogent reasons. Not that that registration certifies virtue, but while the fact of belonging to a recognized association cannot guarantee a member's professional integrity, the association can discipline black sheep incautious enough to enter the fold. Packard, after examining the American Psychological Association's list of rules of conduct, decided that they did not cover all the activities of 'motivation researchers'. He asserts that certain American academics, when they addressed an advertisers' conference, may not have realized that rough players might be in the audience. Were some academics old-fashioned enough to believe that, because they are scientists, the public now absolves them from responsibility for the use made of their advice?

One advertiser's reply to *The Hidden Persuaders* should be read seriously, since the editor of the *Atlantic* chose it for the issue of January 1958. In 'Advertising is not a Plot', Fairfax M. Cone casts doubt on some of Packard's assertions; e.g. that an advertising agency persuaded eight leading social scientists to spend a twelve-hour day looking at TV. Cone comments 'Not many advertising agencies could afford so fantastic an undertaking, even once—and none that I know of could re-bill the cost to its clients'. This does not disprove the statement, merely allowing the conjecture that the writer's range of acquaintance with advertising agencies and their clients might be extended. Though the prospect of twelve hours' exposure to a lighted screen is bleak, long stints are conceivable. Longer and duller ones happened in war-time. The special interest to the social scientists of this day's work may have made them content with a low fee. The article contains a thought-provoking sentence: 'To know more about people, and how they think, and what they want and why, is only to make advertising serve better.' The value-claim in the last word of the sentence does not halt Mr Cone, or the question 'Serve whom?' He answers simply, 'Everybody.' Comment seems needless.

It is a commonplace of experience that the public may become aware of scientific fact only when it is used or abused for commercial purposes. A visit to an exhibition showing the history of the 'moving picture' will suggest that at the start there can have been few Jeremiahs to prophesy that the zoetrope and its progeny would be developed into a social menace. But fairly recently a newspaper—English, as it happened—headlined a threat to mankind—'1984' type—called 'subliminal communication', a sinister method by means of which the individual might be influenced without his knowledge. There followed a flood of articles and a 35-page brochure[83] published by the Institute of Practitioners in Advertising, to be quoted later. From it and similar reports the public may have drawn several conclusions, not all in agreement: (1) whatever this queer phenomenon might be, it was useless to advertisers, who (2) might take comfort from this thought, since some had burnt their fingers with badly designed and sloppily reported 'experiments', but (3) as Aldous Huxley announced in a TV interview, though subliminal projection is not yet a public menace, an experienced investigator says, 'Once you've established the principle that something works, you can be absolutely sure that the technology of it is going to improve steadily.' Huxley thought it might be employed to some extent in the 1960 presidential campaign, but would probably be used more extensively and effectively in 1964, because 'this is the rate at which technology advances'. He warns us of the danger that we may be persuaded, below the level of choice and reason, to vote for a candidate in ignorance that we are being persuaded. In Chapter 9 of his *Brave New World Revisited*[80] he discusses the political and other social implications of 'subconscious persuasion', and in Chapter 10 of 'hypnopaedia'.

What is this phenomenon, or bunch of connected phenomena? What are the findings of those psychologists who are concerned with the facts; not with their actual or potential social importance?

I am indebted to Dr N. F. Dixon for permission to quote from his thesis 'The Effect of Subliminal Stimulation upon Cognitive and other Processes' (deposited in the Department of Psychology, University of Reading).

Dr Dixon writes:

'An interest in the effect upon the human mind of stimulation so brief or so slight as to fall below the threshold of consciousness is considerably older than the science of psychology. It was Aristotle who first invoked the idea of sensory effects unperceived at the time of their occurrence; when speculating about the nature of dreams. . . . Of more modern philosophers, Leibnitz (1765), the first to write of an "unconscious", dealt at length with the possibility of "minute perceptions" . . . "little noticed, which are not sufficiently distinguished to be perceived or remembered, but which become known through certain consequences . . . it is a great source of error to believe that there is no perception in the soul besides those of which it is conscious." ' (*Critique of Locke*.)

. In 1933 Professor H. A. Murray said: '. . . certain features of the object which the subject does not consciously perceive are nevertheless physically affecting his body, and, though he may be unable to report upon these internal happenings, they are, nevertheless, affecting his conscious appraisal of the object . . .'

As long ago as 1910 H. Ohms, by reducing the loudness of barely audible words, demonstrated a 'subliminal' effect, and psychologists have long known of C. W. Perky's 'banana' experiment, proving that a supraliminal visual perception, even with trained observers, may pass for an image of imagination.[134]

Her experiments caused an important advance in verified knowledge of the relation between perceiving and imaging. Their object was

'to attempt to produce in an observer the impression that he was imaging an object which really was being presented, gradually and with increasing definiteness, to his vision.

'In the wall of a dark room separating it from a light grey-tinted room . . . was a window . . . of ground glass. Facing it, in the dark room, was a projection lantern. The illumination of the grey room allowed the ground glass to appear just noticeably coloured, without any shine upon the glass to suggest the presence of a source of light behind it. The least intensity of light from the lantern which would suffice to bring the particular colour (to be projected) over the borderline of visibility was thus found.

'This flush of colour was then shaped into the representation of some object of perception by a set of black cloth-covered screens in which were cut the forms of certain familiar objects. (The experimental precautions, both of apparatus and procedure, are fully described in the article.)

'The stimuli were a tomato (red), a book (blue), a banana (deep yellow), an orange (orange), a leaf (green) and a lemon (light yellow).

'The lanternist had a table of the changes required to raise the colour stimulus from a definitely subliminal to a moderately supraliminal value. The colour stimulus was exposed, step by step as the table prescribed, and in a tempo that had been standardized by practice.

'That the observer in reporting an image really perceived the stimulus, at any rate in the majority of cases, seems proved by the fact that in only one single instance throughout the entire series of successful experiments did an observer report an image before the stimulus was (1) perceptible by the co-operating experimenter, and (2) of such objective intensity that its perceptibility might be expected from the results of preliminary control experiments.

'(The control experiments are described fully in the article cited. A brief account of the essentials in this investigation and discussion of their significance for psychological theory is given in *Remembering and Forgetting*, P. H. Pear (Methuen).)'

What is the situation today? We refer to the pamphlet mentioned above, 'Subliminal Communication', published in July 1958. As a result of this report the institute imposes on its 243 member agencies a ban on the use of subliminal communication in any form for the purpose of advertising or sales promotion, and directs them to refrain from any experiments furthering its use in professional practice. 'The free choice by the public to accept or reject is an integral part of all forms of professionally acceptable advertising, and does not appear to be available to recipients of subliminal communication.'

At the time of writing this chapter (January 1960) this seems to be the most comprehensive account of the phenomenon in its relevance to advertising, propaganda and persuasion.

For the purposes of the report, the sub-committee adopted the following definition:

'The term "subthreshold communication" refers ... to the sending, reception and effects of physically weak visual or aural messages which people receive in a physiological sense, but of which they are not consciously aware.

'The stimuli comprising these messages are weakened—by restricting their duration to very short periods of time, or by decreasing their intensity, or by other means—so that although they fall above the point at which their physiological reception first becomes possible, they are below that at which the audience becomes aware of their presence.

'The reception and effects of subthreshold messages are inferred from people's perceptual, verbal, emotional or overt behaviour when compared to their behaviour previous to the messages; they may also be inferred from the behaviour of persons whose personal characteristics would cause them to react to the receipt of such messages in distinctive ways.

('Other means' might include transmitting a verbal message just above the hearer's known upper-pitch threshold. With advancing age, there is a cut-off of high tones, e.g. of noises made by grasshoppers and crickets. In this region of pitch there might be a discrepancy between physiological and psychological thresholds. Knowledge concerning the underlying physiological mechanisms and their loss of sensitivity in different conditions is still fragmentary.)

The report defines the physiological threshold as that point at which the individual's organs of perception fail to respond to certain stimuli. If 'failure to respond' means the subject's failure to perceive, as reported by himself, but not measured objectively, e.g. by electrical methods, new problems arise.

The point at which the subject becomes conscious of the existence of the stimulus is the 'awareness threshold': in the report, 'sub-threshold' refers to this point of 'bare' awareness.

'In unpublished work at the University of Michigan, Blackwell has shown that subjects can reliably identify during which of four time-periods a spot of light below the awareness level has been presented upon a blank background. A common feature of (such) experiments is that although the subjects subjectively experience their behaviour as "guessing" and remain entirely unaware of the presence of the relevant stimuli, their "guesses" are more heavily influenced by the subthreshold stimuli as they increase in strength while still remaining below awareness.' (There seems here to be an interesting relation to Perky's findings.)

Both visual and auditory threshold (both 'awareness' and 'physiological') may differ greatly in an individual, even in unchanged conditions over short periods of time.

'If the communicator desires in any case to maintain, below the level of awareness for all members of an audiance, the stimuli comprising a message, he runs the risk that certain members will never receive the stimuli, even unconsciously, due to their lower physiological sensitivity.'

Presumably it may be harder to achieve successful subthreshold stimulation as the subject's age increases. It is not surprising that subjects with higher 'verbal intelligence' are more capable than others of perceiving visual stimuli presented near the awareness-threshold.

Professor R. C. Oldfield suggests that the moment-to-moment alteration of awareness-thresholds within the same individual may prove more important than variations in thresholds between individuals.

It seems probable that many stimuli below the absolute threshold operate continually. The stories about 'rather' deaf persons who, apparently not hearing a remark, behave in ways which make it probable that they did, are usually told in illustration of 'None so deaf as those who won't hear'. The subject of 'defensive perception' is relevant here: the connection with 'Listeners never hear good of themselves' is hardly obscure.

Since the present report concerns chiefly the purposeful use of subliminal stimuli for special purposes, the interpretation of experiments is limited. It offers little evidence bearing on the possibility of long-term effects, or of the systematic use of subthreshold techniques to alter significantly, in the long run, perceptions which are established, unambiguous or emotionally involved.

A defensive attitude of the public to subthreshold advertising may be easily understood. An American 'projection company' found that operators of a theatre in which a 'germinal experiment' had been carried out did not wish their house to be identified, because they did not want to be 'subjected to the risk of crackpot liability suits by patrons. They have not yet found a US insurance company willing to cover such suits'.

Scientific investigation of 'subception' has not been helped by the reckless way in which a few self-styled 'experimenters' prosecuted their inquiries and published their inferences. The psychologist's head will be cooler if he avoids novels dealing with the subject. Not for the first time he may envy the physicist, whose data cannot conspire to deceive him. The assertion that even if a suspected 'fact' is proved to exist it will not be 'useful' is neither here nor there. The release of atomic energy produced results with surprising rapidity.

Abatement of the agitation caused in recent years by popular articles on 'subliminal persuasion' may have suggested that it was a will-o'-the-wisp. They were wrong: from several sources satisfactory proof is available that subception exists; that events of which a person is not consciously aware may yet influence his thoughts and actions.*

In 1955 Dr N. F. Dixon

'obtained evidence as to effects produced by stimuli below threshold intensity, but only just below. His observers were asked to say the first words that came into their minds when each of the stimulus words was presented subliminally; and often they responded with words which had some meaningful association with the stimulus words. With the sexual words, this sometimes had a Freudian character. Again, the observers were frequently able to associate their responses to the corresponding stimulus words when these were shown them subsequently. In

---

* For this summary of recent experimental results I am indebted to Professor Magdalen D. Vernon's 'Perception, Attention and Consciousness'; Presidential Address to Section J, British Association for the Advancement of Science, 1959. *The Advancement of Science*, No. 62, September 1959.

other experiments Dixon found that such associations occurred only when they had been long established by use and familiarity. All these effects were more likely to occur if the observer had been instructed beforehand to expect that he was being stimulated in this way. Even when there was no such instruction, the observers were concentrating upon the task of guessing, so that there was little competition from other sources of conscious perception.

'He also obtained evidence of psychogalvanic reflex responses to sexual words which were presented below threshold intensity, and were therefore never consciously perceived.

'R. Jung showed[83b] that even in sleep psychogalvanic responses may appear not only with loud noises, but also with faint but significant sounds such as the whispering of the observer's name. This may happen without the observer waking, or if he does wake, he does not remember what stimulated him. The psychogalvanic response is nevertheless accompanied by changes in the natural brain rhythms of sleep, as shown in the electroencephalogram, changes such as characterize the transition from sleep to wakefulness. Thus clearly there is a mechanism in the brain which can respond to certain types of stimulation, of potential importance to the individual, and although he does not become aware of their precise nature, yet his autonomic nervous system may react to them as to an alarm or emotional threat.'

Let us return to consider motivation research in more detail, remarking here that the term covers many different kinds of investigation, some of which antedated considerably the inquiries which advertisers prosecute. In *Motivation Research*[73b] Mr Harry Henry, recording many important facts about advertising, asserts that motivation research is concerned with the question of why people behave as they do. To this naïve use of 'why', the philosopher might object that scientists stop at asking 'how'. Mother love, for example, is a very profitable theme on which advertisers play, yet any researcher who proclaims that he has discovered why mothers love their children will be uncomfortably reminded that some do not. Mr Henry seems to be too anxious to 'sell ideas' (an advertiser's phrase) to business men, or to students assumed to have no time, or inclination, to read a book on psychology. Even they may wonder if such a statement as 'Motivation Research is also concerned with *personalities*— what sort of people they *are*, psychologically speaking' is not playing down to them. This technique of approach resembles that of the early salesmen of radio-receivers, whose handouts told me that the set I ought to buy *must* have an efficient aerial and earth: an elementary knowledge of physics would have hampered the writer by suggesting that even then the goal of current research was to abolish both external aerial and earth. When Mr Henry admits that motivation research has drawn many of its methods from psychology and sociology but adds that it should not be an academic exercise for its own sake, he might reflect on the fact that nuclear physics developed as an academic exercise for its own sake, and no engineer forbids its development in university laboratories.

Many different inquiries into motivation, by teachers, doctors and criminologists, are ridiculed by critics who proclaim that they would hate to be questioned about their own motives. Yet people are always asking, in curiosity or despair, 'Why did he do it?' An answer to such a question is often demanded for legal reasons, as in cases of treason or stealing. 'Why' does one type of juvenile thief concentrate on one kind of article, and perhaps abandon it later? What makes a rich woman steal goods of little value from a store where she has a credit account? If no easy answer is forthcoming, it is often invented by persons with no special knowledge of the subject: reports of the outbreaks of swastika-daubing in England were followed by imposing pronouncements by important persons who had no time, little desire, or no ability to conduct motivational research.

Mr Henry's assertion that (using the analogy of a clock) motivation research is concerned not with the mainsprings of human behaviour but with the escapements and regulators which can be adjusted in the interests of a manufacturer or advertiser ('In other words, it is concerned only with such motives as are *manipulable*') would make not only psychologists but students of ethics and politics prick up their ears. And when later he refers to 'the inescapable conclusion that Motivation Research is now out of its infantile stage and must accept adult responsibilities', he should not complain if Mr Vance Packard agrees with him, and criticizes the claims of advertisers to manipulate the public mind. The brief 'summary' of *The Hidden Persuaders* is so unfair that it suggests the discomfort which reading it may have produced in Mr Henry, who could find a better director for any future studies of psychiatry than Mr Sam Goldwyn.

To summarize: The dictionary meaning of 'advertise', 'to give notice generally to the public', is wider than that usually accepted today, yet ceremonials in which representatives of the royal family, the churches, the universities and forces appear publicly in picturesque costumes and are photographed for the mass media are effective advertisements. But advertising by poster, press, radio and television is usually the subject of discussion, often unsatisfactory, since there is undue generalization from facts, and many essential facts may be known only to one side in the controversy. There is a widespread tendency to advertise advertising.

A social psychologist may be forgiven for believing that nearly all the issues of advertising, even economic ones, are ultimately psychological, since no advertising is likely to be financially supported unless the holders of the purse-strings believe in its effectiveness.

Since both attackers and defenders of a particular branch of advertising employ deceptively simple 'psychological' terms, often narrowed in meaning, and 'humour' is freely used, the issues are often confused. But from serious discussions several truths, important for students of social patterns, have emerged. Advertisers have increased their skill in manipulating symbols: visual (pictures, diagrams, words) and auditory (words spoken with special emphasis, repeated, sung in 'jingles'). An intimate manner of approach is often cultivated by radio and television actors when recommending a particular product. Scientific investigators ascertain the value, for a particular purpose, of vividness, 'shock', repetition and habit formation. Eventually those who deal with the manipulation of words, e.g. 'brainwashing', 'prestige', may come to regard them as things.

The advertiser seldom or never replies specifically to specific charges: the early form of behaviourism was 'sold' by advertising techniques.

Since in advertising it is difficult or impossible to carry out a rigidly scientific experiment, to change factors singly and to control conditions, it is impracticable to gauge accurately the result of a change of policy. Knowledge of this impossibility may tempt the researcher to occasional over-statement. An aspect of this over-compensation is the claim, heard less often as time goes on, that advertising is an art, and cannot be helped by science.

Motivation research, like dream investigation, with which it has much in common, may bring up findings which seem opposed to common sense, yet the advertiser does not always appeal to this trait in purchasers. Such practices are repellent to anyone desiring that his private life shall be free from investigation, yet the concepts of man's right to privacy may be changing. Many leading persons and young people today do not desire it intensely. The increasing number of ordinary persons who appear in Press notices and photographs and on television may decrease the wish for privacy.

Subliminal persuasion is not yet useful in large-scale advertising, but the history of inventions is full of instances of ideas which were not utilized for years after they had been publicized.

Let us now consider Public Relations. Any member of a profession with a specific label—interpreted too liberally by the public—be he doctor, lawyer or clergyman, often reads of a blunderbuss attack on it. He may be tempted to rush into print to defend the majority of his colleagues, or to remind readers that there are lawyers and lawyers, bishops and bishops. In the council of many a professional body the question may be raised: must the society suffer in silence and get a bad name by default, or should it arrange for malicious lies by important persons to be exposed promptly and publicly?

This problem cannot be solved by simply quoting 'Qui s'excuse . . .', by references to Caesar's wife or reminders to ex-cricketers of the sin of arguing even with an inattentive or unintelligent umpire. One solution is to appoint a Press Officer to supply reliable information, or to put inquirers in touch with well-known, trusted experts. The excellent Press service of the British Association for the Advancement of Science has reduced perceptibly the number of bad jokes about its meetings which used to circulate when this 'rabble of philosophers' met during the Silly Season.

Yet members who believe that more facts about their society ought to be publicized may be uneasy about recent developments in the 'image industry', on which Tom Baistow reported in the News Chronicle of April 23, 1960.

'Not only has every Government department, big city and industrial group of any pretensions got a PRO, but the Boy Scouts, the Lord's Day Observance Society, the Institute of Chiropodists, the Scots Guards, bright London boroughs like Hackney, Tottenham, Willesden and Woolwich, and, of course, the Prime Minister himself, have all organized their public relations.

'Today PR is a booming, expanding industry with about 2,500 practitioners, ranging from the part-time information officer to a handful of experts in the art of "engineering consent", who wield considerable—and, in the opinion of some observers, a disturbing amount of—power.'

The public relations of Public Relations are cared for by its institute, whose PRO offers a definition of public relations : 'the deliberate, planned and sustained effort to establish and maintain mutual understanding between an organization and its public'. A client may have several publics—employees, trade unions, other members of the industry, buyers, and finally the consumer.

By far the greatest number of PROs, who are former newspapermen, provide 'straight' information, mainly to the Press and similar media. The warmth of their invitations, however, may make some pressmen feel indebted for the news which otherwise they would have had to find by their own efforts, and a naïve pressman, if one exists, might be misled into thinking that he is being courted.

In some quarters, here as well as in America, the view is held that in England public relations was once a ludicrously inefficient game, too often played by men whose sole function apparently was to say no, blandly, to inquisitive reporters, or, as it has been phrased, in Britain the war had bred PROs whose instinct was to block information. But the PRO's present task is 'to get clients to open up so we can put over the story'. An ex-reporter, once in General Bradley's 'psychological warfare' outfit, says, in words so plain that they puzzle anyone trying to determine how much they express and hide, 'Ours is the basic global propaganda approach.' (A 'plain man' statement, heard on the radio : 'Advertising can't sell a lousy product twice,' puzzles me. What if the product is the personality of a politician ? Or does the advertising agency expect to sell him only once ?)

M

Trained observers of skilled movement are sceptical about any expert's description of his own performance. They usually follow him around, observing every detail of his behaviour. When studying the PRO, this procedure is seldom practicable. He often blushes unseen, and seldom invites anyone desiring to erect a monument to his profession to look around. Consequently, many writers emphasize his inscrutability, and some, perhaps unconsciously, helping to create his image, describe him as 'a flamboyant, fabulous and delightfully eccentric individual'.

Most writers on public relations relate true sixty-year-old stories of the innovator Ivy Lee, 'who hit upon the dramatically simple thought that a good Press depends on being nice to reporters'. In 1906, when there was an accident on the Pennsylvania Railroad, Mr Lee, the company's PRO, 'threw the usual suppressive machinery into reverse by inviting the Press to travel on free passes to the scene of the accident'. His successors in America may now be paid up to a thousand dollars an hour for advice.

Any animal so naughty as to defend itself when attacked usually receives much sympathy. Many PROs intelligently foresee possible directions of attack and prepare for them : the squid's defensive measures, however, are not unknown to them.

Not all British PROs are inclined to accept unquestioningly an American view that in this field we have almost everything to learn. Some Englishmen think they detect at times a Germanic thoroughness which may contain the seeds of its own defeat. A Scot is quoted as saying 'British methods, more effective, more subtle and less extravagant than the American techniques, are being exported to the USA.'

Whether members of the general public ought to feel flattered or warned by such assertions is a question seldom raised. If things change in the British PR industry at their present rate of acceleration, what will be the power of the PRO in a year or two? In the next general election? Already a book which severely criticizes 'Public Relations' can be advertised by just these methods.

Instances of the necessity of watching and improving public relations are easy to find. The PRO can improve labour relations within an industry. In a university (as distinct from a collection of colleges differing perceptibly in size, status and power) a special information officer (not PRO) could handle many inquiries, either singly or after consultation with the persons concerned and the principal administrative officer. Such functions seem obviously useful, and many of them are carried out as matters of routine, yet the sound of the words 'public relations officer' angers many temperate persons. It will not allay their suspicions to hear the term 'image-making', and to learn that image-makers can fabricate an image of their own profession. Needless to say, one would not wish to help to indict a whole group, ill-defined, with international branches, but accusations like the following are commonly made, and I quote from recent writings:

'They create for a highly commercial, not to say rapacious, enterprise, the benevolent corporate image acceptable in a Welfare State.'

They claim to 'engineer consent', relying on the public's ignorance of this manipulation. At times in America, success of this kind has involved the cold, calculated exploitation of human ignorance.

At the heart of one kind of public relations lies the principle of guilt by association, and its inversion—virtue by association.

The 'serviceable, dubious aim is public acquiescence in the *status quo* of society as it suits big business'.

Denunciatory statements like the above are not applicable to all the public relations outfits in this country. The PR side of the World Refugee Year here was looked after by a small firm. Movements like this, indisputably desirable, make one wonder if in future any competitive project except the smallest can be launched without PR activities. If we have to live with them, the public ought to know more of their workings than it does at present.

CHAPTER TEN

Mass Culture and Persuasion

Culture is currently defined in very different terms: it will be regarded here as 'a way of life'. Recent rapid developments of 'mass media' and 'mass culture' produce important social problems. Some critics of mass culture base their beliefs on 'an image of man in past ages' or party-political attitudes. The attack on mass culture, as increasingly 'homogenized', threatening the individuality of readers, listeners and viewers. The accusation that radio and television decrease interest and time spent in reading: the counter-claim that these media direct thousands of persons to valuable books, new and old, of which they would not otherwise have heard, and that there is a revival in the arts of speaking and listening as means of discovering, imparting and learning new facts.

The mention of 'culture' arouses different ideas, with corresponding emotional fringes. It is the chief concern of the BBC's Third Programme, on which, however, the possible meanings of the term do not seem to have been discussed.

To think of culture as a 'way of life' satisfies many. W. H. R. Rivers's description of culture as allowing increased discrimination of stimulus and gradation of response can serve as a launching platform for thought, since it allows many kinds of culture to be considered psychologically. Current meanings of the word have been examined by the present writer in *English Social Differences*.[130]

The term 'Mass-Culture' seems fairly clear. Long ago, J. B. Priestley insisted that the 'people' are not the 'masses': his later coining of 'Admass' suggests that he likes the concept of 'masses' even less. Unlikely to smother critical thought is the concept of 'mass media': it covers films, radio, TV, posters and newspapers, especially those with gigantic circulations. Though *The Times, Guardian, Observer, Sunday Times* and the chief literary weeklies appeal to relatively fewer readers, the proportion of these who actively modify public opinion is high. As an opinion maker, sound radio is important in Great Britain, where competition in this medium is not yet serious. Years ago, I heard an exchange of opinions on the question 'If you were cast ashore on a desert island with X (a person of very high rank), what could you discuss freely with him for more than a few minutes?' 'BBC programmes' was judged the best answer. The Third Programme is a refuge for 'non-Admass' listeners. TV seems the most obvious example of a mass-medium. The BBC's present competition with ITV lowers the cultural standards of both.

In this country little has been written by observers trying to assess cultural gains and losses due to mass communication. Few critics of culture comment on the increased accessibility of good music, through VHF sets and high fidelity recordings, and of great pictures through good reproductions. Sneers at the popularity of prints of 'Sunflowers' do not help, or the assertion that 'people' (in country districts or small towns) 'ought' to attend concerts and not stay at home to hear great music. Soon after a famous English orchestral conductor had publicly castigated producers of 'canned' music, he directed a concert: the centre pages of its programme were monopolized by advertisements of records made under his direction. In J. S. Bach's time, even Germans living far from Leipzig could appreciate his music only on local instruments. Today, the owner of a good radio receiver is helped to compare and contrast renderings, by different artists, of the same work, and is familiarized with music possibly not yet performed in his country.

In America, a large-scale attempt to assess characteristics of mass culture has been made.[145] Reviewing it in an essay,[157] Professor Edward Shils discusses the 'daydreams and nightmares' of critics of mass culture. He maintains that though intellectuals (he mentions only Americans and Germans) who decry mass media seldom have to work in them, and regard those who do as 'merchants of *kitsch*', savage attacks on mass culture come from some of its creators and promoters. He asserts that few critics of this new culture of the 'lower classes' possess the knowledge of them which results from real contact and empathy.* Their bases for criticism

---

* On the important distinction between empathy (*Einfühlung*) and sympathy, a colleague comments: I know a number of efficient psychiatrists who possess the quality of empathy—some of them lack sympathy! In *Freud and the*

are derived from 'an image of Man in past ages'; it is almost entirely doctrinal and has little factual basis. He describes the historical background of their culture, maintaining that examination of mass culture has been carried out by speculative sociologists, existentialist philosophers, publicists and literary critics.

Are not *empirical* sociologists engaged in what might seem their proper study? Shils says 'No', implying that if continued their present attitude is unlikely to be useful:

'Precise and orderly as their observations might be, they are made outside a matrix of intimate experience, without the sense of empathic affinity which would enable the events which they observe to be understood as they actually occur in the lives of those who experience them.'

Some sociologists may be disturbed to read that a professional colleague declares empathy to be a desideratum, not a temperamental weakness to be overcome by ascetic training in objectivity.*

Bernard Rosenberg asserts that the political position of an assessor of mass culture is closely correlated with the views expressed about it. For different reasons, radicals and conservatives are repelled by what they regard as vulgar, exploitative influences; liberals seem to occupy a position between these extremes. The die-hards' growl; 'nothing new under the sun' cannot apply to mass culture, which 'unites a resident of Johannesburg with his neighbours in San Juan, Hong Kong, Paris, Bogotá, Sydney and New York'. (An aspect of this world-unity is illustrated by a globe-trotter's complaint to me that in Sydney women's fashions are New York's, and that coffee served in the world's airports no longer introduces the traveller to interesting local differences of flavour, but is often made from a depressingly predictable powder.)

Crisis of Our Culture, Lionel Trilling seems to ask for sympathy rather than empathy in the study of alien cultures . . . the student of culture should begin by feeling that the culture under scrutiny is somehow or other *justified.* This presumably requires sympathy.

* Dr G. Morris Carstairs[33] has demonstrated the value—perhaps the necessity —of empathy in anthropological work. 'Genuine inter-group and inter-racial understanding will only be possible to the degree that each group's covert pattern of irrational complexes is made the object of study, as well as their history and all the overt aspects of their social life.'

Uncomplimentary epithets describing mass culture include 'homogenized'; its cream is distributed evenly throughout the milk, to treat all customers alike. *Life* magazine is cited as an example. Homogenization is not always deplorable. In the dark days of the war, the BBC's 'Itma' cheered palace and cottage. In the childhood of radio, a farmer in the Fenlands told me of his (unprompted) love of Debussy's music. All the same, the best strawberries demand something better than homogenized milk. There are less flattering comparisons: 'Who can sort . . . the sacred and profane, genuine and specious, exalted and debased, when they are built into a single slushy compost?'

What are the basic assumptions of the promoters and appreciators of mass culture? Ernest van der Haag suggests 'Everything is understandable—and remediable'; Rosenberg: 'Everything had better be made understandable.' In England, success in expounding, on TV, archaeology and meteorology is striking, but psychologists may doubt if many parts of their subject can be homogenized.

Who or what is responsible for mass culture? Different writers blame or praise capitalism, democracy, America, but obviously without the rapid developments of technology, mass culture could not have arisen. Engineering, not cultural considerations, determine the 'Regions' into which the BBC divides England.

Many forms of mass culture discourage solitary reading and writing, which, perhaps more than anything, can sustain the belief that one's own thoughts and opinions are of value. A radio set can be silenced as a book can be shut, but the book can be reopened to enjoy or criticize a single paragraph. Whatever claims children make for their ability to do homework with the radio on, they cannot perceive attentively a page and the TV screen simultaneously. Yet many recent developments of science, announced and explained on TV,* are not mentioned in the prescribed text-book, which may have taken three years to write, and two more before it became popular in schools. It is unsporting to suggest that a teacher who at night is too busy or too tired to hear talks and discussions on the air may next day lag behind some fifth and sixth formers. He may not be able to afford both a sound-radio and TV set. Though examiners in schools and uni-

* In America there have been early morning broadcasts on fairly advanced physics and on psychology.

versities may feel at present that it would hardly be playing the game to set questions which could be easily answered by listeners and viewers, but not by the unassisted reader of text books; that day may come. Does it seem like lying down before the Juggernaut of mass culture to admit that a broadcaster-historian may be more informative than his predecessors, who, when they wrote their books, had access to fewer sources of facts and criticism? If a professional historian does not wish to listen to a new assessment of the escape of the *Scharnhorst* and *Gneisenau*, or of a battle in the last war, his successors may criticize his aloofness. Some of Charles Darwin's views on religious belief were first published in 1958; what if he had broadcast and upheld them in critical radio discussions?

To some early commentators it seemed probable that as a result of their new leisure activities, listeners and viewers would read less. In America, however, 'librarians and teachers report that the cultural values communicated by TV programmes are responsible for much wider exploration of the world of books by children than in pre-TV days'. 'In England, at first, TV adversely influences reading and reading-skill, yet in the long run it increases book-reading (as opposed to "comic" reading) with an increased range of books and no loss of skill.'[75]

'Homogenized' and 'composted' can be easily understood when applied, fairly or not, to mass culture. The going is stickier when *kitsch* appears. What is it? Is it inevitably bad? 'Blossom Time' (*'Dreimäderlhaus'*), the musical play based on Schubert's melodies has been described as 'good kitsch'. A dictionary translation is 'trash', which seems a near-miss. Dwight Macdonald cruelly equates it with mass culture. 'Academicism' (not defined) is 'Kitsch for the élite' and—English readers should pause for breath—an example of sophisticated kitsch is the 'bogus intellectuality' of Dorothy M. Sayers's *The Nine Tailors*.

Clement Greenberg considers that kitsch operates deceptively at different levels, some of these high enough to endanger the naïve seeker of true light. The *New Yorker* is 'fundamentally high-class kitsch for the luxury trade'. It converts and waters down much *avant-garde* material. A technique used to defend High Culture against Mass Culture is Avantgardism; a withdrawal from competition: Rimbaud, Joyce, Stravinsky, Picasso 'simply won't play'.

The scientific and artistic technicians of mass culture are blamed for regarding that collective monstrosity, the 'masses', or the 'public', as a norm, and for using as the criterion of reality its level of taste and ideas:

'A questionnaire-sociologist, describing how he will "set up" an investigation, seems to regard people as . . . mere congeries of conditioned reflexes. He calculates which reflex will be stimulated by which questions. Like the Kitsch lords, he is wholly without values, willing to accept any idiocy if it is held by many people.'

If this critic had stated the imaginary sociologist's aim, his point might have been sharper. May the sociologist be studying the spread of an idiocy?

Many sociologists, whatever their personal and political attitudes, are touchingly loyal towards past theorists. *The Crowd*, by Gustave Le Bon, is often cited, though its author did not benefit by seeing orderly Saturday crowds at a huge soccer match, or those in London at the time of the 1953 coronation. Gunther Anders says that the obsoleteness of Le Bon's views on crowd behaviour is emphasized by the fact that today a person's individuality can be erased, and his rationality levelled down, not in a crowd, but in his own home: with powerful, continuous conditioning disguised as fun. The victim may even regard himself as preserving privacy and individual freedom in his own four walls.

Questions concerning different kinds of privacy arise with rapid changes in our country's spending habits, one instance being the social results of television. The physical privacy of a solitary viewer is indubitable, yet since appeals from the screen are usually made to him personally, he is not mentally private, but half of a pair. Seldom does he feel himself part of a crowd.

But television, asserted Mark Abrams, managing director of Research Services Ltd, in a broadcast on November 6, 1959, is only one of the factors rapidly increasing the tendency towards a home-centred society. The last few years have seen a big swing in consumer expenditure: 'after a post-war burst of spending on ephemeral luxuries' (alcohol, tobacco and commercial entertainment) 'people are turning to a wide range of more durable commodities' (better heating and lighting, furniture, fittings, apparatus, gadgets). The 'Do It Yourself' movement helps here. The husband spends more time in his home, withdrawn from direct contact with the outside world; less in the pub, the cinema, the trade union or political meeting. Owning a car—today one family in four has one—he adds to his house a movable room, and drives privately in it to and from his workplace, deliberately avoiding physical and social contact with passengers in trains and buses. At weekends he may transport the family in this 'room' to the seaside, where, again, the car possibly serves as their private house. For long holidays he may prefer the caravan to the seaside lodging-house, with its enforced sociability.

It is possible to contest a comfortable claim that TV has caused a rebirth of the Victorian family pattern. The large dining-table, now banished from many old houses, and too large for many new ones, acted as a centripetal force. Across the table, diners faced and—parents permitting—conversed with each other. The 'telly's' influence is centripetal: viewers facing the screen images, which often talk or sing to them as separate persons. To answer back would be fatuous. Viewers seldom feel—they are not meant to—that they are private: for people are apt to 'drop in'. *Fortune* reports that in some new middle-class American communities it is virtually impossible to keep neighbours from invading one's living-room with or without the pretext of TV.

Does mass communication threaten the individual's experience of self? What is happening to the average young person's 'valuation of the factors which define his identity'? What is the effect of continually hearing and reading comments which denigrate the identity of public persons? Many 'write-ups' of personalities by gossip columnists are intended to be feline, and editors who hire the journalist may specify this.

Marshall McLuhan asserts that oral communication is less concerned than before with literary culture. There is renewed reliance on speaking as a method of discovering new truths. One thinks of researchers who, aided by air travel, speak frequently at distant conferences, and of the few printed papers which issue from these meetings. During the war, 'the atomic physicists found that only by daily face-to-face association could they get on with their tasks'. Few lamenters of the decline in the habit of reading good or 'solid' books consider the extent to which new ideas are acquired and old ones modified as a result of listening to radio discussions between experts: these are increasing in number and quality, and the Radio-Link exchanges between distant countries are a new, impressive feature.

Ernest van der Haag believes that in moral and aesthetic matters authority and individual judgment are being supplanted by group acceptance. The person with individual talent is now encouraged to share rather than to cultivate it. A successful author is paid to give a course on writing, a scholar to lecture or write popularizations, the beautiful woman to 'model' or appear on TV, the singer to desert the concert hall for the juke-box. Even universities and foundations . . . 'can't quite resist infiltration by popular culture . . . they imprison high culture as much as they shelter it'.

Twenty years ago, a writer on a subject of psychological interest was often content to describe observations about his own narrow milieu. This short-focus view has its defenders: 'Jane-ites' assert that she displayed admirable sense and taste by ignoring battles being fought abroad by her countrymen. Today, in considering mass persuasion, one seems ashamed not to try to keep up with contemporary developments of thought 3,000 miles (1/60 sec.) away, even if the books cited will not be on one's desk for months. A book which modifies an Englishman's earlier impressions of American mass culture is Reuel Denney's *The Astonished Muse*.[39]

Many scholars imply that 'real' education and real culture can affect the individual only through the written word, yet professional educators allow that words spoken in classrooms by teachers who in written examinations have demonstrated unusual knowledge of printed words may be educative. Denney asserts that there exists a whole population of Americans who have lost all competence to listen to the well-spoken word: they were print-trained out of auditory competence just before the Ear Age of the modern mass-media began. High respect for print as such, especially among the oldsters, allows certain English newspapers to imply that the whole of Fleet Street shares their opinions, and to ignore, attack or guy radio talks and discussions on today's problems. Yet how many professional writers know the facts about popular tastes in reading in America? Denney writes:

'It appears that about half the adults of the USA never or rarely buy even a paper-back book. This is not surprising, in view of the probability that 50 per cent of the college graduates in the US read less than seven books a year. On the other hand, the decline of book-club sales in the total book market is a sign that many readers make more of their own reading decisions.

'In Europe, the educated are the book-educated: the book is the sign of intellectual freedom and superiority.'

Some scholars may regard 'the aesthetics of full employment and general welfare' as a subject unworthy of academic consideration, but Professor Denney reminds us that if we desire (some don't) a rich popular culture, it cannot be built up by default, e.g. by such negative attitudes as are expressed by conspicuous non-ownership of TV sets.

To summarize: few critics of mass communications in this country have assessed the cultural gains and losses which these may cause: more information from American sources is available. Mass culture tends to be homogenized: some aspects of this process do not seem wholly deplorable. Many forms of mass communication impede or discourage solitary reading, writing and thinking, yet radio and television disseminate information which could appear in books only after long delay. Contemporary developments of thought can be discussed on the air by speakers in widely separated countries. The view has been expressed that in moral and aesthetic matters group acceptance supplants individual judgment and authority. A person with marked talents is encouraged in many ways (e.g. offers of money and personal publicity) to share rather than to cultivate his gifts. The aesthetics of full employment and general welfare are important: 'if we desire a rich popular culture, it cannot be built up by default and by conspicuous non-ownership of television sets'.

CHAPTER ELEVEN

Concepts of Progress

Modern views of the nature and desirability of progress:
C. P. Snow, J. Z. Young, Jacquetta Hawkes, Arnold Toynbee,
C. S. Lewis. One man's progress—another's regress? Was
there progress between Sumerian, Egyptian, Minoan,
Hellenic, Inca and our own Western civilization? The
common belief that progress and technical advancement are
synonymous. The illegitimate insertion of value-claims into
accounts of a handful of scientific findings. The belief that
manipulation and control of cultural practices and human
behaviour are necessary features of any civilization, and the
road to progress towards a better life. The criterion of survival in determining the desirability of imposing a social
change.

A reply, now famous, to the question 'Why do men want to climb
Everest?' was 'Because it's there'. Conflicting opinions have been
expressed about extensions of this simple attitude towards any
challenging task. For a long time our island has been there, but
its inhabitants have seldom regarded this fact as justifying invasion. A burglar, seeking to excuse his action, does not cite the
mere existence of the booty. Only twenty years ago some scientists
viewed any attractive problem as an Everest, and offered reasons
as pure as any mountaineer's for attacking it. Since then, Nazi
doctors' desire for physiological knowledge caused them to vivi-
sect healthy Jewish women.

'You can't stop Progress' is sometimes urged to shrug off the
increasing slaughter on the roads, in part due to progress in producing more vehicles and persuading more people to buy them.
Did the effort and money put into the now abandoned 'Blue
Streak' rocket constitute progress? A popular subject for debate
today is the rise of the 'meritocracy' in Britain: if it eventually
dominates our society, will this be progress?

For centuries the nature of progress has been discussed, though
never with today's sense of urgency. Survival is sometimes re-

garded as a biological criterion of utility, but is today's progress not tending towards extinction? Are there writers today who profess to regard the death of humanity with resignation, even boredom?

In 1958 the *Observer* invited experts to discuss the nature and possibilities of progress. They were Sir Charles Snow, scientist, civil servant and novelist, Professor C. S. Lewis, mediaeval scholar, Professor J. Z. Young, zoologist, Miss Jacquetta Hawkes, archaeologist and poet, and Dr Arnold Toynbee, historian. The relevance of this symposium to the present book's theme appears in Toynbee's approval of Lewis's definition; 'Progress is movement in a *desired* direction.' Progressing deliberately involves choice between rival aims. The underlying issue, the tug of war between individual souls and a collective humanity, has never been more critical in earlier times.*

Sir Charles Snow, who straddles the gulf between 'intellectuals' and 'scientists', appeared to imply in his contribution that the individual doesn't matter much. As a novelist, Snow is less tightly shackled, yet his individual 'Lewis Eliot' reflects and refracts impersonal forces.

Jacquetta Hawkes considered that Snow's picture of survivors of an atomic war, achieving, soon afterwards, an exalted liberalism, is unrealistic. In her view, one man's progress may be another's regress. One believes that society exists for the individual; another, that the individual must be sacrificed to society. Among these latter thinkers there will always be a fanatic, like Karl Marx, certain that the direction he has chosen is the only right one. That is why the concept is so dangerous. Can one say that there was progress between Sumerian, Egyptian, Minoan, Chinese, Hellenic, Inca and our own Western civilizations? Or is each to be regarded as unique, with its own strengths and weaknesses? What the late Gordon Childe described as the 'upward curve' of history, in which no trough ever declined to its predecessor's low level, and each crest out-tops its last precursor, is,

---

* Today a radio-speaker, who sounded like an officer briefing troops before battle, proclaimed to a captive audience, breakfasting, and with little time for thought, that since atomic power cannot be stored, and at present, for 64 per cent of its life, expensive machinery lies idle (he did not consider if this stand still might save us from annihilation) 'in the national interest' 'we' must 'agree' to stagger our holidays and buy certain specified expensive apparatus to warm ourselves. If this is Little Brother, what will Big One sound like?

she maintains, illustrated by today's spectacular advance in technology. Is this increasing complexity a cultural equivalent to biological evolution, or do we just hope that it is? In her view technical elaboration is not progressive, but neutral, able either to serve or to endanger the quality of individual life.

It might have been useful to consider the fact that not only many scientists but those who control their activities and administer funds for their support believe and preach that progress and technological advancement are synonymous. Their strongest argument is the increasing mastery over certain diseases. They sometimes urge that any discomforts and austerities which technological advancement may entail for the average citizen— though the life of many applied scientists is very comfortable— are worth enduring for posterity's sake, and that the remedy for any ills science may cause, incidentally or accidentally, is to produce more and 'better' scientists. Jacquetta Hawkes writes of the scientists' fantastic productivity and speeding of communications, and of the dire threats and losses already offsetting undoubted improvements in health, material prosperity and the status of women. She emphasizes the importance, when considering whether in any one civilization real progress has been made, of the time-scale on which the assessor is working. Snow's and Lewis's vistas hardly extend beyond the last century. Young shows 'the vast impersonal perspectives of a zoologist'. Hawkes's own time-scale, derived from the long view of history exposed by archaeology, falls somewhere between these two.

(If, with respect, a social psychologist may indicate the standpoint of one seeing life as it affects him here and now, even the time-scales of Snow and Lewis seem on the long side. 'It doesn't seem fair,' said a member of one of Shackleton's Antarctic teams to me, when he read that scientists were taking photographs of a coast-line which he and others had mapped by months of dangerous work. Politicians rush hither and thither in jet planes, but are they, when they arrive, as fit to discuss difficult matters as when a ship gave them days to study and think over their briefs? Some people believe that the exploitation of the internal combustion engine has given unprecedented scope to wickedness, and that the struggle for oil has been ugly, and cleverly camouflaged, from the start.)

Miss Hawkes asserts that ten million years of human history, following on aeons of biological evolution, leave no doubt that what is most distinctively human is 'heightening of consciousness'. To my mind, 'heightening' suggests a spatial arrangement of consciousness, and this concept is regarded by many psychologists as slippery. 'Clarification of awareness' might convey the meaning better to a psychologist. This awareness includes increase in sensory discrimination and mystical experience, which, unless induced experimentally by a drug, shocks some scientists. Yet airmen can experience a type of awareness which, to some of them, seems mystical, and so may an experimental subject deprived of the normal amount and variety of sensory excitation. As Miss Hawkes says:

'. . . although knowledge can be valuable and intellectual achievement almost always admirable and awe-inspiring, man is at his greatest and most complete in imaginative creation. That is to say, in all the visual arts, in music, literature, the highest scientific vision, and in the expression of religious myth and symbol, which I believe to find its proper place in the same category. In this realm of experience, the only one where we have a sense of possible relationship with levels of being beyond our small comprehension, there can be no progress. There is not progress between the paintings on the walls of the Altamira caves and those on the walls of the Sistine Chapel, or between either and the work of Picasso. There can be greater complexity as a result of the accumulation of experience, but no "movement in a desired direction".'

She remarks upon:

'. . . the enormous increase in the number of human beings, with the resulting tendency towards mass-life and conformity under absolute government. In the East, political power-lust, and in the West commercialism gone mad, are destroying our hard-won freedom of thought. Then there is the horrifying spread of depersonalization in work and recreation; loss of the conditions favouring peace, privacy and peculiarity.

There are psychologists who apparently believe that of these, peculiarity at least may often be undesirable. Their views are criticized by Professor Morris S. Viteles, a pioneer in the application of scientific methods to the study of human behaviour. He reproves certain psychologists for illegitimately inserting value-claims which they approve, into their account of only a few scientific findings: [174] 'a foundation of scattered, splintered and splinter-like data that could fall apart with the most meagre essays in the way of further exploration through the use of available scientific techniques'. He cites Professor A. V. Hill's warning: 'Scientists should be implored to remember that, however accurate their scientific facts, their moral judgments may conceivably be wrong.'

Viteles quotes examples of certain psychologists' unbounded faith in the moral right of a scientist of human behaviour to subordinate 'natural man' to the socially adaptive and conforming influences of scientific methodology, and the belief that deliberate manipulation and control of cultural practices and human behaviour is a necessary feature of any civilization and the road to progress towards a better life.

Some scientifically-minded thinkers who put forward this view do not tell us who is to manipulate, and who will manipulate the manipulators. What would be their interpretations, in this context, of 'civilization', 'progress' and 'better'?

In evaluating control practices, one criterion used is survival, though there is litle evidence to suggest that scientific controllers are much concerned with the survival of the individual. One psychologist proclaims that experimentation involving control of cultural practices may yield findings distasteful to Western thought, which has emphasized the importance and dignity of the individual. We note that an overriding value is claimed for science. Sometimes this seems but another way of asserting the predominant importance of the scientist; even, in some contexts, of certain scientists. But as Aldous Huxley has asked,[80] is not 'Science', as used thus, only the opinions and guesses (not always unchallenged and uncriticized) in a certain month, of Professors and Doctors X, Y and Z? J. B. Priestley writes[140] 'I . . . wonder about these New Men . . . now exercising such power over us, incidentally without having received any mandate from most of us . . . if these are the sort who should have so much power.' He suggests that we ask ourselves if they are the human beings in whose hands the future of the world can be safely left.

N

It is difficult to believe that the world's future is not being left in their and their masters' hands. But today scientists' relations with their employers are ambiguous, unpredictable, often secret; Hiroshima and Nagasaki being examples.[cf. 5a] In America the implementation of naval, military and air policies, often conflicting and nakedly competitive, depends on the particular group of scientists swaying the politicians, who often have their party's axe to grind. Who supposes that a prime minister or president can do any more than to obey his scientific advisers, even if he knows, as he ought to, that their judgments may have been questioned by equally 'sound' scientists? In Britain, the repeated under-estimation of the cost of a new weapon of 'defence' or 'deterrence' seems to be regarded as another bad joke, to be placed alongside the incorrect political prediction of its usefulness. Our civilization is even more lopsided and top-heavy than it was when William McDougall applied those epithets to it thirty years ago.

Professor Hyman Levy writes (*Monthly Record* of Conway Hall, vol. 65, March 1960) 'Science, one of our greatest social achievements, is internally directed, consciously and deliberately, to the pursuit of truth. Externally . . . it serves social ends in a confused and fumbling way'. Here he seems to reify or personalize 'Science'. Social ends are being served by individual scientists, many of whom do not consider themselves to be confused or fumbling. Politicians complained recently that the money spent on the abandoned 'Blue Streak' had gone down the drain. Surely not all of it: how much went into the pockets of highly intelligent and skilful persons, eager to work on still another fiasco if well paid?

A well-known authoress writes to me of the grave, depressing change of attitude in this country towards the idea of an annihilatory war:

'Whereas all the articles making crazy plans for missile warfare used at least to pay lip service to the idea that it would never come to pass, now it seems to me that the assumption is that it will.'

One sign that the danger is perceived, even regarded as already approaching, is the frequent reaction with grim humour. The announcement that the base at Fylingfield will afford the nation four minutes' preparation was received by many people with the uneasy smile which greets the sandwich-board wearer who on festive occasions warns the crowds to prepare to meet their doom. In the serious film *Seven Days to Noon* this got a big laugh. *Punch* depicted a clergyman preparing a shortened form of service. A BBC humorous programme featured an interview with a 'scientist' who by wearing a Heath Robinson collection of gadgets hoped to get an extra minute's warning.

Any suggested parallel between this 'humorous' attitude and that of civilians hearing the sirens in World War II is unjustified, since most of them knew what they were supposed to do, and were partly reassured by knowledge of the presence of AA guns and fighter planes. The methods of attack by the enemy had been categorized, and the civilian often knew something about the corresponding techniques of defence. In the four minutes now promised we are encouraged to hope—how many will?—that 'they' at least will be suitably punished—but who will they be, and shall we care?

Study of the psychoneurotic has shown that in the face of danger, real or imagined, his characteristic behaviour is to deny it, and compulsively to repeat actions which, though intended to ward off or to cope with the peril, are useless. We see such behaviour on a national scale today.

Let us assume that progress is movement in a desired direction: what is the social cost of our present progress? Never before have so many persons been offered data on which to base individual opinions: never before have the social forces making it hard to do this been so powerful and their attack so many-sided. Not only the habitual sceptic but the ordinary well-educated citizen frequently realizes that the 'facts' he is vouchsafed come from unreliable sources.

There are baffling differences in public attitudes today. One can observe innumerable kindnesses of person to person (unless they are driving cars). Nations behave towards each other with gross immorality; as Dr J. C. Flugel remarked, they are like the nastiest type of small boy: they swagger, brag, grab, lie, cheat and betray their supposed allies. There is an increasing number of people who believe that modern war is always likely to raise more problems than it settles, but unfortunately this attitude in

N*

many persons seems contemporaneous with apathy towards the possibility of another great war. Yet we do not forget the numbers who took part in the two Aldermaston marches, admired by many who did not share the chief aims of its leaders.

Who in 1960, observing the dismay and disorder of the summit conference, can disagree with Professor William McDougall's assertion, made in 1930, that the disproportionate rate of progress between the physical and the human sciences is due in part to the fact that the study of inanimate matter is relatively easy?

CHAPTER TWELVE

Conclusion and Afterthoughts

In the present book, I have discussed, from a psychologist's, not an educationist's or politician's standpoint, important ways in which dominating persons continually influence our minds, with or without our consent or even our knowledge. Some of these moulding techniques merely extend long-accepted manipulations; others are new, and being frequently and violently discussed. Since some large-scale persuasions operate in early life and are unusually powerful, let us take a few examples, beginning with strict versus permissive methods of child-rearing, and the relations of the disputants' justifications to attitudes, often ambivalent, towards their parents. A topic related to this is the social desirability of sending a young child away from family influences to those of a boarding school. Opinions on this matter are considerably influenced by national and class differences, due largely to early indoctrination. Supporters of the idea of conscription, who, in this country, usually avoid the tricky question of conscripting females, urge the general desirability of 'getting the boy away from Mum'—a non-U term—seldom waiting to hear comments from the lady herself. But we are moving towards a social pattern in which girls will marry in the expectation of going out to work: will the Mums in the twenty to thirty age-group be quite as angry as their parents were at the suggestion that the boy should not stay at home until he is grown up?

There seems little agreement concerning the educative value to the individual young man of peace-time army service, voluntary or not. The army claims to mould his character and make a man of him: so do most armies. Some even make men out of women. In our peace-time army, the youth learns a trade, some methods of fighting, and is taught toughness and discipline. Yet the ss were disciplined: so were the inventors and users of the Nazi gas-chambers and those who, pushing women and children into railway trucks, left them to freeze to death.

Now that either side of such debatable questions is often 'put over' by public relations techniques and advertising, even highly critical minds can be moulded if the suggestion comes often enough from a source regarded by the reader or listener as authoritative.

Some problems raised in this book are really new, not unusual aspects of old ones. For some persons, the consciousness of the empirical and social Self may alter in ways which would surprise the average man. The 'social envelope' of an air pilot who regularly visits several continents in the course of a few days, dropping off for holidays in countries distant from each other, will differ amazingly from that of his grandfather. Problems like this deserve closer study. Recent observations of the attitudes and sentiments of American airmen and their wives stationed in England could be valuably supplemented. The selves of subjects of space-ship 'mock-ups' are modified so extensively in a few hours that conventional criteria of normality are quite inapplicable.

Such alteration of personal self-consciousness, even by 'negative' means—sensory deprivation can produce disturbing hallucinations— may take place simultaneously with changes in social self-consciousness: this is alarmingly manipulated by 'brainwashers'. But writers who advocate that every civilized person should strive to have a room of his own are inclined to assume that privacy is not only the right of most normal persons, but that they intensely desire it—or ought to. Yet this is not true of numerous people; e.g. those moved from slums to housing estates. Often many of them long to return to the bustling streets and the matiness of the public houses. Perhaps, indeed, the younger generation in England does not want much privacy. It is not experienced by the middle-class and upper-class boy at boarding school. His sister, even before she leaves school, may dream of 'modelling', appearing on television or in 'Miss Middletown' contests. In villages, few social events are unattended by photographers and reporters from the local papers.

News is assiduously personalized. In most papers, details of the private lives of personalities are offered, and often it is clear that these widely advertised 'confessions' have been paid for. Popular holiday camps, crowded seaside resorts and the success of motor coach tours suggest that privacy is not extensively desired.

The power of advertising increases alarmingly. It seems impossible to discuss it objectively: because of the bad temper often shown by the disputants and the difficulty in obtaining hard facts. Some of these are now being publicized by Consumer Research and similar organizations. Whether advertising, on the whole, reduces the cost to the consumer is an economic question of frightening vagueness, and the answers are usually to match.

Both the Church of England and the Roman Catholic Church use modern methods of persuasion and information, to supplement the traditional bell-ringing, preaching, posters and processions. In America the Methodist Church has its PRO. The Moral Rearmament Movement is spending huge sums on a pamphlet 'Ideology and Coexistence' and its wide distribution. Occasional exhortations to increase the advertising of religion arouse hotly conflicting attitudes.

Perplexing questions arise concerning 'public relations' and managed publicity. Some critics cannot contemplate coolly the idea that now the world has shrunk and messages span it with the speed of light, many trustworthy information officers are indispensable if the truth is to be circulated quickly and extensively. Soon after any great event we expect to receive an authoritative statement of the facts: if they prove to have been censored, by falsification as well as omission, this will be news, widely discussed in the Press and on the air.

Yet troubling doubts arise. If many persons complain in identical terms of the unsatisfactory service alleged to be rendered by a large firm or corporation it is usually answered, and it is important that it should be, by an information officer. But the ordinary member of the public has no way of learning about the general principles governing this particular man's function. In what instances is it true that 'public relations is the craft of arranging truths so that people will like you', and that the PRO's ambition is to achieve complete anonymity; to become 'a wordsmith without a name'? Few leaders of public opinion make, or would be permitted to make, a speech entirely composed by themselves. 'Politics is a chancy business . . the Senator's oratory is suspect, so Junior may be right after all.'* Of a recent book of memoirs, a responsible critic complained that the famous English author had insufficiently acknowledged his indebtedness to his ghost-writers: readers were assumed to know that, in the nature of things, such a busy man would work against a background of

* S. Gorley Putt, *View from Atlantis*; London, Constable, p. 134.

ghosts, some fairly well known.

Are the PROs then, 'the lineal descendants of the Sophists, whose craft in the fifth century BC enabled them (for pay) to make the worse appear the better cause'?

Advertising is an activity which attracts, and pays well, many bright young people, but are members of university staffs, particularly those deeply concerned with the teaching of the undergraduate as well as with the quality of research, happy about this?

The inventor of the term 'brainwashing' deserves no thanks from anyone trying to understand the techniques, some hamhanded, some astute but sporadic, and others cleverly integrated, which are given that name. The word, misleadingly descriptive, attracts those who believe that the only way to unravel the mind's workings is to grasp the activities of the brain: presumably, to explain the physical events occurring when a gramophone record is played may lay bare the whole story of Verdi's *Requiem*, including his temperament and the religion which inspired him, not to mention the mental processes of the singers and the conductor. In serious writings one reads silly extensions of the image, e.g. 'a mere rinse'. Like 'subversive', it is often used to indicate any form of suggestion the aim of which the writer, often noted for professional success in a similar activity, disapproves. To substitute for 'brainwashing' 'forcible indoctrination' is unsatisfactory unless 'force' is extended to include, say, the subtlest arts of sexual attraction. The indoctrination methods of the Chinese Communists, modified to suit civilian and soldiers respectively, which combined cruelty with apparent friendliness, are difficult to compare with subtler ones intended to alter the victim's whole character.

Such success in using psychological knowledge might be brought to the notice of certain publicists who, with bulging cheek, frequently assert or imply that psychology is rubbish, comical, fantastic and just common sense. They have many credulous readers: when one of the world's greatest scientists seriously asked me if I 'believed in' hypnotism, I inquired, knowing that he was a teetotaller, if he believed in alcohol.

Moral and religious exhortations to resist brainwashing may move the converted, yet persons who can stand up against repeated threats are often uncursed with imagination. To pit body and mind successfully against some brainwashing techniques may require not only knowledge of their nature, but also capacity to acquire, and quickly, skill in applying some of them in opposition.

Can brainwashing, advertising, propaganda and public relations be regarded as belonging to the same category? 'Stratospherically' seen, yes: they employ both suggestion and persuasion. To many mouldings of our opinions techniques of resistance could be devised by elaborating counter-suggestions and means for implanting them: for centuries religious and military systems have done this. In many people, as in existentialists, general attitudes of scepticism could be inculcated. They are fashionable in some quarters at present: but who wishes to produce thousands of stumbling half-educated philosophical anarchists?

Here arises the many-sided problem of the nature and limitations of strictly rational thinking. To distinguish sharply between reasons of the 'mind' and 'heart' plays into the hands of lazy thinkers by accepting question-begging popular concepts rejected by physiologists and psychologists alike. We respect the purely rational thought of the physical scientist which makes it possible to construct and launch an earth-satellite, but what physicist, on the basis of his specialist knowledge, could tell a national leader whether to try to use this achievement as a bludgeon at a summit conference?

I see no way in which the ordinary citizen can judge any top-level question on the basis of his own knowledge. The science which he learned at school twenty years ago will be insufficient to enable him to judge even a great non-human issue. But in political matters? On the day that the Press disclosed the issues of Suez, I heard a serious political discussion (in a private house) closured by a polite question 'Don't you think the Government has good reasons, but hasn't told us of them?'

Forces which are moulding our knowledge and actions have been described and discussed. What can we do about them? To this question no psychologist could contribute more than part of an answer. We should insist on verification of important claims more often than we do, and acquaint ourselves with the techniques of the smoothy's answers. We should ask more questions than we do before choosing an adviser or leader. We should carefully examine their sentiments and ideals as they have been shown in action, and distrust the technique of the 'build-up'. Though the scientific study of man cannot tell us whom to choose, it can help more in this direction than obscurantists suggest.

BIBLIOGRAPHY

1. ADLER, D. L., 'Some Recent Books on Personality', *Psychol. Bull.*, 1954, 51, pp. 283-96.
2. ADORNO, T. W., FRENKEL-BRUNSWIK, E., *et al*, *The Authoritarian Personality*, 1950, New York, Harper.
3. ALLPORT, G. W., *Personality; a Psychological Interpretation*, 1937, London, Constable.
3a. ALLPORT, G. W., *The Use of Personal Documents in Psychological Science*, 1942, New York, Social Science Research Council.
3b. ALLPORT, G. W. and POSTMAN, L., *The Psychology of Rumor*, 1947, New York, Henry Holt.
4. ALLPORT, G. W., *The Nature of Personality*, 1950, Cambridge, Mass., Addison-Wesley.
5. ALLPORT, G. W., 'The Trend in Motivational Theory', *Amer. J. of Orthopsychiatry*, 1953, 23, pp. 109 f.
5a. AMRINE, N., *The Great Decision*, 1960, London, Heinemann.
6. ANNAN, N., 'The Intellectual Aristocracy'; in PLUMB, J. H. (ed.) *Studies in Social History*, 1955, London, Longmans.
7. ANON (ed.), 'Factors Used to Increase the Susceptibility of Individuals to Forceful Indoctrination', Symposium No. 3, Group for the Advancement of Psychiatry, Dec. 1956. (1790 Broadway, New York 19.)
7a. ANON, US *Fighting Man's Code*, 1955, Nov., Office of Armed Forces and Education, Department of Defence.
8. ANON, 'Give-up-itis', Editorial, *Guardian*, Nov. 25, 1957.
9. ANSBACHER, H. L. and R. R. (ed.) *The Individual Psychology of Alfred Adler*, 1958, London, Allen and Unwin.
10. ARON, R., *The Opium of the Intellectuals*.
11. ASCH, S., *Social Psychology*, 1952, New York, Prentice-Hall.
12. AT SSU-CH'I, 'On Problems of Ideological Reform', *Hsueh Hsi*, 7, Jan. 1, 1951.
13. BARZUN, J., *The House of Intellect*, 1959, London, Secker and Warburg.
14. BASKOWITZ, H., PERSKY, H., KORCHIN, S. J. and GRINKER, R. R., *Anxiety and Stress*, 1955, New York, McGraw-Hill.
15. BAUER, R. A., 'Brainwashing—Psychology or Demonology?' Symposium, Amer. Psychol. Assoc., Sept. 3, 1956.
16. BEACH, F. A. and JAYNES, J., Review of work on dependence of psychological development on stimulation from the environment, *Psychol. Bull.*, 1954, 51, pp. 239 f.

17. BEAUVOIR, Simone de, *The Second Sex*, 1953, New York, Knopf.
18. BEAUVOIR, Simone de, *Memoirs of a Dutiful Daughter*, 1959, London, André Deutsch.
19. BEAVAN, J., 'The New Intellectuals', *Spectator*, 6707, Jan. 11, 1957, pp. 38-9.
20. BECK, S. J., 'The Science of Personality; Nomothetic or Idiographic?', *Psychol. Rev.*, 1953, 60, pp. 353-9.
21. BERNAYS, E. L., *The Engineering of Consent*, 1955, Univ. of Oklahoma Press.
22. BETTELHEIM, B., 'Individual and Mass Behaviour in Extreme Situations', *J. Abn. Soc. Psychol.*, 1943, 38, pp. 417-52.
23. BEXTON, W. H., HERON, W. and SCOTT, T. H., 'Effects of Decreased Variation in the Sensory Environment', *Canad. J. Psychol.*, 1954, 8, pp. 70-6.
24. BIDERMAN, A. D., 'Communist Attempts to elicit False Confessions from Air Force Prisoners of War', 1957, July, *Bull. N.Y. Acad. Med.*
25. BIRD, C., *Social Psychology*, 1940, New York, Appleton.
26. BOLTON, J., 'The Organization Scientist under Fire', BBC broadcast, April 26, 1958 (sound).
27. BONE, E., *Seven Years' Solitary*, 1957, London, Hamish Hamilton.
28. BRIDGEMAN, W. and HAZARD, J., *The Lonely Sky*, 1955, New York, Holt.
29. BROOKES, R. C., 'The Difficulty of Interpreting Science', *Listener*, Oct. 1, 1959.
30. CANTRIL, H., *The Psychology of Social Movements*, 1941, New York, Wiley.
31. CANTRIL, H., GAUDET, H. and HERZOG, H. *The Invasion from Mars*, 1940, Princeton Univ. Press.
32. CARRINGTON, C., *Rudyard Kipling*, London, Macmillan.
33. CARSTAIRS, G. M., *The Twice-Born*, 1957, London, Hogarth Press.
34. CARSON, G., *Cornflake Crusade*, 1959, London, Gollancz.
35. CHITTY, S. (ed.), *The Intelligent Woman's Guide to Good Taste*, 1958, London, MacGibbon and Kee.
35a. CHURCH, R., *Atlantic*, Oct. 1958.
36. CLARK, B. and GRAYBIEL, A., 'The Break-Off Phenomenon', *J. Aviation Med.*, 1957, 28, pp. 121-6.
36a. COHEN, J., in *Psychological Factors of Peace and War*, ed. PEAR, T. H., 1950, London, Hutchinson.
36b. CUNLIFFE, M.

36b. CUNLIFFE, M., 'The Intellectuals—The United States', *Encounter*, IV.5 May 1955, pp. 23-33.

37. DALE, H. E., *The Higher Civil Service of Great Britain*, 1941, Oxford Univ. Press.

38. DANINOS, P. and OGRIZEK, D., *Savoir-Vivre International*, 1950, Paris, Odé.

38a. DAVID, H. P. and BRACKEN, H., *Perspectives in Personality Theory*, 1957, London, Tavistock Publications.

39. DENNEY, R., *The Astonished Muse*, 1957, Cambridge Univ. Press.

40. DIXON, N. F., 'Symbols in Associations Following Subliminal Stimulation', *Int. J. of Psychoanal.*, 37, Parts II-III, 1956, pp. 1-12.

41. DRUCKER, P., 'The New Tycoons', *Harper's*, 210, May 1955, p. 39.

42. ERIKSON, E. H., *Childhood and Society*, 1950, New York, Norton.

43. ERIKSON, E. H., 'On the Sense of Inner Identity', 1953, *Health and Human Relations*, New York.

44. ERIKSON, E. H., 'The Problem of Ego-Identity', *J. Amer. Psychoanal. Assoc.*, 1956, 4:56.

45. ESTES, S. G., 'Judging Personality from Expressive Behaviour', *J. Ann. Soc. Psychol.*, 1938, 33, pp. 217-36.

46. EYSENCK, H. J., *Dimensions of Personality*, 1947, London, Kegan Paul.

47. EYSENCK, H. J., *The Structure of Human Personality*, 1953, London, Methuen.

48. EYSENCK, H. J., *Sense and Nonsense in Psychology*, 1957, London, Pelican Books.

48a. FADIMAN, C., *Party of One*, 1955, Cleveland, NY World Publishing Co.

49. FAULKNER, W., 'The American Dream', *Harper's*, 1956.

50. FIELD, J., *A Life of One's Own*, 1934, London, Chatto and Windus.

50a. FISHER, M. and J., *Shackleton of the Antarctic*.

51. FISHER, N. G., 'The Intellectual Individual in Contemporary Society', *Mem. Manch. Lit and Phil. Soc.*, 1954-5, 96, pp. 71-88.

52. FISHMAN, J. A., 'Some Current Research Needs in the Psychology of Testimony', *J. Social Issues*, 1957, 13.2, pp. 62-6.

53. FISHMAN, J. A. and MORRIS, R. E. (eds.), 'Witnesses and Testimony at Trials and Hearings', *J. Social Issues*, 1957, 13.2.

O

54. FLANAGAN, J. C., 'The Critical Incident Technique', *Psychol. Bull.*, 1954, 51, p. 327.
55. FREUD, A., *The Ego and the Mechanisms of Defence*, 1946, New York, International Universities Press.
56. FROMM, E., *Man for Himself*, 1947, New York, Rinehart.
57. GINSBERG, M., *On the Diversity of Morals*, 1956, Heinemann.
58. GINSBERG, M., 'German Views of German Mentality', in *Reason and Unreason in Society*, London, Heinemann.
59. GOFFMAN, E., 'On Face-Work', *Psychiatry*, 1955, 18, 3, pp. 213-31.
60. GOTTSCHALK, L., KLUCKHOHN, C. and ANGELL, R., *The Use of Personal Documents in History, Anthropology and Sociology*, 1945, Bull. 53, Social Science Res. Council, 230 Park Av., New York, 171.
60a. GREY WALTER, W., 'Mirror for the Mind', *Listener*, Oct. 1, 1959, pp. 521-2.
61. GRIFFITH, T., *The Waist-High Culture*, 1959, New York, Harper. 1960, London, Hutchinson.
62. GUETZKOW, H., *Multiple Loyalties*, 1955, Publication 4 of Center for Research on World Political Institution, Princeton Univ., N.J.
63. GURKO, L., *Crisis of the American Mind*, London, Rider.
63a. HALL, G. S. and LINDZEY, G. (ed.), 1957, *Theories of Personality*, London, Chapman and Hall.
64. HALMOS, P., *Solitude and Privacy*, 1952, London, Kegan Paul.
64a. HAMILTON, M. A., *Remembering My Good Friends*, 1944, London, Cape.
65. HAMMERSCHLAG, H., *Hypnosis and Crime*, 1957, London, Rider.
66. HARDING, D. W., *Social Psychology and Individual Values*, 1953, London, Hutchinson.
67. HARDWICK, E., 'The Classless Society', *New Yorker*, Jan. 19, 1957, pp. 30-48.
67a. HARRINGTON, A., *Life in the Crystal Palace*, 1959, New York, Knopf.
68. HARRIS, R. and SEEDON, A., *Advertising in a Free Society*, 1959, London, Inst. Economic Affairs, 7 Hobart Road, SW1.
69. HAWKES, J., *Man on Earth*, 1954, London, Cresset Press.
70. HAYEK, F. A., 'The Facts of the Social Sciences', *Ethics*, LIV, Oct. 1943.
71. HAYEK, F. A., 'Individualism, True and False'.
72. HEBB, D. O., 'On Human Thought', *Canad. J. of Psychol.*, 1953, 7, pp. 99-110.
73. HEBB, D. O., 'The Mammal and his Environment', *Amer. J. of Psychiat.*, 1955, 111, pp. 826-31.

73a. HEBB, D. O., 'The Motivation Effects of Exteroceptive Stimuli', American Psychologist, 13.3, March 1958.

73b. HENRY, H., Motivation Research, 1958, London, Crosby Lockwood.

74. HEYWORTH, Lord, Advertising, 1958, London, Unilever Ltd.

75. HIMMELWEIT, H. T., OPPENHEIM, A. N. and VINCE, P., Television and the Child, 1958, Oxford Univ. Press.

76. HOGGART, R., The Uses of Literacy.

77. HOLLINGSHEAD, A. B. and REDLICH, F. C., Social Class and Mental Illness, 1958, New York, Wiley.

78. HOMANS, G. C., The Human Group, 1950, New York, Harcourt Brace.

78a. HUNTER, E., Brainwashing, 1956, New York, Farrar, Straus and Cudahy.

79. HUXLEY, A., Brave New World, 1932, London, Chatto and Windus.

80. HUXLEY, A., Brave New World Revisited, 1959, London, Chatto and Windus.

81. HUXLEY, A., Science, Liberty and Peace, London, Chatto and Windus.

81a. HYMAN, H., 'The Psychology of Status', Arch. Psychol., 1942.

82. INBAU, F. E. and REID, J. E., Lie Detection and Criminal Investigation, 1953, Baltimore, Williams and Wilkins.

83. INSTITUTE OF PRACTITIONERS IN ADVERTISING, Subliminal Communication, 1958, London.

83a. JONES, H. M., (ed.), 'A Humanist Looks at Science', Daedalus, 1958 (Winter).

83b. JUNG, R., in Brain Mechanisms and Consciousness, 1954, Oxford, Blackwell.

84. JUNGK, R., Brighter Than a Thousand Suns, 1958, London, Gollancz.

85. KARP, D., Leave Me Alone, London, Gollancz.

86. KAHL, J. A., The American Class Structure, New York, Rinehart.

87. KATES, S. L. and JORDAN, R. M., 'The Social Stimulus Self and Self-Image related to Personality and Psychotherapy', J. Soc. Psychol., 1955, 42, pp. 137-46.

88. KEATS, J., The Insolent Chariots, 1958, New York, Lippincott.

89. KEEHN, J. D., 'The expressed Social Attitudes of leading Psychologists', Amer. Psychologist, 1955, 10, p. 208.

90. KELLER, H., The Story of My Life, 1903, New York, Doubleday Page.

90a. KENNEDY, A., 'Scientific Lessons of Brainwashing', Royal Institute Discourse, Feb. 1960.

91. KINKEAD, E., 'The Study of Something New in History', New Yorker, Oct. 26, 1957, pp. 102-53.

92. KINKEAD, E., Why They Collaborated, 1960, London, Longmans.

92a. KLINEBERG, O., Social Psychology, 1940, New York, Henry Holt.

93. KOESTLER, A., The Yogi and the Commissar, 1947, London.

93a. KOHR, L., 'The Brainwashers', Spectator, April 15, 1960.

94. KRONENBERGER, L., Company Manners, 1951, New York, Bobbs-Merrill.

95. KUBIS, J. F., 'Instrumental, Chemical and Psychological Aids in the Interrogation of Witnesses', J. Social Issues, 13.2.1957, pp. 40-9.

96. LA BARRE, W., 'Some Observations on Character Structure of the Orient; The Chinese', Psychiatry, 1946, 9, pp. 215-37.

97. LANG, D., 'Man in Space', New Yorker, Nov. 15, 1958, pp. 106-28.

97a. LEWINSKY, H., 'The Nature of Shyness', Brit. J. Psychol., 1941, 32, pp. 105-13.

98. LIFTON, R. J., ' "Thought Reform" of Western Civilians in Chinese Communist Prisons', Psychiatry, 1956, 19, pp. 173-95.

99. LIFTON, R. J., ' "Thought Reform" of Chinese Intellectuals, a Psychiatric Evaluation', J. of Asian Studies, 1956, Nov. No. 1.

100. LILLY, J. C., (Moderator of) Symposium No. 4, 'Methods of Forceful Indoctrination, Observation and Interviews', Group for the Advancement of Psychiatry, 1956 (1790 Broadway, New York 19).

100a. LINKLATER, E., Private Angelo, 1946, London, Cape.

101. LITWINSKI, L., 'Towards the Reinstatement of the Concept of Self', Brit. J. of Psych., 1951, 42, pp. 246-9.

102. LITWINSKI, L., ' "Belongingness", as a Unifying Concept in Personality Investigation', Acta Psychologica.

103. LYNES, R., The Taste-Makers, 1954, New York, Harper.

104. MACKINNON, D. W., 'The Use of Clinical Methods in Social Psychology', J. Social Issues, 1946, 2, 4, pp. 57-54.

105. MACLEOD, R. B., 'The Phenomenological Approach to Social Psychology', Psychol. Rev., 1947, 54, pp. 193-210.

105a. MACLEOD, R. B., 'The Place of Phenomenological Analysis in Social-Psychological Theory', in ROHRER, J. H. and SHERIF, M. (eds.), Social Psychology at the Crossroads, 1951, New York, Harper and Bros.

106. MANDELBAUM, M., 'Societal Facts', *Brit. J. of Sociol.*, 1955, 6, pp. 305-17.
107. MARQUAND, J. P., *Point of No Return*, London, Hale.
107a. MARQUAND, J. P., *Women and Thomas Harrow*.
108. MARTIN, H. G., 'Locating the Trouble-Makers with Guilford-Martin Personnel Inventory', *J. Appl. Psychol.*, 28, pp. 461-7.
109. MAYER, M., *Madison Avenue, USA*, 1958, New York, Harper.
110. McCLELLAND, D. C., 'Towards a Science of Personality': Chapter V in DAVID, H. P. and BRACKEN, H., *Perspectives in Personality Theory*, 1957, London, Tavistock Publications.
110a. MEAD, M., *Cultural Patterns and Technical Changes*, Paris, UNESCO.
111. MEERLO, J. A. M., 'The Crime of Menticide', *Amer. J. Psychiat.*, 1951, 107, pp. 594-8.
112. MEERLO, J. A. M., 'Pavlovian Strategy as a Weapon of Menticide', *Amer. J. of Psychiat.*, 1954, 110, pp. 809-13.
112a. MEERLO, J. A. M., *The Rape of the Mind*, 1956, Cleveland, World Publishing Co.
113. MICHEL, R., 'Intellectuals', *Ency. Social Sciences*.
114. MILLER, J. G., 'Brainwashing—Present and Future', Address to Amer. Psychol. Assn., Sept. 3, 1956.
115. MOOREHEAD, A., *The Traitors*, 1957, London, Hamish Hamilton.
116. MURPHY, G., 'The Boundaries between the Person and the World', *Brit. J. of Psychol.*, 1956, 47, 2, pp. 88-94.
117. NEWMAN, E. B., 'Public Relations—for What?', *Amer. Psychologist*, 1957, Aug. 12.8.
118. NICOLSON, H., *Good Behaviour*, 1955, London, Constable.
119. NICOLSON, H., *The Development of English Biography*, 1928, New York, Harcourt Brace.
120. NICOLSON, H., 'Intellectuals in the English World', *Listener*, Oct. 5, 1956.
121. OBSERVER, 'Is Progress Possible?', 1958, July 13, 20, 27, Aug. 3, 10. Symposium; Jacquetta Hawkes, C. S. Lewis, C. P. Snow, A. Toynbee, J. Z Young.
122. ORGLER, H., *Alfred Adler, the Man and his Work*, 1939, London, Daniel.
123. ORWELL, G., *Nineteen Eightyfour*, 1949, Penguin Books.
124. PACKARD, V., *The Hidden Persuaders*, 1957, London, Longmans.
125. PACKARD, V., *The Status Seekers*, 1959, New York, David McKay Co.

125a. PACKARD, V., *The Waste Makers*, 1961, London, Longmans Green.

126. PEAR, R. H., 'America Through Foreign Eyes', *Brit. J. Sociol.*, 1956, 7, p. 158.

127. PEAR, T. H., *Remembering and Forgetting*, 1922, London, Methuen.

128. PEAR, T. H., *Voice and Personality*, 1931, London, Chapman and Hall.

129. PEAR, T. H., *The Psychology of Conversation*, 1939, London, Nelson.

130. PEAR, T. H., *English Social Differences*, 1955, London, Allen and Unwin.

131. PEAR, T. H., *Personality, Appearance and Speech*, 1957, London, Allen and Unwin.

132. PEAR, T. H., 'The Psychological Study of Tensions and Conflict', in *The Nature of Conflict*, 1957, Paris, UNESCO.

133. PEAR, T. H., 'The Gap between Scientists and Intellectuals', *Monthly Record of Conway Hall*, Dec. 1959.

134. PERKY, C. W., 'An Experimental Study of Imagination', *Amer. J. Psychol.*, 1910, 26, pp. 422-52.

135. PERELMAN, S. J., 'La Plume de mon Ami . . .', *New Yorker*, Oct. 11, 1958, pp. 38-41.

136. PLEKHANOV, G. V., *The Role of the Individual in History*, 1940, London, Lawrence and Wishart.

137. PONCINS, G. de, *Kabloona*.

138. PONSONBY, A., *The Decline of Aristocracy*, 1912, London, Fisher Unwin.

139. PRIESTLEY, J. B., *Low Notes on a High Level*, 1950, London, Heinemann.

140. PRIESTLEY, J. B., *Thoughts in the Wilderness*, 1957, London, Heinemann.

140a. RENIER, G. J., *The English, are they Human?*, 1947, London.

141. RIESMAN, D., *Individuality Reconsidered*.

141a. RIESMAN, D., DENNEY, R. and GLAZIER, N., *The Lonely Crowd*, 1950, New Haven, Yale University Press.

141b. RIESMAN, D. and GLAZIER, N., *Faces in the Crowd*, 1952, Oxford University Press.

141c. RIESMAN, D., 'Books; Gunpowder of the Mind', *Atlantic*, Dec. 1957.

142. ROBERTSON, A., *Man His Own Master*, 1948, London, Thinker's Library.

143. ROBERTSON, A., ' "Brave New World"; 25 years after', *Monthly Record of Conway Hall*, 62.3, March 1957, pp. 6-8.

144. ROGERS, K., 'The Motivation of the Motivators', *Bull. Brit. Psychol. Soc.*, 1958, 35, p. A.2.

145. ROSENBERG, B. and WHITE, D. M., *Mass Culture: The Popular Arts in America*, 1957, Glencoe Free Press, Ill., USA.

146. ROSENFELD, E., 'Social Stratification in a Classless Society', *Amer. Sociol Rev.*, 1951, 16.6.

146a. ROSS, I., *The Image Makers*, 1960, London, Weidenfeld and Nicolson.

146b. ROVERE, R. H., *Senator Joe McCarthy*, 1960, London, Methuen.

147. SALZMAN, L., 'The Psychology of Religion and Ideological Conversion', *Psychiatry*, 1953, 16, pp. 177-87.

148. SANTUCCI, P. S. and WINCKUR, G., 'Brainwashing as a Factor in Psychiatric Illness', *Arch. Neur. Psychiat.*, 1955, 74, pp. 11-16.

149. SARGANT, W., *Battle for the Mind*, 1957, London, Heinemann.

150. SCHEIN, E. H., 'The Chinese Indoctrination Process for Prisoners of War', *Psychiatry*, 1956, 19, pp. 149-72.

151. SCHEIN, E. H., Review of *The Hidden Persuaders*, *Contemp. Psychol.*, 1957, Sept., pp. 308-9.

152. SCHEIN, E. H., 'Patterns of Reactions to Severe Chronic Stress in American Army Prisoners of War of the Chinese', *see* LILLY, J. C., pp. 253-69.

152a. SCHEIN, E. H., 'Brainwashing and Totalitarianization in Modern Society', *World Politics*, 1959, vol. xi.

152b. TAPLIN, W., *Advertising: A New Approach*, 1950, London, Hutchinson.

153. SCHILDER, P., *On the Image and Appearance of the Human Body*, 1950, New York, International Universities Press.

154. SCHOFIELD, W., 'Psychology, Law and the Expert Witness', *Amer. Psychologist*, 1956, 11.1.

155. SEGAL, H. A., 'Initial Psychiatric Findings of Recently Repatriated Prisoners of War', *Amer. J. Psychiat.*, 1954, 3, pp. 358-63.

156. SHILS, E., *The Torment of Secrecy*, 1957, London, Heinemann.

157. SHILS, E., 'Daydreams and Nightmares; Reflections on the Criticism of Mass Culture', *Sewanee Review*, 1957, 65, 4, pp. 587-608.

158. SHORT, P. L., 'The Concept of the Brand Image', *Bull. Brit. Psychol. Soc.*, 1958, 35, p. A2.

159. SIMON, C. W. and EMMONS, W. H., Review of Subconscious Persuasion Literature, *Psychol. Bull.*, July 1955.

160. SKINNER, B. F., *Walden Two*, 1948, New York, Macmillan.

161. SKINNER, B. F., *Science and Human Behaviour*, 1943, New York, Macmillan.

162. SNOW, C. P., 'The Two Cultures', *New Statesman and Nation*, 1956, LII, 1334, pp. 413-14.

163. SNOW, C. P., 'The Two Cultures and the Scientific Revolution', 1959, Cambridge Univ. Press.

163a. SNOW, C. P., 'The Moral Un-Neutrality of Science', 1961, Lecture to the American Association for the Advancement of Science.

164. SOROKIN, P., *Facts and Foibles in Modern Sociology and Related Sciences*, 1956, Chicago, Henry Regnery Co.

165. SPROTT, W. J. H., *Human Groups*, 1959, London, Pelican Books.

166. STRASSMAN, H. D., THALER, M. B. and SCHEIN, E. H., 'A Prisoner of War Syndrome: Apathy as a Reaction to Severe Stress', *Amer. J. Psychiat.*, 1956, 112, pp. 998-1003.

167. STRAUSS, E. B., 'The Anatomy of Treachery', *Bull. Brit. Psychol. Soc.*, 1957, 32, pp. 1-13.

168. STUART, G., *Narcissus; a Psychological Study of Self-Love*, 1956, London, Allen and Unwin.

169. SYKES, C., *Three Studies in Loyalty*.

170. TRILLING, L., *The Opposing Self*, 1955, London, Secker and Warburg.

171. TRILLING, L., *The Liberal Imagination*, 1950, New York, Viking Press.

171a. TROTTER, W., *Instincts of the Herd in Peace and War*, London, T. Fisher Unwin.

171b. TURNER, E. S., *The Shocking History of Advertising*, 1952, London, Michael Joseph.

172. VERNON, P. E., *Personality Tests and Assessments*, 1953, London.

173. VERNON, M. D., 'Perception, Attention and Consciousness', *The Advancement of Science*, 1959, Sept. No. 62.

174. VITELES, M. S., 'The New Utopia', *Science*, 1955, vol. 122, 3181, pp. 1167-71.

175. WALD, R. W., 'The Top Executive: a First-hand Profile', *Harvard Business Review*, 1954. Aug.

176. WARD, T. H. G., 'The Psychological Relationship Between Man and Aircraft', *Brit. J. Med. Psychol.*, 1951, 24, pp. 283-90.

176a. WEITZENHOFFER, A. M., *Hypnosis, an Objective Study in Suggestibility*, 1953, London, Chapman and Hall.

177. WELLS, H. G., 'Experiment in Autobiography', 1934, New York, Macmillan.

178. WEST, R., *The Meaning of Treason*, 1949, London, Macmillan.

179. WHYTE, W. F., *Street Corner Society*, 1943, Chicago Univ. Press.

180. WHYTE, W. H., Junior, *Is Anybody Listening?*, 1952, New York, Simon and Schuster.

181. WHYTE, W. H., Junior, *The Organization Man*, 1956, New York, Simon and Schuster.

181a. WILSON, E., *Europe Without Baedeker*, London, Secker and Warburg.

182. WINDELBAND, W., *Geschichte und Naturwissenschaft*, 1904, Strassburg, Heitz and Mündel.

183. WINOKUR, G., 'The Germ Warfare Statements; a Synthesis of a Method for the Extortion of False Confessions', *J. Nervous and Mental Disease*, 1955, 122, pp. 65-72.

184. WINOKUR, G., 'Brainwashing; a Social Phenomenon of our Time', *Human Organization*, 1955, 13, pp. 16-18.

185. WOOLF, V., *A Room of One's Own*.

186. WOOTTON, B., SEAL, V. G. and CHAMBERS, R., *Social Science and Social Pathology*, 1959, London, Allen and Unwin.

187. WORDSWORTH, W. (ed. LANG, A.), *Selections from the Poets*, 1897, London, Longmans.

188. WRIGHT MILLS, C., *The Power Elite*, 1956, Oxford Univ. Press.

189. WRIGHT MILLS, C., *The Causes of World War III*, 1959, London, Secker and Warburg.

190. YOUNG, M., 'Advertising: Good or Bad?' *Guardian*, Jan. 25, 1960.

SUBJECT INDEX

INDEX OF NAMES